Passionate Spirits

A History of the Royal
Canadian Academy of Arts,
1880-1980

Rebecca Sisler, RCA

Passionate Spirits

Clarke, Irwin & Company Limited
Toronto/Vancouver

Dedication

To my colleagues with love
and infinite respect

© **1980 Clarke, Irwin & Company Limited**

Canadian Cataloguing in Publication Data

Sisler, Rebecca.
Passionate spirits

Includes index.

ISBN 0-7720-1308-X

1. Royal Canadian Academy of Arts — History.
I. Title.

N17.C36S57   706.071   C80-094805-X

1 2 3 4 5 6 85 84 83 82 81 80

Printed in Canada

Contents

Acknowledgements

The emergence of this history has been dependent on the good will and active contribution of many individuals across Canada. On behalf of the artists of the Academy I would like to make particular mention of the following sources of both moral and practical support:

Charles Hill, Curator of Post Confederation Art, National Gallery of Canada, for his unfailing assistance in locating material; Dennis Reid, formerly with the National Gallery, who kindly allowed research access to the manuscript (since published) of his book *Our Own Country Canada*; the staffs of the photographic departments of the National Gallery of Canada, the Art Gallery of Ontario and the Montreal Museum of Fine Art, whose institutions house so many of the works of the early RCA members; the staffs of the reference libraries of the National Gallery of Canada, the Art Gallery of Ontario and the Montreal Museum of Fine Arts; Alan Suddon, Fine Arts Department, Metropolitan Toronto Public Library; Moncrieff Williamson, Director, Confederation Centre Art Gallery and Museum, Charlottetown, both for his assistance in fund-raising and for the wonderful original research on the early days of the Academy, made available in his book *Robert Harris, 1948-1919: An Unconventional Biography*; the Ontario Archives, which houses much original material, including the early records of the Ontario Society of Artists; the staff of the Manuscript Division of the Public Archives of Canada, the depository of both the RCA archival material and of the Lorne files; Nan Girard, Secretary of the Academy in the late sixties and early seventies, whose work at that time in producing a typewritten transcript of ninety years of handwritten RCA minutes (my bible), made the writing of this history immeasurably easier; Dorothy Aitken, my assistant in the RCA office, for her painstaking retyping of the manuscript and unfailing sensitivity to all manner of relevant detail. A special thank you to my friend Evelyn deRostaing McMann, formerly with the Fine Arts Department of the Vancouver Public Library, who contributed the List of RCA Presidents and Members.

The Academy's warm appreciation to donors to the History:

Mrs. Sonja Bata, Toronto

Mrs. W. E. Blatz, Toronto

The Samuel and Saidye Bronfman Family Foundation, Montreal

Mrs. J. F. Crothers, Toronto

The Government of Newfoundland

The Government of Prince Edward Island

Gulf Canada, Calgary

The Hamber Foundation, Vancouver

Mr. and Mrs. W. C. Harris, Toronto

Polysar Limited, Sarnia

Seven-Up Canada Limited, Toronto

Shell Canada, Calgary

Mrs. A. H. Squires, Toronto

Star Oil and Gas, Calgary

Mrs. O. D. Vaughan, Toronto

Mr. G. M. Williamson, Charlottetown

Wintario, Heritage Branch

And finally, my own gratitude to the President of the RCA, John C. Parkin, and to the Chairman of the Centennial Committee, Fred Fletcher, for their seeming unquestioning of my ability to carry through with the undertaking.

Rebecca Sisler, RCA
Toronto, 1980

Foreword

The Royal Canadian Academy of Arts in 1980 is Canadian art in synthesis: painting, sculpture, architecture, printmaking, graphic design, industrial design, textiles, ceramics, photography, film, yacht design—in effect potentially all areas of the contemporary visual and environmental arts.

The Academy's story as an integral part of Canadian art has been one of continuing evolution. Founded in 1880, its practical contributions have been considerable—the founding of the National Gallery, the establishing of the first Life Drawing Classes in the country, the encouragement of excellence through the awarding of various prizes and scholarships. And most important to the fostering of standards, the sponsoring of the annual open-juried RCA shows, through which for over ninety years the finest Canadian art has surfaced in a continuous and changing stream, reflecting the rich texture of Canadian talent as one generation after another has sought to interpret the feeling of the times.

In writing the History of the Academy, sculptor Rebecca Sisler, herself an Academician, has chosen not to write a history of Canadian art in the literal sense, but rather to approach her subject from the inside, to view events through the eyes of the artists themselves. Indeed in the interests of historical integrity we invited her to tell the story, blemishes and all, and she has done so.

The result is a revealing interplay of relationships between artists and their work, artists and their fellow artists, artists and their contemporaries, artists and the society in which they lived, artists and the politics of their profession. I believe that much of the material will be new even to art historians, and as such will make a major contribution to the understanding of the development of Canadian art.

Plainly, the History shows the Academy and its members to have been a vital cultural influence over the years. One hopes that future generations of artists will continue with the same sense of creative responsibility to society.

John C. Parkin, CC, D.S.C., D.ENG.
President, Royal Canadian Academy of Arts/
Académie royale des Arts du Canada
Toronto, 1980

A Short Perspective on Academies

The Canadian Academy, as it was first called, is generally considered to have been patterned after the Royal Academy in Britain. Which is true. But the Royal Academy was patterned after the French, which in turn grew out of the earlier Italian system.

Recent history does not deal kindly with academies. They are almost irrevocably branded as the reactionary force that barred the great Impressionist painters from the prestigious French Salon exhibitions over a century ago. The romance of scorned genius dies hard, although in truth a number of the Impressionists would seem to have lived fairly comfortably during a substantial part of their careers. Nevertheless, it was certainly a disastrous gaffe on the part of the academic art world to have been caught so deeply napping as to be unable to recognize the most innovative and committed art movement since the decline of the Renaissance. Posterity has never forgiven them. Academies are institutions that perpetuate stereotyped repetition of art forms from the past. Academicians are grey-bearded fossils.

However, there is more to know.

Although Italy was the birthplace of the modern academy, and certainly of the art academy, the academy's roots were in ancient Greece. Plato and his followers had met in the Grove of Akademeia near the Acropolis in Athens, and they gradually assumed the name of that vast garden that hosted their famous discourses. Hundreds of years later when Greek scholars sparked a rebirth of Platoism while on a religious mission in Italy, the term academy was revived. By 1500 as the Renaissance came into full swing the term had become very fashionable.

The earliest academies were not connected to art in any way, but were informal gatherings where philosophic issues were discussed in a sympathetic milieu. The academies spread like wildfire through Italy however, and very soon broadened their base to include groups who met to generate excellence in writing, speaking, acting, music. The concept eventually extended even to groups dedicated to gourmet feasting according to precise rules, and to card games and shooting. Art academies were bound to come into the picture.

It would be pleasant to swallow oyster-like the tale that Leonardo da Vinci formed the first art academy. But since the sole evidence is a series of prints attributed to Leonardo or one of his pupils bearing the inscription "Accademia Leonardo Vinci," scholars are still wrangling the issue. Leonardo's theories on the training of young artists do survive however, and are known to have laid the foundations for all future systems of academic training up to the nineteenth century.

Under the new system, disciplined knowledge was more important than manual skill. Anatomy, perspective, theory, and practice of proportion. Drawing from drawings, drawing from casts, drawing from nature. A pattern still not unfamiliar to students of European academies in the first half of the twentieth century, but a revolutionary system in a society that for several centuries had totally controlled the development of artists under the old guild system. Under the guild system, an artist's social position was that of a house painter or stone mason. A twelve year old would begin his career as an apprentice to a painter and was put to work at everything from tool-making and colour-grinding to serving as his master's valet. There was no other route to the guild certificate that would allow him to practise as a professional. When, around 1490, as the new wave of thought began to sap at the roots of the guild system, young Michelangelo was sent by his master Ghirlandjo to study at Bertoldo's experimental school for sculpture in the garden of Lorenzo the Magnificent, he became one of the first artists to receive a modern art education.

Seventy years later, in 1563, the more formalized Accademia del Disegno was founded in Florence under the protectorate of Cosimo de Medici. It was in effect the first true art academy. Although concerned with education, it was primarily an honours society recognizing artistic achievement with a detailed code of professional ethics laid out in forty-seven articles, and was committed to freeing artists from guild restrictions. By 1593 when the Accademia di S. Luca was founded in Rome, partly because of continuing guild intransigence, priorities had shifted to focus on the training of beginners, and this was to become the major direction of most academies of art. These studio academies fanned out quickly across Italy to Bologna, Genoa, Milan and other cities, and it was in this form, around 1600, that they migrated north into the rest of Europe. By 1740 there were twenty-five legitimate art academies and numerous lesser establishments scattered across the continent, and the roads to all led from Paris.

The Académie Royale de Peinture et de Sculpture was founded in 1648, one of a network of French academic institutions under direct royal patronage. Its early members were young men between thirty and thirty-five years of age and they had the same battle on their hands as had their predecessors in Italy. The French guilds still controlled painters under regulations set out in 1260 for "Peintres et tailleurs." Within the context of its times the new academy was an avant-garde movement and as long as it was battling the guilds it was a liberal and constructive force in the development of French art. Its schools evolved a complex and rigidly imposed discipline meant to arm the young artist with every possible theoretic and aesthetic advantage. At the same time there was considerable leeway in development since up until the nineteenth century a student still lived in his master's house and worked regularly in the studio learning painting and carving as had earlier apprentices. For those who emerged able to fulfill themselves within the academic tenets, reasonable expectation of official patronage awaited. The terrible weakness lay in the fact that since the throne paid the bills, it was able to dictate direction, and there was little place for artists who were not prepared to follow.

Nevertheless Paris ushered in the golden age of academies. Vienna, St. Petersburg, Dresden, Edinburgh, Stockholm, Copenhagen, London, Mexico City, Philadelphia. They all faithfully patterned themselves after the great French prototype. Most were strictly schools of art adapted with more or less success to local conditions. A few, like the Royal Academy in England, developed strong honours associations with emphasis on yearly exhibitions. All were concerned with continuity and the sacred handing on of the delicate flame of professional commitment from one generation to another. Unhappily the academies would seem to have been so wrapped up in the responsibilities of their mandate that they did not blink an eye when Voltaire claimed loudly that academies fostered pedestrian talent and harmed genius.

"Genius" was a term volleyed about with much abandon by the philosophers of the Age of Enlightenment, but it was considered somewhat hysterical in academic circles. In 1783 Friedrich Schiller wrote, "Do you expect enthusiasm where the spirit of academies rule?" His challenge fell on deaf ears. The anti-academic movement among the artists themselves did not begin to seethe until after 1800.

The golden age came to an abrupt end as the French Revolution and the Industrial Revolution combined to level the traditional structures of artistic support. In place of a leisure class who had time to enjoy and wealth to patronize the arts, artists were at the mercy of an only modestly enlightened middle-class public. Vast numbers of students from the new class enrolled in the academies across Europe, and then flooded the continent with Voltaire's mediocrity. In an attempt to stem the flood, academies atrophied around systems that had spelled excellence in the past. The German schools did respond to the need for reform and developed a liberalized curriculum that gave young artists a thorough basic training towards the end of producing original work. They also made room for the applied arts which had been shunned since the split with the guilds, and in so doing enlisted substantial government support.

But the pendulum was swinging. While in Paris and London the annual exhibitions of the grand academies continued to emphasize historical subjects painted in the grand manner of the siècle Louis XIV, the Romanticists were coming into open rebellion. "Art must feel free and independent, it must rule, as it

13

were, if it is to thrive; if it is ruled and mastered, it is bound to decline and vanish," wrote a supporter. The cry was still ringing when the Impressionists appeared on the scene full of wilful heresy. Art for art's sake! Not only the Salon of the French Academy but critics and all the art institutions of the day dismissed the Impressionists as a group of madmen.

It was at this interesting juncture in art history that the Canadian Academy loomed into view on the fringe of the New World wilderness. Rather appealingly unaware of the major art upheavals in Europe, it was definitely late in the day as academies go. As a result it was very much a grass roots movement that gave only nodding acknowledgement to traditional artistic polarizations. But like the earliest academies it filled an urgent and legitimate need. It was the vehicle through which a handful of aspiring artists were able to work to graft professional standards on a resisting pioneer culture. Basically an honours and exhibiting society, it became part of the fibre of developing Canadian art. For decades young artists first surfaced through its annual, open-juried shows, and election to membership was coveted as the ultimate recognition.

Historically, in spite of periods of atrophy, academies have been major contributors to the art of the western world. It is true that, varying from country to country, they have often lagged behind the swing of the artistic pendulum. Still, aside from those artists who have always found an inner balance within the classic academic structure, the fact remains that most of today's avant-garde artists are also academically trained. For the implication of the academy goes far beyond the walls and formal codes of institutions that so easily lapse into hibernation. It is rather a philosophic precept that links the future to the past and the past to the future. An evolutionary core that for over five hundred years has spawned the individuals, sometimes kicking and screaming, who in each age strike out alone into the unknown. And it is the jealous preservation of this core *by the artists themselves*, that justifies the continuity of the academy as a practical, living concept.

Artists on the New Frontier

An Academy in the wilds of nineteenth-century Canada? On the surface it scarcely sounds plausible. The spirit of the day was surely reflected in the clearing of land, the widening of frontiers, the establishing of solid communities. The most generous estimate could list only a miniscule percentage of the population as interested in art. From where then, could sufficient artists have surfaced to form an Academy?

In fact, history shows that artists have emerged, survived, even thrived under the most unlikely conditions. This is not to say that education, environment, influence, are not integral tools of development; they are the ladders, the stepping stones, the gusts of wind that fan the ember into flame. But the spark and the flame are the artist's alone, and have been known to insist on life unbidden, under a diversity of circumstances.

Take for instance the seventeenth-century painter Rembrandt, son of a Dutch miller, who showed a natural aptitude for drawing and painting as a child. He studied literature at university but the earlier gift asserted itself and he became an artist. After spectacular early success he found himself drawn in his work along paths not readily acceptable to the public. Portraits that bared the soul? Not for sturdy Dutch burghers. It was said of Rembrandt that when he was in front of his easel he would refuse an audience to the greatest sovereign in the world. He died a pauper, his brilliant legacy of paintings obscured by more popular trends for several generations.

Paul Cézanne, the father of Cubism, was born into a middle-class family in provincial France. His boyhood interest in painting was discouraged at home. "Child!" cautioned his banker father. "Think of the future. With genius you die; with money you eat." He enrolled in law school but after a year announced to his astounded family that he could not go on. Not an impetuous youth, he petitioned his father for a further year before he was finally allowed to go to Paris to study painting.

Berthe Morisot and Mary Cassatt, one French and one American, were both from privileged, cultured homes and were educated to be ladies. Both learned painting as all privileged young women learned painting, and both were strongly supported by their families when they showed signs of serious intent. Käthe Kollwitz, on the other hand, daughter of a master mason in Königsberg, Prussia, was warned by her father when, at seventeen already a gifted art student, she became engaged to a young medical student: "You have chosen. Be wholly what you have chosen." But she did not. She was wife and mother and totally committed artist until the end of her days. During the First World War she saw her work confiscated and destroyed — and still she worked.

Van Gogh, that tortured spirit, was the son of a Flemish clergyman and came to art through a trial of fire. The sculptor Jacob Epstein was the product of a prosperous family in the Jewish ghetto of New York. His childhood aptitude for drawing was mocked by his father. Modigliani, from a dreamy, pampered, bourgeois youth in Leghorn, Italy, was trajected out of himself in Paris like a self-destructing comet, leaving behind a glowing trail of original accomplishment.

By coincidence these randomly noted artists had several things in common. Unbidden, from varied backgrounds, all had shown marked interest in art from childhood, often to the complete bafflement of their parents. Most later sought out at least some formal art training. When the time came, all entered their profession without reservation. No choice was involved; for them there was simply no other route.

Lucius R. O'Brien, ca. 1885, photographer unknown. Archives of Ontario, Ontario Society of Artists papers.

It is scarcely surprising then that in yet another context, a number of painters and sculptors should have been working determinedly in the near wilderness that was Canada at the time of Confederation in 1867. They surfaced chiefly from three distinct sources. One, out of the established cultural framework that had taken root in the earlier settled French-speaking Canada. Two, from among the immigrant artists who arrived as settlers in various parts of the country, armed with the unlikely tools of formal training from the art schools of England and the continent. Three, as manifestations of those classic romantic spirits who in this case, born or at least raised from childhood in the austerity of frontier life, against all odds knew that they were artists and in the end could not be denied their natural bent.

Lucius O'Brien, who was to be the first President of the Royal Canadian Academy of Arts, was one of the last group. His mother, Mary O'Brien, like a number of other transplanted English gentlewomen of her day, kept a journal of her daily life in the wilds. The entry of February 12, 1834 reads like a first checkpoint in the course ahead for her son:

> I don't say that my son is a born artist, but he sometimes torments me very inconveniently to supply him with the implements to "dera, dera." Sometimes by the same passion I get him off my hands for an hour together. The productions of his pencil as far as I can judge are very like and quite equal to those of any other young gentleman of a year and a half old. Just now nothing will serve him but a pen and ink which is not quite convenient.

The O'Briens were not run-of-the-mill settlers. Captain Edward O'Brien was a young Irishman of ancient and respected lineage. He had come out to Thornhill, north of Toronto, as a half-pay officer after serving in the British Army, and as such he was offered the appointment to superintend the settlement of the Kempenfeldt area on Lake Simcoe. He and his bride established the village of Shanty Bay in 1830, near the present-day city of Barrie. Their family was born in a log house that was spoken of by a family friend as "...a perfect gem of civilization set in the wildest natural surroundings."

Nevertheless, the O'Briens seem to have thought very much as Paul Cézanne's father at the prospect of their son actually following an artistic career. Like a proper Ontario boy of breeding Lucius was sent to Upper Canada College in Toronto and then was directed towards a sensible profession. He spent time in an architect's office and then went on to study civil engineering. Although his career was dotted with evidences of his real bent, he was middle-aged before he was able to commit himself unequivocally to his art. Meanwhile he had served time managing a family-owned gravel pit, and as a young man of twenty-six had been elected reeve of the town of Orillia. It was during this period that he shocked his Toronto connections by marrying a local "widow of forty." After a further decade of provincial obscurity he spent time sketching in the south of France before settling permanently in Toronto. While it was some years before he was actually earning his living from his vocation, at every opportunity from the early 1870s onward he was off painting in the hinterlands. The wild grandeur of the receding frontiers appealed greatly to his artistic instincts, and as the railroads pushed relentlessly through geographical barriers, he followed with his water colours and oils.

For all his pioneer background O'Brien seems to have struck an elegant debonair note on the Toronto scene. A colleague, Robert Harris, described him in a letter in 1879 to his own folks back in Charlottetown:

O.R. Jacobi, Notman Photographic Archives, McCord Museum, Montreal.

Mr. O'Brien is a very tall, slight man with aquiline features, long black and grey whiskers and probably forty-five years old about. He is very quiet and deliberate in his manner, an exceedingly good talker and a refined man generally. He is a landscape painter exclusively, choosing generally marine views. He is a very enthusiastic boatman. He is a Canadian by birth, his father was a Colonel in the army and he is related to Lord Dufferin. He has money and an interest in a wine merchant's business here, *which enables him to keep good prices for his pictures.* His landscapes are among the very best done here, for he gets a good deal of the real character of Canadian scenery with them, and they are frankly painted.

High praise from Harris who was a European-trained portrait painter and a bit of an elitist on that score. In the same letter he described Otto Jacobi, a German immigrant who had come recently to Toronto from Montreal:

...the best there is in landscape; he is a German...an old man between seventy and eighty, but as lively as a cricket. He was court painter to one of the German princes and had a studio with the best men of his time in that country. *He is about the only regularly educated artist here.* Jacobi has been in Canada about twenty years and talks English very well and fluently. He is a very witty, clever old fellow, as full of practical feeling as ever could be. I went to spend last evening with him and his "olt wife" as he calls her. We smoked like chimneys, he drank "rye mit vater" and I drank "lemon mit vater" and Mrs. Jacobi looked upon us with complacency. It was a great treat to go through his old sketchbooks, many of them having been drawn by one of the most celebrated continental artists, Kraus....Jacobi is so full of quaint sayings and sarcastic hits at people that I don't know what to tell of him....He is as much removed from the commonplace as can be.

In fact, Otto Jacobi was forty-eight years old when he arrived in Montreal in 1860, and he had been painting for most of his life. His father had been a malt brewer in Königsberg, Prussia, and the family appears to have recognized the boy's talent from the start. He was thoroughly trained in Königsberg, Berlin and Düsseldorf. Later he spent twenty years at Wiesbaden as court painter to the Duke of Nassau before seeking out a more adventurous life as a portrait painter in New York. Even that was too tame and when he was invited to Canada to paint a presentation canvas of Shawinigan Falls for the Prince of Wales, he simply stayed for the rest of his working life.

Although he first settled in Montreal, when the Ontario Society of Artists was organized in 1872 Jacobi was among the first exhibitors. He was also one of the early teachers in the OSA school. However, by all accounts teaching was not his forte. His basic instructional method was to paint a picture in front of a clustered circle of students. When finished he would step back and exhort, "Now you haf seen me make a vater colour. It is very simple. Make one yourself."

From neither his teaching nor his painting could Jacobi be said to have had great influence on Canadian art. His work was too deeply rooted in the traditions of the old country to capitalize on the challenge of the new situation. But he was professional to the core, which in a milieu that offered local artists few established bench marks, was an inspiration in itself. Crusty, kind, eccentric, he was perhaps the best loved among the Canadian painters of his day.

Napoléon Bourassa, on the other hand, was a prime example of the Quebec bred and influenced artist.

Quebec of course had nurtured traditions in painting and sculpture from the earliest times. The cultural life source was the church but by the mid-nineteenth century the religious base had broadened to make room for a rich stream of portrait and landscape painters and architectural sculptors. When the new influx of artists began to arrive from Britain and the continent with increasing frequency in the mid-nineteenth century, they found thriving artistic activity both in Montreal and Quebec City.

Bourassa was born in 1827 at L'Acadie, southeast of Montreal, and received a classical education at the St. Sulpice Seminary. Like a

John Fraser, ca. 1875, Notman & Fraser Studio. Archives of Ontario, Ontario Society of Artists papers.

surprising number of colleagues from similarly advantaged backgrounds the world over, he prepared for the law. However, in no time his passion for art won the day and against his parents' wishes he threw the laudable career to the winds and apprenticed himself to the portrait painter Théophile Hamel, a route that was not open to artists in less developed Ontario. His art training included a period of travel in Europe—to Rome, Naples, Venice, Florence—but by 1858 he was back in Montreal and established in his own studio. He is said to have at one time remarked that in Quebec, portraiture and religious decoration would provide an artist with an adequate living, and while this might have proved constricting for some artists, it was not so for Bourassa. His well-known ecclesiastical murals and sculptures and even church designs were a perfect form of expression for a deeply religious man who saw art as a great philosophical vehicle through which viewers might expand the horizons of their own thinking.

Bourassa married the daughter of the Quebec patriot Louis Joseph Papineau and as the quintessential French-Canadian gentleman—distinguished, erudite, accomplished not only in his own work as a visual artist but as a musician and particularly as a writer—he was very much a part of the cultural fabric of French Canada.

At this same time Ontario had much less to offer artists either in the way of a living or a sympathetic milieu. When Anna Jameson, the accomplished English wife of Upper Canada's Attorney General arrived in Toronto for a brief sojourn in 1836, she described the growing capital as "A little ill-built town on low land, at the bottom of a frozen bay." And as for culture, "Books there are none, nor music and as to pictures!—the Lord deliver me from such! The people don't know what a picture is." Had Mrs. Jameson stayed longer—she cared neither for the country nor for her husband the Chancellor—she would have been on hand for some fairly encouraging developments.

Actually two years earlier in 1834 the Society of Artists and Amateurs of Toronto had put together a show of 196 works at the Parliament Buildings, then near the Toronto waterfront. Along with seventeen other artists of varying note, the work of young Paul Kane was shown. Financial problems discouraged the society, but by 1847 art matters had developed to such a degree that when artists regrouped to exhibit as the Toronto Society of Arts, all the participants were professionals. Portraits predominated in the exhibition (the first of three before this society too dissolved) and the landscapes in water colour reflected the gentle, pallid style of contemporary English tradition. But there were indications of things to come; Cornelius Krieghoff sent several works from Montreal and Paul Kane was represented by his first Indian paintings.

More important, in the previous year the Upper Canada Provincial Exhibitions had come into being and for many years—until the Art Association of Montreal was formed by art lovers and patrons in 1860—these exhi-

Allan Edson, 1870, William Notman Studio. Notman Photographic Archives, McCord Museum, Montreal.

bitions were to offer the only on-going forum in the country for Canadian artists. On the surface the exhibitions sound scarcely plausible. They were part of annual agricultural fairs, forerunners of the Canadian National Exhibition, which rotated among the major Ontario cities. As the fairs became established each city acquired a permanent building and allotted a section to the fine arts. An early critic gave an apt assessment of what, in more sophisticated times, seems a dubious setting. "Although a shed at the Agricultural Show can never be a Gallery of Art, it will be the best opportunity the bulk of the population have for acquiring correct ideas on the subject."

The Canadian painter Robert Gagen has written of the significance of the fairs both as a place for artists to show their work, and to see the work of other professionals. He mentions the pictures hanging from wooden slats nailed on the bricks and window frames. Portraits were hung with portraits, landscapes with landscapes, etc., and there were both professional and amateur categories. The hanging committee was usually a local carpenter. The judges handing out the prizes were appointed from among the local art authorities. Amateurish, but not so. Very soon work was coming in from Otto Jacobi and Allan Edson from Montreal, Daniel Fowler from Amherst Island near Kingston, William Cresswell from Seaforth, James Griffiths from London, Ontario—and these men, mostly European trained, were anything but amateurs. Gagen, who was a younger painter at the time, describes the

William Raphael, photographer unknown. National Gallery of Canada.

gatherings of whatever artists were on hand for a show, in the hotel or boarding house where some of them would be staying. They would talk art on into the night, discussing the pictures, heaping abuse on the judges, often with the current prizewinners present. They were times much valued by all.

Meanwhile, Montreal was definitely the centre of action. Not only did it have the base of an indigenous Quebec culture that through its master-apprentice system had already produced a glowing lineage of full-fledged artists that spanned several decades—Joseph Legaré to Antoine Plamondon to Théophile Hamel to Napoléon Bourassa—but the parallel blossoming of a prosperous merchant class provided a growing market. Adding to this ferment a number of the most talented of the new wave of immigrant painters were enlivening the scene as well. William Raphael, Adolphe Vogt and of course Jacobi were German and steeped in art before they came to the new country. The Bell-Smiths, father and son, arrived from London in 1886, and brought with them both the well-honed skills of the professional painter, and a perception of the artist's place within society that was to contribute greatly to the coming move toward organization among the artists for mutual advancement. It was a two-way exchange. The newcomers brought a sophisticated, old-world professionalism. In return they were stimulated in their work by the buoyancy of the new country.

In contrast Henry Sandham was born in Montreal of Yorkshire parents and grew up in the Eastern Townships. His introduction to the art world was via association with fellow workers, artists who were earning a living by tinting photographs and painting background scenery for photographic montages in the studio of the well-known commercial photographer, William Notman of Montreal. Allan Edson, the painter of enchanted, light-filtered forests, was raised in his parents' hotel in a village in the Eastern Townships. Like Sandham he gleaned his early art training through brushes with older artists in the metropolis.

John Fraser was a pivotal figure almost from the time he arrived in Canada with his bride and his immediate family in 1856. The Frasers were Scottish but had settled in London, England, some time before John was born. As a boy Fraser was determined to be an artist and at fourteen years old began to work during the day to pay for evening classes at the Royal Academy Schools. The elder Fraser, however, was a member of the Moral Force Chartists, an extreme liberal group, and was beginning to make himself vastly unpopular with the powers-that-be through his intransigent and audible views. The time came when it seemed prudent to emigrate and the clan set out for Quebec. After a false start in the Eastern Townships where John painted kitchen chairs, wagons and cutters to help support the family, he accepted an invitation to join Notman's stable in Montreal. He was an immediate success at the craft of tinting photographic portraits, and within a few years he was promoted to the position of art director in the firm. A brilliant if temperamental artist, he adapted the photographic elements of clarity of light and image to his own landscape painting, and in this approach was a major influence on the younger men such as Sandham who worked with him.

It was Fraser too in 1867 who was one of the prime movers when the Montreal artists banded together to form the Society of Canadian Artists under the maternal eye of the Art Association of Montreal, which had been formed seven years earlier. Several exhibitions were organized with the particular aim to show for sale the work of Canadian artists. This had become an urgent prerogative since many Montreal patrons were zealously committed to gloomy and mediocre European pot boilers, familiar Dutch windmills and uninspired French landscapes that were turned out by the dozen to please an uninformed public. Unhappily, a period of deteriorating economic conditions was developing in Quebec and as usual art circles were the first to suffer. When in 1872 the AAM and the SCA attempted to economize by combining their annual shows, their efforts were dismissed by a waspish columnist. "The co-partnership is to be regretted because it is an acknowledgement of the decadence of both societies."

Be that as it may, times became so desperate that public art activity came almost to a standstill, with artists scattering in their attempt to find means of survival. By 1873 the SCA had petered out and the art focus began shifting to Toronto.

John Fraser, meanwhile, had earlier been posted to Toronto to open a branch office for Notmans. Even before the demise of the SCA he was urging Toronto artists to organize to improve their lot. But since by all accounts Fraser was a floridly egocentric man, given when viewing his own work to tossing off such epigrams as, "A man who can paint like that should wear a gold hat!" it was difficult to rally his new colleagues to the cause. In the end they had to face up to the reality that if they were ever to move out from under the aegis of the agricultural fairs as the main theatre for their work, it was going to be up to themselves. Good sense prevailed. In June of 1872 a meeting was at last called at Fraser's home on Gould Street in Toronto, and the first of two great art societies, the OSA and the RCA, was founded.

The formation of the Ontario Society of Artists was a vital first step in the coming of age of Canadian artists and art. Its formal concepts were a reflection of the responsibility felt by the artists themselves towards their profession: the fostering of original art, promoting the interests of its members, and when the opportunity offered, the establishment of a School of Art and a Public Art Gallery. They also planned to conduct an Art Union, a sort of art lottery meant to cultivate public desire to own pictures. There were existing prototypes both in Glasgow and London. In essence subscribers paid a modest sum for a ticket which entitled them to a draw for prizes, which were selected works of art from a current exhibition. An attractive lure for a reluc-

Henry Sandham, ca. 1882, Notman Studio, Boston. Notman Photographic Archives, McCord Museum.

tant public, since included in the price of the ticket was a small reproduction of a painting as well as free admission for the duration of the exhibition. For the new art society the Union was to prove a very effective means of involving prospective patrons.

In a practical sense these ambitions and professional goals were a framework upon which the artists were able to stretch and pull themselves up into a more creative and committed sphere of achievement. Their annual exhibitions began in 1873. Three years later they opened their first Art School in leased premises at 14 King Street, the modest forebear of the Ontario College of Art. And after years of unremitting concern, in 1900 they were instrumental in founding the Art Gallery of Toronto.

This does not mean that all went by the book. John Fraser was chosen as the first Vice President (the position of President was honorary and in this first instance was conferred on W.H. Howland, a young art collector who was President of the Queen City Insurance Company). But by the time the first annual meeting swung around, in spite of his acknowledged contribution, Fraser had so alienated his fellow members that they could stand him no longer. They nominated and elected Lucius O'Brien in his place. Fraser resigned in a dark rage and took with him those members who had joined from Montreal, such as Sandham (by now his brother-in-law) and Hammond. As a result the Society lapsed into being a purely provincial group. Adding to the absurdity of the situation, the first treasurer, another local businessman, was found to have been embezzling the funds, leaving unpaid bills totalling $1,023.75.

Nevertheless the extent of the changes resulting from the Society's efforts in its early years, and what improvements evolved in terms of opportunity and stimulation to the artists themselves, are clearly underlined in a letter from O'Brien to Robert Harris in the summer of 1879. Harris, after an excellent training in Boston and in Europe was back home in Charlottetown and was finding the going rocky. He wrote to O'Brien for advice on Toronto prospects. O'Brien's reply, to a young artist known to him only through his work, is a remarkable example of the sense of fraternity and common cause, the almost blood relationship that ideally links professional artists.

My Dear Harris, — as brothers in arms we will drop the Mr. I received your letter on my return from my summer trip and am glad to give you what information I can. Toronto is the best art centre in Canada, at present, and there are more artists here than anywhere else, and no lack of portrait painters or rather colourers of photographs. Still, judging from what I have seen, your work would be among the best, if not better than anything we have here and you would have a fair chance with the others. Success in portrait painting seems to be very much a matter of push and business attack and of your capacity in this way I cannot judge.

Our Society does a good deal by the Art Union and Exhibitions to sell pictures and sketches for saleable and interesting work, not too high in price, as there is some demand. In our Art School and proposed extension of Art Education there is room for a good teacher and I should think your training in Europe would *enable you to help us*. This also would be a source of some revenue, in addition to painting. Of book illustration there is not much at present. Professional models are scarce here, but you can easily get subjects for most things, and in all these facilities we are improving.

The seven years of our Society had done a good deal in cultivating art feeling in the Country and we think, from the arrangements I have just made in Ottawa and Montreal, that we may reckon upon Exhibitions every year to which your pictures may be sent for sale.

Our Society meets once a month and the gatherings are pleasant and our rooms are always open...While I would not lead you to expect any great return from a residence in Toronto, yet I think you might get on here and we would gladly welcome you. *This and the country around it, are growing fast and promise to have a great future*.

Harris came, and did indeed "get on." At thirty years of age he was already a gifted, dedicated portrait painter and on the brink of a remarkable career. And he was thus on hand for the somewhat turbulent birth of the second great art society.

Since the formation of the SCA in Montreal there had been an instinctive urge among artists to shepherd their common needs for the advancement of opportunities in their very tenuous profession. The times had defeated the fledgling national organization and although the OSA was launched on a much more stable course, in spite of early aspirations, because of internal personal disputes it had been unable to move beyond its regional base.

But the country was changing.

As the railroads rolled back frontiers it became possible to conceive of Canada as more than a series of remote outcroppings of civilization strung along the limits of vast intractable barrens.

Soon communities would be linked from sea to sea, rivers, forests, plains and mountains harnessed as the backdrop to the new Dominion. It was romantic, heady stuff and as the geographical scope of their work indicates, the artists were not untouched by this national vision. Further, according to painter Robert Gagen, who would have been twenty-eight years old at the time, when he and his Ontario colleagues visited the Philadelphia Centennial Exhibition in 1876, they were somewhat shocked to find that their own earnest, English-style water colours were out of step with the times. The Exhibition, a great general fair featuring practical displays calculated to underline America's coming of age one hundred years after Independence, also provided an enormous building to house an international collection of fine art. England, France, Germany, Italy, Spain, the Scandinavian countries, the Netherlands, Brazil, Mexico. The United States alone showed several thousand pictures. And while the general tenor of the exhibit reflected a strongly academic official line, it was a great visual feast for America's country cousins from above the forty-ninth parallel, whose modest individual contributions were lost in the rich mélange. They returned home very much aware of their own inadequacies, and with a growing conviction that they, the artists, would have to make a united effort to lift themselves beyond their present provincial imitations.

By the late 1870s then, enthusiasm and sense of urgency for a national organization were fomenting quietly. It needed only a catalyst to bring elements to a head.

Chapter Two

Founding of the Academy

Sir John Douglas Sutherland Campbell, Marquis of Lorne, heir to the eighth Duke of Argyll, was thirty-four years of age when he arrived in Canada in January of 1879 as Queen Victoria's representative. A sensitive man, a poet who loved drawing, a friend of the celebrated British painters Landseer and Millais, as far as Canadian art was concerned he was the right man in the right place at the right time.

The appointment as Governor General did not come as a complete surprise. Several years earlier Lorne, whose Highland family was known for second sight, had a clairvoyant vision of himself being offered the Governor Generalship of Canada. When the position was in fact conferred by the British Prime Minister Lord Beaconsfield, it was said to be almost the only action ever taken by that Prime Minister not criticized by his implacable foe, Gladstone, then leader of the opposition. The Queen had approved as well, although she had given her permission with some reluctance since she could hardly bear to allow her daughter, "poor dear Loosey," to go so far from home.

The Princess Louise, Lorne's wife, was of course a daughter of Queen Victoria. Preceding their marriage in 1871, Lorne, a Liberal member of Parliament and a "subject," had not been wholeheartedly welcomed into the Royal family circle on the grounds that Louise should preserve the royal strain by marrying, like her mother and sister before her, yet another Prussian Prince. But the Queen championed Lorne to the family and her private secretary advised the Household, "This is the best Briton. Uphold him—and make the best of him." There was shortlived concern over precedence. Should Lorne go up or Louise down? But the feisty Duke of Argyll had no time for suggestions of a new title for his son, and he won. The country approved the choice and by the time the young couple set out for Canada, nervous reservations about Lorne as a departure from Royal tradition were long resolved, although the Queen reportedly remained doubtful that her daughter's bohemian tendencies (Louise was something of a painter and sculptor) were to be cured by a husband who wrote poetry.

It must surely have been a refreshing relief for Lorne to escape for a time to the colonies.

The couple's reputation as aesthetes had preceded them to Canada. Lord Dufferin, as the out-going Governor General, had suggested that the Marquis of Lorne and Her Royal Highness the Princess Louise would give warm support to the development of the fine arts, and at the opening of the sixth annual exhibition of the OSA in May of 1878, had even alluded to the formation of an art Academy. "After all, we must remember that the Academy of Great Britain began pretty much like this Society. . . ."

It would be with considerable confidence then that Lucius O'Brien, as Vice President of the OSA, set out for Ottawa in February of 1879 to petition the new Vice-Regal couple's patronage for the Society, and particularly requesting that they open the coming OSA exhibition. Not only was he received with marked warmth at Rideau Hall, but Lorne put to him a proposal for a new society that would link artists throughout the Dominion. The OSA Minute Book records the special meeting called on March 17 to report the news to the membership:

Sir John Douglas Sutherland Campbell, Marquis of Lorne, 1879, Notman & Sandham Studio. Recent print from original negative, Notman Photographic Archives, McCord Museum, Montreal.

> The chairman [L. R. O'Brien] reported the result of his late visit to Ottawa and the New Governor General also HRH the Princess Louise. He said the visit was most flatteringly received and his Excellency and HRH had promised to open our coming Exhibition. His Excellency spoke of a scheme he had in view for the formation of a school and Society and on comparison it was found that our own system coincided remarkably with his views.

The artists may well have been slightly puzzled by this apparent overlap of enthusiasm, which if implemented would appear to challenge the position of the existing OSA school. On the other hand they must have wondered if more would even be heard of the scheme. However, Lorne was absolutely sincere in his interest, and during the opening of the new building of the Art Association of Montreal near the end of May, he left no doubt as to the wider vision of his concept.

Excitement began to mount. It was to be the beginning of four years of unfailing Vice-Regal moral support and joint plotting with the artists in the cause of Canadian art.

The occasion of the Montreal opening could not have been more suitable for the public launching of the Academic kite. The Vice-Regal pair themselves exuded cultural authority, and the cream of society was present. The official party swept through the door into the Art Association's grand new gallery. All eyes strained to catch sight of the real, live Princess. She was dazzling in white satin with lace draperies and diamond ornaments, while his Excellency wore evening dress, adorned with the Order of the Thistle and the ribbon sash of the Order of St. Michael and St. George. The papers next day gave much prominence to his address in which he had embedded the new proposal:

> . . . I think we can show we have good promise, not only of having an excellent local exhibition, but that we may, in the course of time, look forward to the day when there may be a general art union in the country, and when some more fortunate successor may be called upon to open the first exhibition of a royal Canadian academy to be held each year in one of the capitals of our several provinces. . . .

Following the opening Lorne continued on to the summer residence of the Governor General at Quebec City. Obviously not content to leave the realization of his plan to a successor, he immediately wrote a letter to O'Brien outlining his impressions, "for what they are worth," of what might be attempted. Noting his position as a comparative stranger to the Canadian situation, he was obviously using O'Brien as a sounding board to ensure credibility in his direction. Certainly he could not have been more fortunate in his collaborator.

O'Brien was a dedicated artist, fully aware of the limitations imposed on his profession by what had been until lately a pioneer culture, and he had long proven his deep-rooted respect for his fellow artists. And he was a statesman. In all the exhibitions of bad temper that were to erupt between the artists in the coming months, there was never a whisper questioning O'Brien's integrity and sense of concern for his colleagues' aspirations.

The extent of the exchange between the two men over the summer is not documented, but by September arrangements had been made for Lorne to attend a special meeting in the OSA rooms in Toronto. It was a curious affair. The Princess, keenly interested in art, accompanied her husband and the members were so overwhelmed by their distinguished guests that discussion following his Excellency's concise outline for the formation of a Royal Canadian Academy of Arts was minimal. It was left for O'Brien to move and J.A. Fraser to second the Society's approbation of the new organization, and to indicate their intention to take practical steps towards moving the concept ahead.

Fortunately the officers had recovered sufficiently by the following day to meet again with Lorne to edit his draft paper of specific proposals, to be submitted to the OSA general membership and to the Art Association of Montreal. Provision was made for annual exhibitions, and, doubtless influenced by the interest in the applied arts generated in the 1850s by his late father-in-law, Prince Albert, Lorne was anxious to include a category of drawings for machinery, industrial design, house decoration and furniture. Dispelling

possible uneasiness of local groups, the new association would leave existing societies intact. It would be called "The Canadian Academy," pending application to the Crown for permission to prefix the name with "Royal." The initial membership would be chosen by agreement of the officers of the OSA and the AAM, "...being the only important Art Societies existing in the Dominion."

Five days later the OSA membership gathered to formally discuss Lorne's paper. All proceeded smoothly at first. There was no dissenting voice over the basic fact of an Academy. Nor had anyone trouble agreeing that nominations for Charter membership be limited to artists presently residing in Canada. But as the motherhood issues were cleared from the agenda, the real concern loomed and hackles rose perceptibly.

Indeed, *who* were to be the Charter members of this grand new society? Obviously artistic sensibilities, particularly those of the more numerous and contentious painters, were about to be severely tested.

With the key question smouldering in their midst like a disturbed wasp's nest, several impractical motions were placed on the floor and shot down one by one. Everyone who had shown in OSA exhibitions should be included in the Academy; nonsense, this was selection by default. Members should be chosen through submission of unsigned works to a jury of the British Royal Academy or the American National Academy of Design; but few artists cared to risk such impersonal finality. A further special meeting should be called to again discuss the issue; an out-and-out stalling tactic, supported only by the most insecure. Finally a practical, responsible proposal disentangled itself from the haze, hung for a

Opening of the Canadian Academy of Arts at Ottawa; His Excellency Declaring the Exhibition Open, Canadian Illustrated News Vol. XXI, No. 12, March 20, 1880, cover. Public Archives Canada, Ottawa.

period of indecision, and then was put to the vote. Moved by painter William Revell and seconded by architect Frank Darling that the present nominations from Toronto members be limited to eight painters, with the number of places open to the other professions to be left for further consideration. The present nominations would be determined by adoption of the eight names receiving the highest number of votes by ballot.

It was to be a clean cut of the scalpel and not wholly attractive to the mixed bag of painters, but in a sudden burst of ethical resolution names were placed on the slate and voting was underway. Stunned though the gathering may have been by their spontaneous action, there could be no quarrel with the resulting list of eight: Fowler, Fraser, Jacobi, O'Brien, Cresswell, Sandham, Raphael and Perré. They were the core of the most respected and professional of the OSA artists, and on September 20 O'Brien conveyed the results by letter to the AAM who were meanwhile supposedly overseeing a similar process in Quebec.

Predictably, an attempt was made to overthrow the decision at the following OSA meeting, but without success. A further special meeting was then called at the request of five still disgruntled members, but it aborted when not all of the five appeared themselves, and those that did refused to sign the roll. Since no motion was put to the floor the meeting was adjourned before it began. It was the final gasp of resistance and the Academy was left to develop as a leavening influence in Canadian art as opposed to a comfortable, common interest club.

From his seat of comparative calm at Rideau Hall, the Governor General had viewed the battle with considerable philosophy. "There is a marvellous amount of bitterness and bad language. Half the artists are ready just now to choke the other half with their paintbrushes."

Sensibly the brushes soon reverted to their normal use and the organization developed by leaps and bounds over the late autumn. According to Robert Harris, that indefatigable writer of letters home, by December the main topic of conversation on everyone's lips was the inaugural exhibition to mark the founding of the Academy. O'Brien had just returned from Ottawa where he had stayed as a guest at Government House. "The details of the projects were talked over. Mr. O'Brien says the Marquis is quite enthusiastic about the affair. I wish I had something worthwhile ready to send, but I shall have to send some old things I'm afraid. . . ."

But like almost every other prospective exhibitor in the country, Harris immediately threw himself into preparing the best work possible for the show.

Towards the end of the month copies of the new constitution and laws were circulated to the press and were found to be closely adapted from those of the British Royal Academy. Reaction was mixed but the *Gazette* of Montreal gave full and sympathetic coverage, quoting generously from the material:

The objects which are sought are the encouragement of design as applied to painting, sculpture, architecture, engraving and the industrial arts, and the promoting and support of education leading to the production of beautiful and excellent work in manufactures.

To accomplish these a National Gallery was to be installed at the seat of government, exhibitions held in the chief cities of the Dominion, and schools of art and design were to be established. Membership was to be limited to not less than forty artists who should be called "Academicians of the Canadian Academy." Of these not more than ten were to be architects, three engravers, six designers. There was also to be an order of members who would be Associates, not less than twenty in number, but left indefinite.

Members were to be "men of fair moral character," a clause that had to be altered as one of the initial acts of the organization at their meeting on March 6, 1880. The word "men" was struck out, presumably in deference to Charlotte Schreiber, the one woman on the Charter list. It was a pleasant gesture but there was not to be another female Academician for over fifty years.

Oddly enough, the Art Association of Montreal had done little to supplement the original OSA list of eight painters. Only three painters were added from Quebec. Napoléon Bourassa and Allan Edson from Montreal, and Eugène Hamel from Quebec City. The Association's minutes from the period are not available for reference, but it may be that as an organization of laymen interested in the arts rather than an organization of working artists, and more apprehensive of controversy, they decided to skirt the issue by simply recommending these few incontestable names for consideration by the Governor General.

The process for completing the list of Charter Academicians and Associates is not clear, but would seem to have been the result of wide consultation by Lorne with various knowledgeable sources, with undoubted professional appraisal from his lieutenant in the field, L.R. O'Brien. In the end, twenty-five artists appeared on the list of Charter Academicians, including eighteen painters, six architects and one lone sculptor, F.C. van Luppen, a Belgian emigré who had settled in Montreal. In addition there were fifty Associates. Future Academicians would be elected by the members from this group until the full complement of forty was reached, and after that when vacancies became available through death of members. Associate ranks would be renewed by nomination and election of younger artists as the first step towards full membership. It was definitely a paternalistic system, identical in principle to that followed by the Academies of Great Britain and France, and in a new and growing country was to prove a source of considerable discontent in later years when the Associates, who had no voting privileges, rebelled against an overtight rein. But for the time there was nothing but excitement and approbation from the artists concerned.

As for the national scope of the new organization, it was necessarily of a limited nature. Given the underdeveloped state of the country—the railroad had not yet pushed through to the west coast—aside from a handful of artists from the Maritimes, inevitably the bulk of the membership was enlisted from Quebec and Ontario, where indeed most artists had settled.

In spite of general enthusiasm from both the public and the artists, some of the press reaction was skeptical, even derisive, with one wag proposing that the artists might more appropriately look forward to incorporation in 1980. Inevitably other critics questioned the selection of names, an open affront to the Governor General since his was the official word confirming the line-up of the seventy some painters, sculptors, architects and designers as Academicians and Associates. O'Brien was finally obliged to respond with a letter to the editor of the Montreal *Herald* pointing out that indeed Canadian artists did realize their modest place in the larger scheme of things, but that the Academy would surely assist them in promoting the higher standards espoused by some of the doubters.

However, Lorne and the artists were coming down the home stretch. At the end of January Harris was writing home: "The Academy is now formed, and the Officers appointed. You may see notices in the paper about it." He himself had been nominated by the Governor General as an Academician. Like the other nominees Harris was much concerned with preparing a creditable Diploma Work for presentation to the Academy as a qualification of full membership. These Diploma Works were so called because as each member reached the stature of Academician he would not receive his Membership Diploma until he had presented an original piece of his art — his Diploma Work — to the Academy. Again, it was a practice adopted from the Royal Academy, but in this case it was considered particularly important since the works were to remain in Ottawa to form the nucleus of the collection of the proposed National Gallery. The first Academicians set the tone for what was to become the accepted attitude of suc-

ceeding generations of Academy artists by offering, for the approbation of their governing Council, a representative piece of what each considered to be his finest work.

As for the first slate of Officers, they were chosen by Lorne, and there had never been any question in anyone's mind but that Lucius O'Brien would be the first President. Napoléon Bourassa was Vice President. Toronto architect James Smith was Treasurer, with Toronto painter Marmaduke Matthews (an Associate) named as Secretary. They were to serve for five years, with their successors then to be elected by the Academy itself.

As events developed, when the time for the exhibition approached Robert Harris was appointed one of the jury of selection. He met in Ottawa on March 1 with his fellow jurors — Napoléon Bourassa and Henry Sandham, Thomas Scott, the government architect, and James Griffiths, an elderly painter from London, Ontario. On the following day the Ottawa *Free Press* reported them hard at work, saying that they had juried the show with "unsparing severity...whatever the victims may feel at the moment the public will gain."

And as usual, Harris had something to say:

We have had an awful lot of work, [the jury had also to hang the show] and have rejected an awful lot of pictures, which of course makes some people very wild. The Government has been very good in the way of fittings. Mr. Scott, the Government architect, managed all the matter for us in good style. The Marquis came to chat and consult with us and we all went to Rideau Hall. He is quite pleasant and nice to get along with!

In spite of his gracious exterior, the entire period of the founding of the Academy was undoubtedly one of considerable stress for the Marquis, for he had serious domestic problems. Official allusion places his wife the

Princess Louise faithfully at his side throughout Academy proceedings, but in fact she had returned to England in mid autumn amid much speculation in the British press that she was suffering from depression settling into melancholia, and it was expected that Lorne would be recalled. No such thing happened and the rumours were denied, but the New York *Tribune* continued to find her absence from Ottawa unusual. Scoffing at gossip implying that she lacked "warmth of affection for her husband," they leapt into the fray suggesting that the Princess being an intelligent and clever woman, had not found suitable intellects in Canada—an explanation which was even less palatable from the official point of view.

With conjecture flying, the Princess arrived back in Ottawa in early February, but was no sooner there when she was involved in a very unpleasant accident. The Governor General's sleigh overturned immediately after leaving the gate of Government House on the way to a reception in the Senate Chamber. News was brought to the waiting assembly that the Princess had been thrown out and injured. She suffered severe contusions to one side of the head and one badly cut ear. In the Royal tradition, she was reported to have shown a great deal of fortitude under the circumstances.

As March 6, 1880, and the formal opening of the Academy exhibition approached, the Princess was far from recovered and it was feared she would be unable to attend the inaugural ceremony. She did not, and must surely have been excused. But the implications of the gossip columns were considered so serious that first Lorne and then the Princess herself felt called upon to issue statements to the press refuting suggestions that she had not wanted to return to Canada, and insisting that illness alone now prevented her from resuming her place at her husband's side.

Averting their eyes with admirable gallantry and delicacy, officials of the Academy elected not to notice the Vice-Regal drama either at the time or throughout later prolonged absences.

Certainly his personal anxiety did not prevent Lorne from making every effort to launch the Academy in style. He had been able to persuade the government of Sir John A. Macdonald to co-operate and the Clarendon Hotel at the corner of Sussex Drive and George Street—it had been used to quarter troops during the Fenian Raids—was made available for the exhibition. A great sign was painted and fastened to the balcony over the Sussex Street entrance proclaiming: EXHIBITION, CANADIAN ACADEMY OF ARTS

Earlier in the day of Saturday, March 6, the first Annual Meeting of the Canadian Academy took place. Among the initial resolutions was the formal establishment of the National Gallery through the acceptance of the Diploma Works from the Charter Academicians. Of the twenty-five who had been nominated, eighteen had already presented a work, and most of the others complied within the current year, thus forming the core of the Gallery's permanent collection. Several other items were considered and passed, including a resolution from Bourassa and his colleague Eugène Hamel, that the senior Quebec painter, Antoine Plamondon,

Clarendon Hotel, Opening of the Canadian Academy of Arts at Ottawa, Canadian Illustrated News Vol. XXI, No. 12, March 20, 1880, Public Archives Canada, Ottawa.

although elderly and in any case too much the egoist to consider joining the others in full membership, nevertheless be recorded on the list as an honorary, retired Academician, a perfectly legitimate category. The first governing Council was appointed on the simple basis of selection of the first twelve names on the roster, with alphabetical rotation to take place annually. With the historic meeting adjourned, the members proceeded to visit His Excellency at Government House.

Then business aside, as an addendum to the Minutes notes: "In the evening at eight o'clock the formal opening of the Exhibition took place and the annual assembly of members and Honorary members was held."

Everyone was there, the Clarendon Hotel full to overflowing. In spite of inclement weather both artists and patrons had converged on Ottawa, with the OSA cancelling their monthly meeting to accommodate members who were heading for the capital. Academy supporters, who had paid sums between one and twenty-five dollars for the privilege of becoming Honorary members (although Lorne headed the list with a subscription of $500, while one other gentleman, Allan Gilmour, had contributed $100 toward the cause), came in droves to attend the glamorous affair. The Prime Minister and his wife attended as did many government ministers and senators. Lady Macdonald, Lady Tilley and Lady Tupper were elegant in black silk dresses, while the Academy's Charlotte Schreiber was reported handsome in black velvet. In the words of the Toronto *Globe*'s special correspondent:

The rooms were brilliantly lighted, and what with the bright costumes of the ladies in relief against a background made up of the choicest works of our Canadian artists, strains of sweetest music mingling with the hum of hundreds of voices broken by an occasional peal of merry laughter, made up a most pleasing tout ensemble.

Not surprisingly however, as the Ottawa *Citizen* pointed out, "Those present confined themselves more to promenading than to looking at pictures."

Nevertheless, for those who did look the rooms were rich with works that the years were to prove important, and which justified the *Citizen*'s conviction that the high standards set by the jury represented "the cornerstone of the quality of Canadian art in years to come," and that would "elevate incalculably the art of Canada."

The range of subject and style was broad and very much reflected the varied backgrounds of the exhibitors. The now famous "Sunrise on the Saguenay," by virtue of being not only the President's Diploma picture but the finest painting in the show, had been hung by the jury in the place of honour above the dais in the main gallery. There was Allan Edson's "Trout Stream in the Forest," in which the viewer was given a magically intimate glimpse of a gentle, resurgent world of nature. There were the scenic interpretations of the European-trained painters: William Raphael's brooding and evocative "Indian Encampment, Lower St. Lawrence," and John A. Fraser's "Laurentian Splendour," serene but like himself with an air of latent tumult. Charlotte Schreiber and Robert Harris represented the new, less constrained approach to figure painting, while Eugène Hamel's works were typical examples of the traditional establishment portraitist. On the other hand a young, unaffected painter from Doon, Ontario, Homer Watson, had sent in a painting "The Pioneer Mill," and it had not only been accepted, but had been purchased the day before the opening by Lorne for Queen Victoria. Daniel Fowler of Amherst Island showed twenty-seven works, but oddly enough the grand old man of Canadian painters, Jacobi, was almost the most poorly represented. As the time for the exhibition approached he had found himself in the rare but enviable position of having sold all recent paintings. He borrowed a work back for the occasion, but since he was not in a position to present a Diploma painting, his name did not appear on the list of Charter members.

The architects were represented of course, and their thirty-seven submissions gave a view in synopsis of local architecture of the era. Thomas Scott showed a drawing of his Union Station, Toronto; W.G. Storm his renderings of Toronto University (his Diploma drawing), Osgoode Hall, and of St. James Cathedral, Toronto; J.W. Hopkins his Merchant's Bank of Canada, Montreal; James Smith his Deaf and Dumb Institute, Belleville. There was even an ambitious show on the part of Lorne's special interest group, the designers (forty-seven exhibits from carved cabinets to lace curtains). In an attempt to stimulate these applied arts, five awards had been solicited from industry with William Doughtie taking top honours, winning not only a prize of $15 for his design for wallpaper, but a special silver medal offered by the Governor General as well. The sculptors unfortunately were at a numerical disadvantage with only five artists mustering a total of eleven works, and indeed it was to be another decade before this area of the arts began to show signs of marked development.

Hanging Committee of the Canadian Academy of Arts, 1880. Seated (l. to r.) Henry Sandham, Montreal, and James Griffiths, London, Ontario; standing (l. to r.) Robert Harris, Charlottetown and Toronto, Thomas S. Scott, Dominion Chief Architect, Ottawa, and Napoléon Bourassa, Montreal. Notman Photographic Archives, McCord Museum, Montreal.

33

It was a huge show with 388 works of art in the main exhibit alone. This included a special loan section of European masters from private collections, apparently on the grounds that at this early stage the Canadian works on their own would not sufficiently engage the interest of influential patrons who were still reluctant to recognize local talent. There was also a further display of some seventy-seven outdoor, on-the-spot sketches by four painters, O'Brien, Fraser, Verner, and a lesser-known man, Armstrong Scott, as well as small pictures to be redeemed with Art Union coupons. In all the works filled twelve rooms of the hotel.

With the crowd milling and surging through the building, the exhibition's climactic moment came with the arrival of the Governor General, complete with Guard of Honour and all his retinue in uniform. He was greeted with rounds of applause as he made his way through to the dais, "...even the ladies joining in most heartily." Standing beneath O'Brien's splendid painting he gave a lively, thoughtful speech, commenting on the incredibly short time since the project had been proposed, and ardently promoting the cause and justification of Canadian artists, stressing the great possibilities ahead.

O'Brien replied, speaking in the highest terms of Lorne's encouragement, acknowledging his courtesy and his "careful regard for the sensitiveness which is a peculiar feature of artists." It was a gracious speech, mentioning, to more loud applause, that the Queen had been a purchaser (as well as the oil by Homer Watson, Lorne had selected the painting "White Mountains" by Edson, and had commissioned O'Brien for a painting of Quebec City for Her Majesty). Napoléon Bourassa delivered an address in French on behalf of the "Province and nationality which I have the honour to represent." He too spoke passionately for the artists, who with almost no encouragement up until that time had nevertheless managed to carry the flame.

And so the Academy was launched.

It was ten days later when Lorne was able to settle down to write of the event to his father. With typical British reserve he gave a low key summation of the time that in terms of general hope and high ideals among the artists, that for sheer emotional high may never have been surpassed in the history of Canadian art:

The Academy has turned out a great success, there being many very good pictures, and the whole country joining in praise of the initiative of such an institution.

Chapter Three

Early Years

According to popular myth artists are improvident, often whimsical innocents. Not so. On the contrary, they are often particularly down-to-earth if somewhat optimistic examples of humanity. They have to be or few would survive. In the best of times their daily living is entirely without security, and even in the case of the unusually gifted, subject to ebb and flow with the changing tides of "isms" and the mutability of public appreciation. Moreover, considering the constant levelling of the psyche in face of the drain on innermost resources, humility is never far from the surface (however well concealed), and as a group artists probably have more sense of social perspective than most. So that far from being bowled over by the unaccustomed attention in Ottawa, once the dust had settled the new Academicians dispersed quietly back to their studios and their own work. But with a difference, for now they had a new collective confidence.

The first two decades of the Academy's existence were enviable times in many ways. True, the base of support for the organization was tenuous—for years the annual government grant hovered around $2,000—but there was an excitement, an enthusiasm among the artists, a sense of cause. And issues were relatively simple. After all, who could seriously quarrel with a concerted attempt to raise the country's climate of aesthetic appreciation through general fervour in all matters relating to the arts? And the results were tangible. The exhibitions, for example, became established annual events open to all artists who cared to risk their work to the critical judgement of a jury of their peers. And year by year the scope of the exhibitions broadened with successful submissions coming regularly from new, young talent as well as from familiar, established names. Six years after the founding of the Academy the exhibition was back in Ottawa for the first time since 1880, and within that period the very fact of the Academy had stirred enough artistic adrenalin to result in 1886 in a major show composed entirely of Canadian works. Never again were loan paintings from private collections, previously considered necessary to buttress local standards, to be part of Academy exhibitions. And when that same year the Academy was invited to collaborate with the current Governor General, Lord Lansdowne, to prepare for Canadian participation in the Colonial and Indian Exhibition being held in London, England, an eminent British critic, R.A.M. Stevenson, wrote of the result:

When we have excluded from the exhibition the mass of work which is not art at all, we have more paintings to consider among the Canadians than in all the other sections put together.

The artists had surely come a long way in the ten years since the Philadelphia Centennial Exhibition, and their progress had been a step by step move towards maturity. After the initial tour de force at the Clarendon Hotel, plans had gone ahead to hold the second exhibition in Halifax. Again the exhibition was considered a resounding success. Unprecedented provincial attention was focused on the arts, which however superficial helped to make their significance available to a wider public and gave sanction to the rarefied concept of painting, sculpture, architecture and design as an important spiritual balance to everyday material life. In deference to Lorne's involvement, the entire main floor of the Nova Scotia Parliament Building was made available, right up to the anteroom of the Assembly itself. Lord Lorne was present at the opening and Maritime society out in force, with "American, French and British uniforms relieving the sombre array of black coats, and harmonizing with the rich dresses of the ladies." Much press coverage was devoted to the event and no Halegonian with any pretence to interest in cultural matters would have been unaffected by the Academy's visit.

At the more serious Annual Assembly next day the first Academician designer, J.W.H. Watts, was elected, a choice that was later disputed by the previous year's medal winner William Doughtie, on the grounds that Watts was really an architect. But Watts had in fact been appointed Associate in the designer class. The Governor General's award for design was again offered, this time "for the best application of any Canadian plant, flower, or leaf to industrial design," and was won by A.H. Howard, an accomplished manuscript illuminator and designer of furniture and fabrics.

Meanwhile the underpinnings of the Society, the housekeeping, was taken care of by the Council. During the first year there had been considerable attention to adjusting the Constitution to actual circumstance. The frailty of women, for instance, was taken into account:

Women shall be eligible for membership in the Royal Canadian Academy, but shall not be required to attend business meetings nor will their names be placed upon the list of rotation for the Council.

The one woman, Charlotte Schreiber, whose stature as an accomplished painter had qualified her for membership, seems by no means to have been a shrinking violet, although she may conceivably have preferred to devote her time to painting rather than committee meetings. Daughter of an English clergyman, she had come out to Canada as a bride in 1875. Her maternal grandfather had been a cousin of Sir Isaac Brock, and doubtless there was a legacy of Canadian lore within the family. As a young woman she had studied art in London under a painter noted for portraits and historical works, and her own work very much reflected this early training, and while highly competent, aroused the respect rather than the enthusiasm of her new colleagues in Toronto. She lived for a time in the suburban village of Deer Park and quickly gained a reputation as an eccentric among her neighbours, one of whom described her as "that pretty Mrs. Schreiber who rides in a haywagon and paints!" She and her husband later built a house in the seclusion of the countryside, on the banks of the Credit River, where she painted diligently for a number of years, exhibiting regularly in both the OSA and the Academy shows. But when her husband died in the late nineties, she returned to England and was almost completely lost from Canadian sight.

As for the other women artists in the early Academy, Mrs. Schreiber was joined in 1893 by both Mary Bell Eastlake and Mary Heister Reid, who were elected Associates. The former was born in Ontario, the latter in Pennsylvania. Both were married to artists, and were committed to lifelong application in their profession as painters. They were followed in 1895 by Laura Muntz, an immigrant girl who had grown up on a backwoods farm in Muskoka, and by Florence Carlyle, a product of the small Ontario town of Galt. By the time they reached the Academy all of these women were Paris trained, widely travelled, winners of awards for their work in international competition. They were by any way of judging, highly motivated, dedicated and accomplished professionals. How they felt about the Academy's attitude to women as a protected species is not known, but chances are they found the ruling hilarious. It was a curious situation. As painters, in the abstract sense, they were welcomed and respected by their male counterparts. Their works made their way on their own merit into the exhibitions, and once there held their own. It was the idea of their presence in the living flesh within the inner sanctum of traditionally male enclaves, such as the committee room, that was difficult to assimilate. In all events, although the restricting clause was dropped

when the Constitution was revamped in 1913, the incipient danger posed no real threat, since a second woman, Marion Long, was not elected full Academician until 1933.

Other housekeeping matters of early Councils were less equivocal. The Queen was petitioned for permission to use the prefix "Royal," and on June 22, 1880, Lord Kimberly (the British Colonial Secretary) conveyed to Lorne the Queen's wish that "...the prayer of the memorial be acceded to." And two years later on May 17, 1882, the Royal Canadian Academy of Arts was officially incorporated by an act of Parliament.

The painter William Revell designed the Academy Membership Diploma. The Diploma was approved within the first year, but due to organizational priorities it was not actually available until 1883. Inadvertently the delay offered a welcome face-saver to the Council. Several Charter members had been slow in presenting their Diploma pictures and as time passed a small core of procrastinators remained. Council was placed in the sensitive and embarrassing position, since the presentation and acceptance of a Diploma Work was prerequisite to membership, of enforcing a motion requiring delinquents to fall back to Associate status and await elevation through the normal elective channel. But because the delinquents included none other than the beloved Jacobi and the ailing Bell-Smith (senior), the Council was most reluctant to press the issue. As the Membership Diplomas at last materialized, forcing the Council to action, to everyone's relief Jacobi was finally able to enter an unsold picture in that year's exhibition. It was forthwith accepted as his Diploma Work. Sadly, Bell-Smith died that same year, leaving only Theodore Berthon, the society portrait painter, and Montreal architect W.T. Thomas as the only unqualified members.

Conspicuous by her absence during this period was the Princess Louise, who had returned to England in the spring of 1880 for treatment of her injured ear. A year passed and inevitably the press drew attention to the unusual length of her stay. Another year slid by and there were persistent rumours of a royal rift over the Princess' refusal to return to Canada. However, return she did in the early summer of 1882, and aside from a further extended absence during a sojourn in Bermuda, throughout the final year of her husband's tenure she was exemplary in her apparent warmth of interest in Canadian affairs. The press however gave up with some reluctance. In one last flicker of outlandish speculation, the Ottawa *Free Press* reported a story that was going the rounds to the effect that the Princess Louise had joined the Roman Catholic Church, scarcely a popular move for a member of the British Royal Family. Snorted the Toronto *Telegram* in reply, "The next thing we will probably hear is that the Marquis of Lorne has joined a baseball club!"

The Academy's position throughout was to take no notice of what must have been a puzzle of considerable public interest. (The Queen's correspondence later revealed that indeed there had been a problem based on an aversion that Louise had developed for her husband—the Queen attributed it to the shock of the accident). Not even Harris mentioned the matter in his letters home. For whatever the artists may have speculated privately, the Princess was after all an official patron. And absent or not, from the beginning she had appeared to hold the Academy in real affection. Each year, as a token of her support that carried great weight with the public, she had gone out of her way to submit several of her own paintings for the exhibitions. When, in 1930, the Academy presented her at Kensington Palace with an illuminated scroll to mark the founding fifty years earlier, she responded in a letter of informal and unaffected friendliness.

The exhibition of 1883 was Lorne's last official Academy function. His term drawing to a close, he was due to leave for England in October of that year. In an effort to convey their joint esteem, the Academy and the OSA decided to combine their annual shows in Toronto in May. Lorne, with Louise recently returned from Bermuda, did the honours at the opening. It was a large and handsome show, a fitting way to underline the gratitude of the artists to the man who had gone so far beyond the normal call of his position to lend prestige and moral support, even donating considerable sums of money, through prizes, purchases and outright donations to their cause. Although there were certainly to be generous and important supporters of Canadian art in the future, Lorne is set apart from all the rest in that he was blessed with a large enough spirit to be able to look with equanimity on the often capricious behaviour of artists caught in the frustrations of their difficult profession. A rare bird indeed among art patrons, who when face to face with rampant sensitivity, not only did not fly for the nearest cover, but was able to maintain his trust in the essential integrity of the artists and to allow them a full voice in their own affairs.

The Academy's growing prestige as an authoritative voice in the arts was brought into unexpected focus at this time during a trip O'Brien made to Ottawa to negotiate for some valuable loan pictures for the 1883 show. The paintings, as it turned out, were not available. But he came upon something much more exciting. Arriving in Ottawa he found talk of the government commissioning a large historical painting of the Confederation Conference, with the young Robert Harris as the artist under consideration. It was evident that in order to pass the debate in the House of Commons the proposal needed all possible backing. O'Brien was advised that a brief from the Academy would carry considerable weight with the government. With no time to spare, without even an opportunity to ask for authorization from Council, he immediately set about drafting a suitable document of support. It was presented by a deputation of members from both sides of the House. The resolution passed, with $4,000 granted for the purpose, and the commission was entrusted to Harris. The finished painting was shown at the Academy exhibition in 1884, and was hailed as a breakthrough from the tired tradition of woodenly posed figures. "The freedom and boldness with which the painting is handled are something new in the portraiture of this country," extolled the Montreal *Gazette*. The painting of course became even more celebrated when it was lost in the fire that razed the Parliament Buildings in 1916.

Of the Academy's three original objectives, undoubtedly the most baffling to the artists was their effort to establish the National Gallery as a living entity. As Lorne had earlier explained to the Prime Minister, "...members elected [to the Academy] will be required to give a Diploma Work, which will be presented to the country. In this way we shall start a National Gallery at Ottawa." All literature related to the founding reflected enthusiastic acceptance of this course, and it was re-affirmed legally at the time of incorporation in 1882. But there matters rested. Once a reality, the National Gallery would appear to have been a distinct embarrassment to succeeding waves of officialdom.

Had Lorne been a year or so longer in Canada, perhaps he might have succeeded in encouraging more generous government commitment. But with him, and with the elusive Princess, departed a great deal of the allure of the arts within official circles. Granted the government had other grave concerns—railroads to build across the country, rebellions to monitor in Manitoba—and support of a national repository for art was well towards the bottom of its list of priorities. The incoming Governor General, Lord Lansdowne, was sympathetically disposed towards Academy aspirations, but he did not have the same depth of interest as his predecessor. In Harris' words, "...a capital man to get on with though I don't say his taste equals his liking for art." His successor, Lord Stanley, Harris found even less promising: "...he is very genial and amiable, but when you have said that, it is all there is to be said about him."

Short of a miracle, at this stage of Canada's development, without a strong voice lobbying from some privileged position, there was no hope for more than perfunctory support for the enterprise or for the arts on any level. And it was to be 1907 before that cultivated and enlightened dynamo, Byron E. Walker, President of the Bank of Commerce and financial mentor to Robert Borden, leader of the Conservative Party, quietly took matters in hand.

In the intervening years the Academy was left to batter away with no authority and very little ammunition, on a system that was tuned to oiling the machinery of material prosperity. To be sure, their neglected offspring was placed under the wing of the Minister of Public Works and assigned a miniscule budget of $1,500 a year. Space was given to house the collection in the old Supreme Court building at the foot of Bank Street, but in 1887 it was removed to the Department of Fisheries on O'Connor Street, where it shared premises with a fish hatchery (in the basement) and a marine display. The second floor of the Fisheries Building was home to the National Gallery for twenty-six years. The paradox had its brighter side. The public enjoyed the marine display, and often tarried for a look upstairs as well. When the Fisheries exhibit was away in Chicago for the Columbian Exposition in 1893, the number of visitors to the National Gallery was recorded to have dropped significantly. Small wonder that as a crowd pleaser it was regarded as an unprofitable political investment.

Somewhere along the way the Academy's J.W.H. Watts, who by virtue of being head draughtsman in the office of the Chief Architect, was an employee of the Department of Public Works, was appointed to the ancillary position of custodian of the National Gallery. But he was given no mandate other than to keep the doors open. The collection grew modestly, thanks to the continuing deposit of Diploma Works and through an Academy program to purchase works from their own exhibitions for donation to the Gallery, as well as through gifts from a few private individuals. From time to time the Academy made concerted attempts to lobby for proper facilities, but until well into the first decade of the new century the National Gallery was virtually neglected by one government after another.

Fortunately the Academy fared better with its Life Classes, although they were not to be the ambitious "Schools of Art and Design" envisaged by Lorne. There was no real call for them. The country could after all absorb only a limited number of trained designers. And as for art schools, for some time the OSA had been making a concerted attempt to establish a bona fide program in Toronto, and regular art classes had long been a part of the Art Association's operation in Montreal. For the Academy to attempt to move in and undercut immediate colleagues in a field of both limited support and application was unthinkable. Their approach was to work with the existing system and to offer the option of higher education within that framework.

It was in this area of art instruction that the Academy most resembled its progenitors of some four hundred years earlier in Renaissance Italy. The classes in Ottawa, Montreal, Toronto—later in Hamilton, Winnipeg and Halifax—had precious little in common with the highly structured schools that had developed in Europe and Britain. But they did resemble those small studio academies that had earlier sprouted throughout Italy to fill a local need, and which from the time the Carraci brothers formed their Academy in Bologna, had held drawing from life as the core of Academy principles.

Life drawing it was. There were no such classes being held in Canada in 1880, and they were badly needed. Almost in the same sense that the mastery of musical scales is the backbone of the true musician, is the honing of powers of observation and the sharpening of the instinctive sense of discipline in the serious artists, through drawing from life. The Academy set about filling this gap.

It was a labour of love. Those members whose background and training fitted them to instruct such classes, gave their time on a regular basis, without pay, over a duration of nearly seventy years. After a tentative start in Ottawa at the time of the first meeting of Council, when $100 was voted to the newly formed Ottawa School of Art for advanced drawing classes, a workable system was developed that could be plugged in with simple economy to local situations as they developed. The procedure was breathtakingly simple and consisted of small grants being made from Academy funds to local committees of Academicians, to be applied as they saw fit towards "higher art education" in their own areas. The grants were used to defray expenses for model, space, light, heat, with tuition provided free to students who were judged capable and far enough advanced to study from the nude. Usually the money was put to use in collaboration with an existing institution, but this was a matter for yearly review, and in isolated cases the classes took place in the studio of one of the instructors.

The key of course was the quality of the instructors and in the early years it was very high indeed. George Reid and William Cruikshank for instance in Toronto, Robert Harris and later William Brymner in Montreal. Between them they stirred the embers of several generations of aspiring artists and influenced scores of fledgling designers and illustrators who came to the classes to sharpen their artistic wits.

In retrospect the concept seems modest and economical to an extreme. But it was right for the times and it worked. The Life Classes offered the classic key to technical facility and gave to gifted students a first glimpse of the cyclical rhythm and order that are the understructure, the bones of all great art. As the years passed A.Y. Jackson was one earnest young artist to catch a whiff of the flame in the Montreal classes conducted by William Brymner. Some fifteen years later, a radical painter in full stride, Jackson himself surfaced as an instructor in the Toronto classes. And so the wheel turned.

But of all the issues that were to concern the artists of the Academy, the one that was closest to them was the exhibitions. Exposure, possible sales, direct means of raising standards. They were the lifeline. Few artists sold with the easy facility of Jacobi in his late years. Sculptors were so straitened that one year Council waived their fees, "in view of the small encouragement given in Canada to sculptors." The Academy exhibitions were the artists' most important forum.

Inevitably they were of greater significance to the painters and sculptors than to the architects and designers, whose professions were by nature made more feasible through a built-in commercial base. And while it was one thing

41

for Thomas Fuller to show a pleasant architectural rendering of a design for the main Parliament Building, it was quite another for Lucius O'Brien that same year, 1882, to show his thundering canvas, "Kakabeka Falls, Kamanistiquia River." Or in 1890 to hang the water colour drawing of a design for the Temple Building in Montreal, by Alexander F. Dunlop (later first President of the Royal Architectural Institute of Canada) in the same show with George Reid's "Mortgaging of the Homestead," an enormous and powerful narrative genre painting that was one of Reid's greatest efforts. Obviously in each case the one was a pale reflection, a bare reminder of the real thing. *The other was very much the real thing.* While the architects (after all the early interest, only four designers were elected by 1900) valued membership and gave depth and often direction to the Academy, in a practical sense the exhibitions were peripheral to their profession. On the other hand, they were integral to the painters and sculptors. Clearly, painting and sculpture were the heart and soul of the exhibitions, and the exhibitions were the Academy's glory.

Year after year—ninety-one to be exact—the shows alternated between Montreal, Toronto and Ottawa, with very occasional forays to outlying centres. Unfortunately the very sparse annual grant never allowed development of the original concept to hold the exhibitions "every year in a different city of the Dominion." After the over-stimulation of the Lorne years, even Ottawa was felt to be a little remote for a successful show. Harris did not mince words when the exhibition was

diverted there from Montreal to avoid the 1886 smallpox epidemic. "Ottawa is empty, and it is like burying the pictures." And there is no doubt that the artists did want the work to be seen.

Certainly it was not financial gain that prompted artists to devote weeks, sometimes months of their time each year preparing the best work they could offer for the Academy exhibitions. For contrary to public perception which, after attendance at an exhibition thronged with admirers and lauded by the press, assumed an accompanying financial advantage for the artists, reality was far less romantic. "This is the best exhibition the Academy has yet made, and it is to be hoped that it would receive that appreciative attention and encouragement which it certainly deserves," praised the Montreal *Gazette* in 1890. But unlike the Royal Academy shows in England where, incredibly, the gate receipts alone formed the backbone of that Society's financial security, and where for years the market at least for academic works had almost exceeded the supply, the Canadian shows were far from a major source of revenue. By 1930 the highest commissions on sales ever realized by the Academy from an annual exhibition had been $300—and that had been an exceptional high. To be sure, there was always great attendance. In covering the opening of the twenty-third exhibition the Montreal *Star* devoted several columns to minute descriptions of the chiffons and laces of those many ladies who were "...among the wearers of handsome gowns." But sales were minimal.

No, the artists' motivation was something altogether more integral to both their common cause and to their development as individuals, and was a spinoff of the philosophy behind the Academy. O'Brien probably spoke for several generations of artists when he addressed the opening of the fifth exhibition in Montreal:

The prerequisite for all successful art work is the personal intercourse and association of those engaged in it. All great and enduring art movements have been progressive and cumulative, each individual artist adding his quota of suggestion or accomplishment to what has been done or is doing around him. His thought and imagination, to be fruitful, must be of the thought and time in which he lives, stimulated and fed by the heritage of the past.

The exhibitions then, offered the artists peer support, cross pollination, and communication with the world. It is all very well for the human soul to call in the wilderness, but there are few spirits hardy enough not to need a human response. And strangely enough, for the artist the approbation of his peers had always been far more important than the praise of a gallery full of patrons in velvets and brocades, and the exhibition openings drew painters, sculptors and architects together with the best of their work. Wonderful to meet, to speak the same dialect without reservation, to warm to a few words of sincere praise from a colleague. Even more, respect for himself is the key to an artist's continuing growth, and the exhibitions created a unique situation where an individual could pit his work, for his own information, against a backdrop larger than the limitations of his own immediate circle and in context with the flow of the times. The resulting revelations might send him hurtling back to the easel or workbench, but it was a stimulus that could only lead to renewed assault on the private forests obscuring his vision.

For a great many years the three important showcases for artists remained the open-juried spring exhibition sponsored by the Art Association of Montreal, and those of the OSA and the RCA. The AAM, in contrast to the other two, was in essence an art gallery with its affairs conducted by a board of laymen. Such boards have traditionally found artists uncomfortable collaborators—they will insist on the relevance of their views in relation to art—and interestingly, from very early on the AAM showed signs of the classic, defensive position that seventy-five years later was to almost totally isolate artists from organizations which in many cases they themselves had helped to found. "It would be wiser not to have artists on the board," the AAM prevaricated when in 1883 the inestimable Napoléon Bourassa was proposed as one of their number, "as in such cases there is always a tendency to jealousy." At the same time succeeding boards were assuredly devoted to the promotion and support of the arts, but from the premise of public interest rather than of the artist.

The OSA and the RCA on the other hand (both of whose internal squabbles did much to reinforce the uneasy institutional attitude) were purely and simply organizations of artists, and their record of inter-relationship was one of respect and reciprocal goodwill. Many painters and sculptors who were elected to the Academy had come up from the ranks of the OSA, whose less cautious exhibitions were usually the first to show the work of new artists. But because the Academy exhibition standards were higher and their base broader than the other venues, they became the artists' ultimate measuring stick. Young people who

RCA Crest designed by A.H. Howard in 1895, and used for many years on Academy exhibition catalogues.

had wet their feet at the shows of the OSA and the AAM, then set their sights on those of the Academy. If their work passed the jury it was shown alongside the best in the country, and to note the appearance of this emerging talent is to trace the history of Canadian art.

From the first the Academy record when under international scrutiny was excellent. The 1886 Colonial and Indian Exhibition in the Royal Albert Hall in London, England, was their first challenge. On invitation from Lord Lansdowne the Academy appointed Homer Watson and Robert Harris to serve on the selection committee under His Excellency, and they began by choosing a core of work from the current RCA show. Their old friend Lord Lorne was on hand on the London side to supervise the installation and promotion of the Canadian display—and as in old times the Dominion government handsomely footed the bill without a murmur. The Canadians were a considerable hit, so that it was perhaps an over-anxious attack of paternalism that prompted Sir Charles Tupper, Canadian Commissioner to the Exhibition, to arrange for a well-known professor from the Royal Academy School, J.E. Hodgson, RA, to review the Canadian section for the edification and instruction of the artists. Actually Professor Hodgson went out of his way to be pleasant in his written report, especially commending L.R. O'Brien as a very considerable and accomplished artist, and speaking highly of John A. Fraser, F.M. Bell-Smith, Paul Peel, Homer Watson, Allan Edson, William Brymner and Robert Harris. A little dismayed however to find some of the Canadians unduly touched by French Academic thought

National Gallery, 1900, photographer unknown. Public Archives Canada, Ottawa.

—at the time considered mannered and sentimental in English circles—he ended on the romantic note that as pioneers in a new world "still struggling to subdue her untamed forces...I should like to see Canadian art Canadian to the backbone." It was a chord that held tremendous appeal for the authorities and was to resurrect itself some twenty years later as the major philosophy underlying official support.

The Chicago World's Fair in 1893 was the second international confrontation and it too was remarkably successful. On a miniscule budget Robert Harris, by now a man with a reputation for getting things done, assembled a show that filled two galleries in the Fair's Fine Arts Building. The work had been chosen directly from that year's RCA and OSA exhibitions, and although the display was limited because of lack of funds to transport the larger works, the Canadians nevertheless carried off a number of awards in international competition. Gold medals went to George Reid, Horatio Walker, Robert Harris, C.V. Ede and S.B. Holden (Ede and Holden were not Academy members), with a silver medal to the young Florence Carlyle.

At home, the ninth annual exhibition stands out as distinct from the rest. Once again the Academy and the OSA joined forces, this time at the curious location of the Granite skating rink in Toronto. The story dated back several years.

Frustrated by inadequate space available for their exhibitions, particularly in light of the lukewarm success of the National Gallery in Ottawa, the members decided to strike out on their own and to build an Academy gallery in Toronto. This was in 1884. A resolution was passed authorizing Academicians in the area to collect subscriptions for the cause, and the government actually allowed them $500 in that year's budget as seed money. Through careful management a residue had built up in the treasury from commissions on works sold at exhibitions, from membership fees and from modest sums donated by the honorary members. By 1886, when a suitable building lot came to their attention at the corner of Wilton Avenue and Victoria Street, Council was able to scrape together $3,000 to pay half of the asking price on the spot, with the balance taken out in a mortgage.

The following year, encouraged by reports of a successful money-raising venture in Montreal, plans went ahead to hold an Art Fair to help fund the building of a gallery on the lot. A distinct gamble involving not only enormous effort on the part of members, but also a cash outlay of $1,000 towards expenses. The OSA, who shared the Academy's enthusiasm for an artist-run gallery — and indeed there was a considerable overlap in membership — gave their support by putting their weight behind a strong, joint annual show, to which the Fair was to be appended. In May of 1888 the Granite rink was engaged for the event and the artists threw themselves into an all-out effort. The rink was transformed into an old English town, with booths selling various artistic bric-a-brac. Some three hundred ladies, gentlemen and children were enlisted to take part in musical and dramatic recreations of Elizabethan entertainments. But although public admiration ran high the practical result left much to be desired. In the words of the committee report:

As a matter of artistic presentation, the fair was most successful, but the cost of fitting up so large a space, and the enormous expenses connected with the entertainments were so heavy as to absorb most of the returns.

In the end, after all their effort, which must have taken a serious toll of artists' working time, a profit of $451.12 was deposited to the Building Fund. Resisting a further OSA proposition involving a joint stock venture, with the Academy throwing in the lot as collateral, gradually visions of a gallery faded from view as the artists resigned themselves to their gypsy existence until more fortuitous times. The lot itself was sold in 1907 at a profit of $3,000.

And then there were the Dinners. The same year as the successful failure at the Granite rink, an important institution was introduced into Academy tradition. "In view of the fact that the members of this Academy come together only once a year...it is desirable that the members and associates of the Academy meet during the times of Exhibitions at a social occasion known as the Academy Dinner...." The Dinners proved to be an unqualified triumph and contrary to dry, minuted references, have tended to be among the more colourful formal gatherings of Canadians right up until the present day.

Apart from the heavy responsibilities of exhibitions, classes, and building programs, as time passed internal changes gradually took place within the Academy. As early as 1885 Napoléon Bourassa had withdrawn from active professional life, and in keeping with that stance, stepped down from the Vice Presidency of the Academy. He spent the last twenty-five years of his life in virtual retirement. And by the end of the first decade both William Cresswell and Allan Edson were dead. John Fraser, continuing obdurate, was in self-imposed exile in New York. When O'Brien moved aside from the Presidency in 1890, there was already a new wave of confident, Paris-trained artists sitting on the Academy's back benches. William Brymner, Franklin Brownell, George Reid, Paul Peel, Percy Woodcock, F. McGillivray Knowles, Wyly Grier. All had been emerging painters or still art students at the time the Academy was founded, and all had managed to get themselves to Paris for their final years of study (Peel actually lived there although he had exhibited with the Academy since 1881). Naturally as a group their work was highly redolent of the romantic high realism of the French Academic school. Most were figure painters, and it was to be yet another generation before they in turn would be overtaken by new concepts in landscape painting. Reid and Peel became perhaps the foremost Canadians in the popular field of narrative genre — the large, technically superb canvases depicting whole scenes from everyday life which a later age would label sentimental, but which were painted with a patent honesty that almost defied the categorization. Grier was still a student at the Slade School of Art in London at the time of the Clarendon Hotel exhibition, but surfaced within a few years as one of the country's finest portrait painters.

They were a gifted lot, their handsome works showing up with impressive regularity in the open-juried shows of the Paris Salon and of London's Royal Academy. But curiously, except perhaps for Brymner who at least recognized the significance of the phenomenon even though it was not his own form of expression, after their years in Paris these artists were almost totally unsinged by the brushfires of Impressionism that for some time had been licking at the foundations of the French Academic fortress.

There were, of course, exceptions. Maurice Cullen, the salty Newfoundlander who became renowned as the painter of pulsing, evocative Quebec snow scenes (and who in later years confounded a prominent Montreal surgeon who was offensive as a dictatorial fellow member of a painting jury, by politely inquiring when the doctor was called away to perform an emergency operation, "And may I help you operate?"). J. W. Morrice, the Osgoode Hall law graduate turned brilliant painter, whose first professional encouragement came when a picture was accepted in the 1884 Academy exhibition, and who went on to carve an international niche for himself as a glowing Impressionist painter — and as a cultivated alcoholic habitué of Parisian cafés. Aurèle de Foy Suzor-Coté, the young Quebecer from Arthabaska who went to Paris to study singing and painting, and opting for the latter eventually returned home to paint shimmering canvases of the countryside around his native village. But these were isolated cases. The general and popular trend was still very much in the classical wake.

Completely outnumbered but nevertheless holding their own with the painters and architects in the affairs of the Academy, were two lone sculptors. The one Charter sculptor, François van Luppen, had returned to his homeland in Belgium by the mid-eighties, leaving the field to Louis Philippe Hébert and Hamilton Plantagenet MacCarthy. Hébert was a former Quebec farm boy whose natural talent led him to eventual apprenticeship in the studio of Napoléon Bourassa, before moving on for academic study of sculpture in Paris. MacCarthy arrived in Toronto from London,

England, in 1885, already an established portrait sculptor with busts of Queen Victoria and King Leopold of Belgium to his credit. Until after the turn of the century these two would appear to have had no serious competition, and in fact when the Academy's fifty year history was written in 1934, records showed that during that entire period only nine sculptors had reached the rank of full Academician. Clearly, sculpture was not an overcrowded profession.

There was good reason. The buying public had had literally no exposure to smaller studio works and felt not the slightest need of them — if they were purchasing Canadian art at all they would choose a painting. Portrait busts and statues were in a rather different category as were historical monuments, since there was a definite official endorsement of the need to pinpoint historical achievement through the erection of monuments to the past and to commend current dignitaries to the future in the form of portrait busts and statues. But despite the high visibility of such public works, pleasant enough to the artists' vanity, because of the disproportionate production costs involved in for instance casting and transportation, very little money remained in the pocket of the artists at the completion of a job. So that although by the physical evidence there would appear to have been a great deal of commissioned work on the go — between them Hébert and MacCarthy were responsible for creating numerous public sculptures scattered from Ontario to Annapolis Royal in Nova Scotia — the total monetary rewards would have been no more than enough to uneasily support a handful of sculptors. Consequently, only those with a most determined calling ventured into the field.

Meanwhile the 1890s were dominated by the vigorous young figure painters. It was natural under the circumstances that when the Academy Presidency became vacant, they would look to the now senior man in their own camp, Robert Harris, to assume responsibility.

Harris, however, was not so easily pinned down. He was actually elected President of the Academy at the 1890 Annual Meeting, but he resisted. "It was not an easy matter, as they were determined to make me take the office." But he had not been well and work pressure was building up as portrait commissions were beginning to flood in his direction, and he was not a man to take on responsibility that he could not honour. He turned down the Presidency. A second vote was taken and somewhat in the role of painter emeritus, the elderly Otto Jacobi was elected in his place. Wrote Harris, delighted, "I don't think anything in his eighty years can have pleased him more. He has the studio next to mine [they were both living in Montreal] and his gratification seems to pervade the building."

Jacobi held the fort for three years, until in 1893, still with reservations, Harris at last agreed to take over. He served for thirteen years, the longest term of any President throughout the Academy's history.

By any measure Harris was a remarkable man, a curious mixture of reticence and witty charm — and the absolute antithesis of the bohemian artist. He was forty-four years of age when he was prodded into office, still young as artists go, and a self-made man who had wrenched his living as a painter since early manhood. Born in the Vale of Conway, North Wales, he had come out to Prince

Edward Island as a child of seven. His family had been near-gentry fallen on difficult times, and while not highly cultured, still they were people who brought with them an awareness of the enriching value of music, books and painting, and this was always part of their home.

Thrift was a household word during his boyhood in Charlottetown, with the milk and honey of the new country more difficult to come by than anticipated by the elder Harris, who tried through various ill-fated schemes to provide for his family as befitted their station. But if comforts were few, family ties were warm and somehow all of the children were soundly educated. And of the five, two were to surface in the fine arts. Robert as perhaps the most celebrated portrait painter of his day, with his younger brother William as a gifted but dreamy architect who became an Associate member of the Academy.

Robert made his own way with only sporadic financial help from home from the time he was fifteen years old. He started working life as assistant to a land surveyor, for whom he also kept the books. But it was a means to an end as he had long before been touched by the muse, and spent most of his spare moments drawing. By the time he was eighteen he managed to finance a trip to England where for the first time he saw real art. He wrote his mother about the National Gallery in London, "Every place grows pale, poor and small beside it." He never looked back. Study in Boston, London, Paris and Italy. It was a long and unrelenting struggle over the years which led to his election as Academy President. And when the responsibility came to him it was not because it was an honour he had sought, but because it was recognized that throughout his career he had thrown every ounce of energy into developing his painting and along the way had acquired practical, organizational talents that made him the most logical choice on the scene.

The remaining years before the turn of the century were ones of consolidation for the Academy. Times were not easy for the artists. On the commercial market Canadian art was moving very slowly. European works, aside from portraits, were still considered de rigueur among the collectors, and of course the hard core buying class was actually very small. William Raphael, back living in Montreal, was quoted in the press as saying that "Without teaching no local artist could live here. If he depended on the sale of his pictures he would starve." The same could have been said of Toronto. So that it was more important than ever for the art societies to hold their ground. And if it had been O'Brien's special gift to be able to unite artists in an awareness of their own worth and capabilities, it was Harris who set that vision firmly on a workable modern base that could resist the erosion and frustrations of difficult times.

As the century closed, one by one the old landscape painters, the founders of the Academy, slipped from view. Daniel Fowler died in 1894, James Griffiths in '96, John Fraser in '98. Jacobi, old and almost blind, his "olt wife" dead, left to spend his few remaining years with a daughter in North Dakota. And respected to the last, a graceful, elegant presence of great integrity, Lucius O'Brien died in the last few days of December, 1899.

It was the end of an era.

William Raphael
Behind Bonsecours Market, Montreal
Oil on canvas 26¹/₂″ x 43″
National Gallery of Canada

Allan Edson
**Mount Orford and the Owls Head
from Lake Memphremagog**
Oil on canvas 36″ x 60″
National Gallery of Canada

Daniel Fowler
Hollyhocks
Water colour 27″ x 18¹/₂″
National Gallery of Canada

Lucius O'Brien
Toronto from the Marsh
Water colour 13½″ x 20½″
Collection Mr. and Mrs. J. A. Grant,
Shanty Bay, Ontario

J. A. Fraser
A Shot in the Dawn, Lake Scugog
Oil on canvas 16″ x 30″
National Gallery of Canada

Henry Sandham
On an Eastern Salmon Stream
Oil on canvas 30″ x 39″
National Gallery of Canada

William Cresswell
Landscape with Sheep
Oil on canvas 23³/₄″ x 35³/₄″
Art Gallery of Ontario

O. R. Jacobi
A Forest Stream
Water colour 22″ x 24¹³/₁₆″
National Gallery of Canada

L. R. O'Brien
Sunrise on the Saguenay
Oil on canvas 34¹/₂″ x 49¹/₂″
RCA Diploma picture, deposited 1880
National Gallery of Canada

Allan Edson
Trout Stream in the Forest
Oil on canvas 23½" x 18¼"
RCA Diploma picture, deposited 1880
National Gallery of Canada

W. G. Storm
Toronto University
Water colour 24″ x 48¹/₂″
RCA Diploma picture, deposited 1880
National Gallery of Canada

John A. Fraser
Laurentian Splendor
Oil on canvas 19¹/₄″ x 37¹/₂″
RCA Diploma picture, deposited 1880
National Gallery of Canada

Daniel Fowler
Dead Game
Water colour on paper 19″ x 27¹/₄″
Exhibited RCA 1880
Art Gallery of Ontario

William Raphael
**Indian Encampment on the
Lower St. Lawrence**
Oil on canvas 23¹/₄″ x 41¹/₄″
RCA Diploma picture, deposited 1880
National Gallery of Canada

Otto Jacobi
Falls of Ste. Anne, Quebec
Oil on canvas 30″ x 23⅛″
Exhibited RCA, Montreal 1880
Art Gallery of Ontario

Charlotte Schreiber
The Croppy Boy
Oil on canvas 35½″ x 30″
RCA Diploma picture, deposited 1880
National Gallery of Canada

L. R. O'Brien
Kakabeka Falls, Kamanistiquia River
Oil on canvas 32½″ x 48″
Exhibited RCA 1882
National Gallery of Canada

Homer Watson
On the Grand River at Doon
Oil on canvas 23⁷/₈″ x 36″
Exhibited RCA 1881
National Gallery of Canada

Thomas Fuller
Parliament Buildings, Ottawa
Drawing, pen and water colour
RCA Diploma work, deposited 1883
National Gallery of Canada

Robert Harris
A Meeting of the School Trustees
Oil on canvas 39¼″ x 48½″
Exhibited RCA 1886
National Gallery of Canada

William Brymner
A Wreath of Flowers
Oil on canvas 47¼″ x 55″
RCA Diploma picture, deposited 1886
National Gallery of Canada

G. A. Reid
Mortgaging the Homestead
Oil on canvas 50½″ x 83½″
RCA Diploma picture, deposited 1891
National Gallery of Canada

Hamilton MacCarthy
Portrait Bust of L. R. O'Brien
Terra cotta 24¹/₄″ high
RCA Diploma sculpture, deposited 1892
National Gallery of Canada

William Cruikshank
Breaking a Road
Oil on canvas 35″ x 68″
Exhibited RCA 1894
National Gallery of Canada

Robert Harris
Harmony
Oil on panel 12″ x 9³/₄″
Exhibited RCA 1893
National Gallery of Canada

Paul Peel
A Venetian Bather
Oil on canvas 61$\frac{1}{2}$" x 44$\frac{1}{2}$"
Exhibited RCA 1893, Columbian
Exhibition 1893
National Gallery of Canada

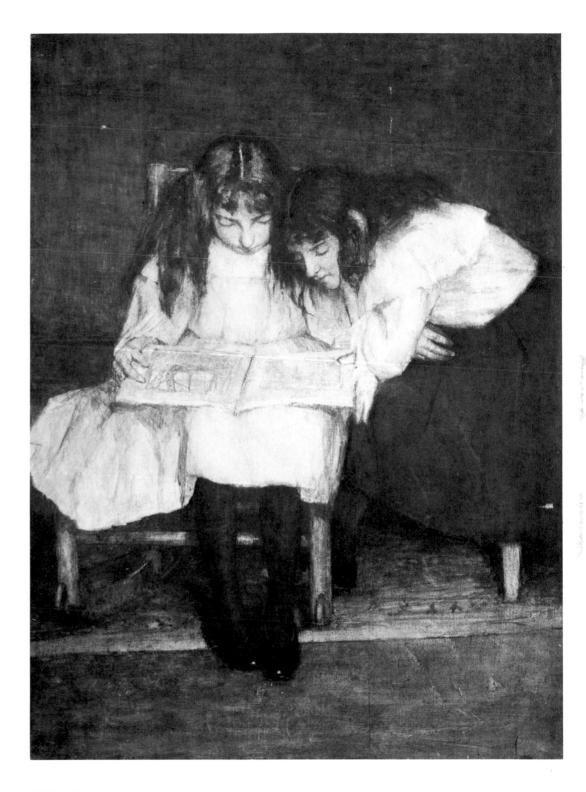

William Brymner
Two Girls Reading
Water colour on linen 40$\frac{1}{2}$″ x 29$\frac{1}{4}$″
Exhibited RCA 1898
National Gallery of Canada

George Reid
The Rye Field
Oil on canvas 17¹⁵/₁₆″ x 24″
Exhibited RCA 1899
Art Gallery of Ontario

Alexander C. Hutchison
Design for McGill University, Montreal
Drawing 24⁷/₈″ x 59″
RCA Diploma work, deposited 1882
National Gallery of Canada

J.W.H. Watts
Design for a Staircase
Pen drawing
RCA Diploma work, deposited 1882
National Gallery of Canada

Chapter Four

Parting of the Ways

Recognition beyond their own borders. A lively developing art scene at home. Masters in their own house. After twenty years of operation the Academy had much to its credit. But almost from the beginning two unforeseen and curiously dependent factors acted as a natural brake on the organization's apparent potential. First, at the core was the inherent absolute that an artist's work is the centre of his being, and therefore his first loyalty. It must be so or neither he nor his work has validity. Secondly, as a matter of course, when faced with ongoing institutional challenges the Academy found itself in direct conflict of interest with the mandate of its individual members: to paint, to sculpt, to design. Thus the kind of consistent political maneuvering and power courting necessary to coerce an unwilling government to more than marginal support of the National Gallery, for instance, would have sapped the artists' whole creative drive. They could not spare the energy. Inevitably, when the time was ripe for cultural expansion the initiative was taken from the artists by influences outside the creative field, leaving the artists in a state of indignant shock.

But the shadow crept over slowly, and certainly in 1900 the implications were only barely discernible, like faintest thunderheads on the horizon. Opportunities unfolded as before and were met with energy and imagination.

Exhibitions remained the central thrust. Here the Academicians were on their own ground—although on the lighter side, according to a columnist who covered the opening of the twenty-first annual exhibition in Ottawa they lacked sartorial sophistication. To begin with Harris, who had a basic antipathy for official occasions, at that particular opening mumbled through a great many pages of manuscript in a voice so low that only those near the dais had any idea what he was saying. And then Lord Minto, who had been appointed Governor General two years earlier, addressed the gathering, "...loud and clear, and though it may have been very much what he said last year when he opened the gallery at Montreal, it was worth hearing again." His message according to the Ottawa *Citizen*, advocated a "Canadian" school of painting. Of the members themselves who flanked His Excellency at the dais, they were classed as "rather shaggy looking than otherwise, not at all like the dapper little artists with pointed beards who frequent New York studios."

79

The Academicians may not have been at all displeased with the assessment. After all they were working men and women. And the following year they proved themselves once again at the Pan American Exposition in Buffalo by carrying off some twenty awards. Sir Wilfrid Laurier as Prime Minister was so impressed that when he filled in for Lord Minto at the opening ceremony of the annual exhibition in 1903, he urged the artists to press their case with his government for increased support. They did so. Harris as President set out a list of specific proposals, one of a number of superb briefs submitted by him during his term of office. For the first time mention was made of an advisory board that could be formed under government auspices to oversee regular purchase of Canadian art from the yearly exhibitions. The government was urged, of course, to provide a legitimate National Gallery to house such purchases. And the inadequacy of the Academy's grant was once again strongly argued. The result? Absolutely no response. Action on an advisory council and the Gallery was still a number of years away — and the Academy grant remained anchored at $2,000 a year. No gain except in the sense of one more blow to the wall of official resistance.

But the artists scored again in 1904 at the Louisiana Purchase Exhibition in St. Louis, and this time after urgent petitioning they did have acceptable government funding. The organization of the Canadian fine art section of what was to be the greatest exhibition ever held in the western hemisphere, was to be Harris' swan song. True to form he carried it off with resounding success. Every detail right down to the packing of the works was handled with the highest professional precision. Even

the customs inspector who supervised the opening of the Canadian crates was impressed. "These are the best arranged things I've had, both as to lists and boxes and method and care, and couldn't be beat!"

The contents of the crates had been chosen with great care from that year's annual show in Montreal which as usual was open to non-Academicians. Very special arrangements had been made to assemble the work for the Academy's exhibition in the first place. Due to space limitations for the Canadians in St. Louis, only paintings could be considered, and commissioners had been appointed from the Academicians in Montreal, Toronto, and Ottawa to visit the studios in their area to discuss with each artist the choice of the finest and most representative of his works. These, along with other key paintings from private collections, including notable work by dead artists, were sent to Montreal to be part of the regular exhibition. The result was probably the finest showing of the Academy in the twenty-five years of its existence. Mileage was offered by the Society to any member from Quebec or Ontario who could travel to Montreal, and from the assembled collection of the cream of the crop, those members present jointly selected the Louisiana show.

In late April Harris, Wyly Grier, and F.M. Bell-Smith accompanied the crate of pictures to St. Louis. Arriving at the enormous grounds of the World's Fair they found labourers on strike, and everything in a state of mad confusion. "Imagine paying carpenters ten dollars a day," wrote Harris, appalled.

Robert Harris, William Notman Studio. Notman Photographic Archives, McCord Museum, Montreal.

Even the walls of their gallery space were totally unprepared for hanging. There was nothing for it but to pitch in and work themselves. One evening they were so exhausted that Wyly Grier fell asleep on his bed with his clothes on. Bell-Smith who was seventy years old appeared to bear up with amazing fortitude, but according to Harris as the tension mounted, relieved the pressure by bursting into recitation of poetry, "like the heading of a cauliflower." Fortunately the three were congenial and were able to work as a very effective team. By May 1 the Canadian art section was completely ready, paintings hung and all in order. But it could not open because none of the other countries' galleries were completed.

When they did open, and the international jury made their rounds, sixteen awards went to Canadian artists. Silver medals to William Brymner, Florence Carlyle, Edmund Dyonnet, Robert Harris and A.C. Williamson. Bronze to Frederick Challener, Maurice Cullen, Clarence Gagnon, John Hammond, William Hope, F. McGillivray Knowles, Laura Muntz, George Reid, Sidney Tully and Homer Watson. And although Canadian art history cannot but applaud the awarding of a further special Commemorative Diploma and Gold Medal of Honour for Distinguished Services in Art to Robert Harris, the fallibility of juries was disturbingly underlined in that in the French section, no such honours were awarded to exhibitors Puvis de Chavannes, Claude Monet, Degas, Renoir, or the master sculptor Rodin. An irony at least of spurious comfort to unsung genius in any age.

Back at home more mundane issues called for attention. The Academy had no official seal and J.W.H. Watts was asked to prepare a suitable design. His handsome presentation was accepted and a seal and press were purchased which have been in regular use up until the present day.

But Robert Harris was tired, in fact ill from the strain of years of overwork. He made it plain when he gave his report on the Louisiana Exhibition that he could not be persuaded to stay on as President beyond another term. And at the Annual Meeting in May of 1906 he stood by his decision. After thirteen years of meticulous attention to building professional fibre into the core of the Academy's structure, in his own words "I left them a good ship to steer at any rate." Unquestionably George Reid, who took his place in office, inherited an organization that was still the major force in Canadian art, and unquestionably the Academy was again in excellent hands.

George Reid's formal ties to the Academy dated back to 1885, when at the age of twenty-five he had been elected an Associate member. He and Paul Peel (elected three years earlier) were the same age and had been close friends in Paris when Reid was there in the late eighties. They were both elevated to full Academician in 1890. Peel was to die two years later, just as his career had taken on spectacular lustre. Reid, whose narrative figure paintings held much ideology in common with those of Peel, went on to become a major figure in Canadian art education.

George Reid, 1907, M. O. Hammond. Archives of Ontario.

Unlike Peel, whose talent had been nurtured through family tradition (his father was a monument maker and teacher of drawing in London, Ontario), George Reid became an artist through a combination of inner conviction and sheer guts. Born on a bush farm near Wingham, Ontario, one of nine children whose Irish father, an inveterate pioneer, homesteaded first one property and then began all over with another, young George was a square peg in a round hole. As a boy of eleven he dumbfounded his family by calmly announcing one evening that he would become a painter. "Girl's work," said his father. "Not any kind of occupation for a robust man." Undaunted the boy smuggled art books, supplied to him by a concerned itinerant bookseller, to the hayloft for secret reading. The story is told that when he was seventeen, hearing of a real painter who lived on a farm near Seaforth some twenty miles away, George walked there and home again in one day. The painter was William Cresswell, one of the Academy Charter members, a crusty old bachelor who dutifully warned the young hopeful that art was "a damned bad trade!"

But nothing could discourge Reid. After a false start as an apprentice to an impecunious architect, two years after his meeting with Cresswell he left the farm with his father's reluctant blessing. His zeal gave him the stamina to work ten hours a day at a reaper works, while attending classes three evenings a week at the Ontario School of Art. By the end of the term he had won a silver medal, and with that encouragement to buoy him, nothing could divert him from further developing his talent. The early eighties found him studying at the Pennsylvania Art Academy, where he met and married his first wife, Mary Heister. Back in Toronto in 1885 he briefly set up a studio there before the two of them went on to study and work in Paris. By 1897, settled in Toronto for good, his prestige as a painter was already such that he was elected President of the OSA. In 1906 he became the third Academy President, and in 1912 he was appointed the first principal of the newly constituted Ontario College of Art.

His first step as President of the Academy was to take the bull by the horns and challenge the apathy surrounding the National Gallery. He was not without informed experience. In 1900 as President of the OSA he had convened a meeting, chaired by Byron E. Walker, to discuss the founding of the Toronto Art Museum, and he was still serving in the role of Honorary Secretary of that institution. After a trip to Ottawa for a first-hand study of the situation, he gave a hard-hitting report of his findings to Council. The National Gallery management was "very slipshod," and the custodian, Watts, without any authority for its control. The collection itself was largely dispersed as decoration throughout the Parliament Buildings.

Reid took immediate action. At last it seemed that the time was ripe for results. By the mid-year meeting of Council, strategically convened in Ottawa, he had prepared a petition for the Governor General, Lord Grey, charting a step by step field plan for achieving a viable national art institution. His three main objectives called for the formation of an advisory council of laymen assisted by a cooperating committee of artists appointed by the Academy, a credible appropriation of funds, and the hiring of a competent, full-time director. His Excellency was cordial in his approval and enthusiastically passed the proposals on to the minister concerned, the Honourable Sydney Fisher. Then came the first lightly rolling peel of thunder. Word looped back via a letter from Lord Grey to Reid, politely but firmly questioning the possibility of too much control by the proposed committee of artists. In the interests of their broader goal, and doubtless assuming that their advice would be sought on an informal basis, the Academy acquiesced their specific role. Their co-operation established, on the opening night of the twenty-eighth annual exhibition, held in Montreal in April of 1907, a telegram was read from Sydney Fisher, announcing that the Laurier government would adopt the Academy proposal and establish an advisory council for art, on whose advice an appropriation would be made for art purposes.

Enter Byron E., later Sir Edmund Walker, by all accounts the most effective force to have hit either Canadian banking or cultural circles. And in view of later developments one wonders if it was perhaps on his advice that objectives one and two were achieved, but at the price of a hands-off policy as far as the Academy was concerned.

In spite of the authority and power that pervaded his adult life, Walker had by no means been born with a silver spoon in his mouth. The son of a watchmaker, he left school at twelve years old to work in his uncle's bank in Hamilton. His rise in the financial world after he joined the fast growing Bank of Commerce in 1868, was solely on the strength of his own methodical, studious, spectacular ability. He was only thirty-eight when he became the

General Manager of the Commerce. By the time he reached the Presidency in 1907, he had also built up a parallel career as a philanthropist. Chancellor of the University of Toronto, President of the Royal Canadian Institute, Director of the Toronto Conservatory of Music, Chairman of the Board and prime backer at the time of the founding of the Toronto Art Museum. When he made his first direct contact with the flagging National Gallery in 1907 as a member of the newly formed Advisory Arts Council, it was as a highly respected, concerned, able, unassuming connoisseur of highest integrity. He was formidable.

The Advisory Council, like every other project with which Walker had been associated, was remarkably successful. Its mandate was to advise the Dominion government on matters of art (as indeed the Academy had done informally since 1880) and to dispense the sum of $10,000 annually for the purchase of works for the National Gallery. Obviously a long overdue reform and one long strongly advocated by the Academy. But these changes were also the beginning of the end of the Academy's direct involvement with the institution they had been instrumental in carrying thus far.

Sir George Drummond was the Advisory Council's first Chairman, with the Honourable Senator Boyer acting as Secretary. Byron Walker was the only other member. Sir George, well known for his own famous art collection, considered the purchase funds so paltry as to be scarcely worth considering, and left activity up to his two colleagues. The more

Sir Edmund Walker, photographer unknown. Arts & Letter Club file, Archives of Ontario.

methodical Walker on the other hand felt that the way to get a larger grant was to show what could be done with a small one, and he recommended purchase of lesser known but distinguished European masters. He also emphasized acquiring work by Canadian artists. His policy was astute. When he took over as Chairman following Drummond's death in 1909, the grant was almost immediately raised to $25,000 annually. Then to $50,000, and finally to $100,000.

The implications of the success of the Advisory Council were probably not immediately apparent to the Academy, although undoubtedly there had been qualms over relinquishing formal input in the Council's activities. But Walker was a patron to be trusted — many of the artists knew him well as a man of unquestionable ethics, who was familiar with and loved art. In his keen interest to learn, he had actually attended classes given by O'Brien in his studio on College Street in the late 1890s, and had further educated himself by visiting world museums whenever he travelled on business. If ever a layman was qualified to serve the arts it was this cultivated banker. What the artists did not recognize or anticipate, was that over his long and demanding career Walker had so often found himself right that he had come to rely almost solely on his own judgement, and opinions once formed were not easily changed, either in banking or in art. Trouble was bound to come.

Meanwhile, having gained a temporary victory in the sense that their strong representation to government had been instrumental in establishing the Advisory Council, the Academy was occupied with its own ongoing domestic affairs. By 1907 the stock of original Membership Diplomas was almost depleted. The Academy decided to hold a competition among its own membership for a new design, a move which brought to light an interesting discrepancy. For until Gustav Hahn, a German emigré, was elected Associate in 1901 and then full Academician in 1905, no designer had been brought into the Academy since 1883, the year that Lorne had returned to England. Looking back, it is not in fact so surprising since until the late 1960s the whole range of modern design professions still remained in a sort of limbo — part of, yet lesser members of the visual arts family. The emphasis on design in the original constitution reflected a particular concern of Lorne's which was probably not applicable to Canada's stage of development. Left alone, any theoretic interest in applied design simply expired through lack of supporting conditions, and did not really come into its own for well over half a century. The immediate effect in the case of the Academy's Diploma competition was that there was very little response to the project at all. In the end architect Frank Darling reported for the committee of selection that they were "of the opinion that none of the designs submitted in competition for the Academy Diploma come up to the standard they think desirable for the response." Finally the longtime design member A.H. Howard was asked by the President to prepare a modified version of the old diploma. This version was to be in use for another twenty-six years, when a more successful competition vindicated the designers' position.

Potentially serious, yet laced with comic overtones of light opera, the exhibition of 1908 unfolded as a uniquely traumatic experience. It was held that year in the OSA gallery over the old Princess Theatre on King Street in Toronto, and somehow a fire broke out in the vestibule, totally destroying twenty works in the blaze, with twelve others damaged to some degree. For some of the impecunious artists it was a blessing in disguise. A sculpture by the young Frances Loring, who had recently arrived from the United States, was among the casualties, and the insurance money constituted her first sale. The windfall was envied by others, even senior artists. Bell-Smith, upon hearing of the fire, was said to have rushed down to King Street and up to the gallery only to find his paintings hanging intact, dry and unharmed. "Just my luck," he exclaimed. "Now I don't even get the insurance!" The Toronto *Star*, obviously aware of the difficulty in mustering public attention towards art exhibitions, certainly took an optimistic view. "This accident should prove something of a drawing card, and once past the charred and blackened entrance the visitor will think only of the pictures."

For all that, Curtis Williamson who did receive $400 in recompense for a burned picture, was not at all enthusiastic since he had entered a particularly fine work that had already been accepted as his Diploma picture. Fortunately, of the twelve pictures that had been purchased by the new Advisory Arts Council, none were harmed.

Then in 1909 after serving for three vigorous years, George Reid who was increasingly involved with teaching, stepped down from the Presidency and was succeeded by William Brymner of Montreal.

Although the adult careers of these two painters were remarkably parallel—both had studied abroad and were rooted deeply in academic standards, and both had become deeply involved in art education early in their development—Brymner, who was actually five years Reid's senior, was definitely the more modern man of the two. Thirteen years earlier, in 1896 when few of his fellow painters seemed really aware of the fundamental shifts of pace emanating from Paris, Brymner had given a lecture to the Women's Art Association in Montreal on the subject of Impressionism. He spoke of the great beauty and breathtaking truth in that school's treatment of daylight and sunlight, and found in Manet, Monet and Degas the sincerity and genuineness in common with all great artists. "...it is the coolness and clearness, and deliciousness of the water fresh from the fountainhead, opposed to the hot unrefreshing drainage from other men's meadows."

It was a perspective that he was to need as confusing times approached. For quite distinct from the fray immediately brewing with the National Gallery, a much more complex and potentially bitter rift was insinuating itself between artists as the latest swell of young painters hove into view, and with their new approach to dealing with landscape, appeared to challenge the precepts of the old, committed pros.

Landscape painting was scarcely new in Canada—it had been in the forefront at the time the Academy was founded and even when the scene was overwhelmed by the more sophisticated portrait and genre painters,

85

there continued to be a quiet swell of artists committed to painting the fields and forests and rivers of the land. Homer Watson had established his pastoral bent from the first and had never wavered in spite of newer more fashionable influences. Cullen and Suzor-Coté appeared in the nineties and established themselves as predominantly landscape painters. Soon after the turn of the century other new talents were making themselves felt. Charles Gagnon from Quebec, Charles W. Jefferys, J.W. Beatty, Fred Haines from Ontario, Horatio Walker, born in Ontario but who painted for the better part of his life on the Ile d'Orléans. Each of these men were artists who followed their own star with little regard for whether their works were or were not part of the current mainstream; they simply painted what they understood and loved.

Horatio Walker at Work, M.O. Hammond. Archives of Ontario.

Of these painters it was Beatty who was the first to foray north for new material. Much in the same sense that the pull of the unknown had drawn O'Brien, Fraser and others two or three decades earlier to penetrate through to wilderness waterfalls and out to the Rocky Mountains, Beatty re-opened the door to the rugged appeal of the northland. Within a few years the challenge of this remote wilderness was to provide the rallying cry for Canada's first group of radical painters. They were not to be welcomed with open arms by their older, traditional colleagues. The Academy exhibition of 1910 was perhaps one of the first barometric indications of the coming unrest. It was noted in the local press as leaning very strongly towards landscape, with the further comment that Canadian artists could no longer be accused of offering foreign subjects or subjects painted from a foreign point of

view. The work of a brash new talent made it into that year's show. A.Y. Jackson, a former pupil in Brymner's Life Class, showed "The Edge of the Maple Wood," a work that in retrospect proved to be a clarion call announcing a feisty career that was to span six decades of Canadian art.

Brymner himself was certainly a traditional painter, although his landscapes in particular showed an Impressionistic sensitivity to light. He often painted delightful studies of children, particularly young girls, and was a fine painter of academic nudes.

He had been born in Scotland but had come to Canada with his parents at an early age. His father became the founder and first archivist in the Dominion Archives in Ottawa, and when the younger Brymner decided upon an architectural career, he was sent to study under the chief government architect, Thomas Scott, who later became a Charter member of the Academy. In 1878 Brymner's duties took him to Paris to help install a Canadian government display at the Universal Exposition. He decided to stay on to study drawing and painting as part of his architectural training. The move proved a watershed. He never returned to architecture. Five years after his arrival in Paris, on the strength of work sent back to Canada for exhibition, he was elected an Associate of the Academy. In 1886 his delicate tonal study of children in "A Wreath of Flowers" was shown at the Colonial and Indian Exhibition in London, and that same year it was accepted as his Academy Diploma Work. He thus arrived home at age twenty-nine preceded by a considerable reputation. Almost immediately he was appointed Director of Art Classes at the Art Association of Montreal, a post he held until illness curtailed his activities in later life. By 1909 he was an obvious choice for Academy President.

Almost contiguous to Brymner's emergence at the helm of Academy affairs, was the appearance of another painter in the midst of the administrative action. Edmund Dyonnet was a native of Crest, France, who after coming to Canada as a boy had returned to Europe for years of intensive art study. Back in Montreal in the early nineties, like Brymner he settled permanently into teaching. Essentially a portrait painter, he was elected an Academy Associate in 1893, and elected to full status in 1901. Along with other respected Academicians—Jacobi, Harris, Brymner, Woodcock—Dyonnet was an early member of Montreal's intellectually exclusive Pen and Pencil Club (an informal group formed in 1890 for "Social Enjoyment and Promotion of the Arts and Letters"), and he was warmly regarded by his contemporaries as a totally dedicated painter and teacher and a delightful if slightly irascible man. He was also, however, an obdurate traditionalist, and in time was to become almost the Academy's nemesis.

He first came into full view under circumstances that presented his most admirable qualities, and they were considerable.

In 1910 the Academy had been invited to send a collection of Canadian art, under government auspices, to the fine arts section of the Festival of Empire Exhibition scheduled to be held in the Crystal Palace in London. Time

was short but a very credible show was hastily assembled and dispatched under the supervision of Dyonnet, who sailed for England on the same ship which carried the fourteen cases of Canadian works. However, at Rimouski word came on board via the pilot boat that King Edward VII had died, and when the ship docked in Liverpool, Dyonnet was given the disturbing tidings that in deference to the circumstances the Festival had been cancelled. He was therefore expected to reload his crates and send them back to Canada. But as the years were to make abundantly clear, it was not in this man's nature to accept defeat meekly. He made up his mind to ignore the instructions.

Acting with characteristic force he immediately contacted the Honourable Sydney Fisher (by this time Canada's Minister of Agriculture), who happened to be in London on government business. Fisher was not unsympathetic, but the King was still not buried and it would be unseemly to make official requests on Canada's behalf as long as England was in a position of formal mourning. There seemed no alternative but to send the exhibit home. Not easily discouraged, Dyonnet set out on his own to locate a private London gallery that would take the show, only to discover that all space was booked ahead for six months, much too long to justify holding the work over in storage. Then by chance he ran into the English landscape painter, Sir Alfred East, who advised him to try the Walker Art Gallery in Liverpool, which had a very good reputation. Racing to Liverpool Dyonnet found the

Walker Gallery authorities not only keenly interested, but that fortuitously space was available if formal application was in their hands within two days. Dyonnet immediately cabled home to Brymner for authorization, and then returned to London to legitimize the arrangement through Fisher. Fisher however had left the city on temporary business and was not expected back until the following day. After an agonizing wait, Brymner's blessing came through only two hours before the deadline. But there was still no sign of Fisher. At almost zero hour he at last returned and immediately gave official consent. With only fifteen minutes to spare, Dyonnet telegraphed Liverpool, and the show was on the road.

When it opened in July the exhibition was a smash hit. Sydney Fisher did the honours and the 113 paintings and five small sculptures were set up to great advantage in three very adequate rooms. Critics from all over Britain came to review the work—the Manchester *Guardian*, the *Morning Post*, the London *Times*, the *Scotsman*, the Glasgow *Herald* and many more—literally every credible journal in England and Scotland. Interestingly, most correspondents wrote from the premise that Canadian art had begun with the Marquis of Lorne (thus allowing it a span of thirty years), and most were aggrieved by the noticeable inroads of the influence of French Impressionism. But while one eminent critic allowed only that "Relatively it is a good show, that is to say, good for Canada," the London *Times* went so far as to predict a prominent place for Canada in any future history of modern art. All

thrilled to the painters of Canadian snow subjects, Maurice Cullen, Clarence Gagnon, Aurèle de Foy Suzor-Coté, and were delighted by the story of sculptor Philippe Hébert, said to have romantically appeared some years earlier out of the wilds north of Montreal, carrying a rough wood carving of his own untutored creation under his arm. In the glare of such overwhelming press attention the public flocked to see the show and enjoyed it immensely.

Dyonnet arrived home triumphant and received a hero's welcome from his colleagues. When, at the Annual Meeting in the autumn, the longtime Secretary-Treasurer James Smith resigned from the secretarial part of his duties, Dyonnet was enthusiastically appointed to the office, which carried not only potential influence, but also a modest salary. He did not retire from the position until he was eighty-nine years old.

In the background of these domestic events, the National Gallery could be seen to be creaking into unaccustomed motion. Sir Edmund Walker (he was knighted in 1910) had definitely taken the institution in hand, and with his usual thoroughness was bringing intelligent order to its state of musty neglect. His first step had been in 1909, when he introduced a recently immigrated young Englishman into Gallery affairs. Eric Brown had come to Canada earlier that year and had been taken on as an assistant at the Toronto Art Museum, one of Walker's major projects. With shrewd instinct Walker picked the young man as his possible future right arm at the National Gallery, and arranged to install him in Ottawa as Secretary to the Advisory Arts Council and Curator of the Gallery. A small salary was arranged and the continuity of the appointment was contingent on results. Brown immediately made good by discovering and arranging for space for the National Gallery in the east wing of the recently built Victoria Memorial Museum, where, bidding a final goodbye to the fish hatchery, the doors finally opened in 1911. Brown's success was acknowledged when he was elevated to the position of Director of the Gallery in 1912.

Eric Brown had been thirty-two years old when he arrived in Canada. He has been described as tall, elegant, with a monocle, but possessed of a simplicity of nature, a shrewdness and enthusiasm that saved him from the role of dilettante. He had been an invalid as a child in Nottingham, and much of his education had been acquired through reading at home. His family was quietly cultured — there was a poet among the ancestors, and his older brother Arnesby Brown was a landscape painter of some repute. Eric himself, always a delicate constitution, had tried his hand assisting a cousin as a cotton grower in the West Indies, and as a farmer in England before coming to Canada to work first for a Montreal picture dealer. The attributes that fitted him for what was to become the central administrative position in Canadian art were his great personal integrity, his absolutely sincere interest in art — and the ardour he came to share with Walker in seeing art develop in Canada. Between them they put the National Gallery on the map.

The first signs of cross-purposes developing between the Academy and the National Gallery were precipitated when Walker took steps to establish the autonomy of his revamped institution, by act of Parliament. It happened that, quite independently, the Academy was at the same time engaged in updating its own constitution, which by now was thirty years old. Since 1911 Brymner, assisted by his predecessor George Reid, had been working diligently to eliminate redundancies that were no longer applicable to Academy affairs. Ahead of its time, for instance, in theory the constitution would no longer bar women from elected office. Through a stroke of irony the new Academy Charter and Bylaws neared completion at the same time that Walker was hammering the nails into his National Gallery Act, and suddenly in 1913 it became apparent that the two bills would come before the same session of Parliament.

Walker's first reaction was mild. After all he was a man who worked from a considerable power base, and he had already made up his mind to the course he was taking. This course did not include input from artists. He wrote to his protégé, Brown, who was drafting the Gallery's Bill, "... I can only hope that the RCA will realize that the National Gallery of Canada is a state institution and that it is not in the true interest of the public that it should be, even in appearance, allied to any other body."

His reaction warmed however at the hint of challenge. Obtaining and studying a copy of the RCA Charter he wrote to Brown in a more aggressive tone. "The statement that the National Gallery was instituted by the Academy in pursuance of its charter, is a very dangerous statement for the Government to admit, even if it is true, which I doubt. ..." Even more offensive was the clause in which the Academy counted itself ready "...to accept, acquire, hold, and exercise such control thereof [of the National Gallery] as may be hereafter offered to, or obtained by it [the Academy]...." Hardly likely that Walker would agree when Brymner wrote requesting that recognition be given in the National Gallery Act to both of these points. Responded Walker with asperity, "Frankly I do not see how you can for a moment suppose that those in charge of the National Gallery would do otherwise than oppose such a proposal."

The artists were astounded. Their position was that they were merely restating their commitments as spelled out in the old constitution, and while they had fought for a Gallery restructure they had, rather naively, never seriously considered the possibility of being cut off completely from Gallery affairs. And there was more to come. It developed that the preamble to the National Gallery Act actually disclaimed the Academy's role in founding the National Gallery, stating that it had been formed by the Marquis of Lorne, "assisted by a number of patriotic citizens." Aghast, Brymner sent a strong protest off to Walker to the effect that the Academy found this a ludicrous statement, "...unless you would designate the members of the Royal Canadian Academy as such [patriotic citizens]."

This was too much for Walker. He was quite unused to having his judgement questioned, and doubtless he was genuinely convinced that neither the Academy nor any other group should be given even a toehold which might provide a base for future interference in Gallery administration. To support this position he was coolly prepared to disqualify all previous Academy efforts and petition to keep the institution alive through years of government apathy. The Diploma Collection? He wrote to Brymner who had quoted it as a major Academy contribution: "...the present National Gallery consists in a very small part of the Diploma pictures and the few gifts which came in its early history, or during that long time when it was almost entirely neglected" — an ungenerous and highly debatable assessment. The founding of the National Gallery? "I think beyond a doubt that the National Gallery was indeed in existence in 1880," thus insinuating, quite erroneously, that it had been initiated independently of the Academy. As for Brymner's plea that the artists should be represented on the board, but would be satisfied if the President of the RCA were made an ex officio member, it was dismissed as incompatible with the good of "the state institution."

And so the Academy lost all say in the affairs of its offspring. After some modification of the more intemperate phrasing, with the Honourable George Perley acting as referee, attempting to make the bitter pill as palatable as possible to the Academy, both Bills passed unopposed through Parliament in June of 1913. The one in effect simply updating the Academy's constitution, the other effectively completely severing the historic link between the Academy and the National Gallery. The Academy, stunned, had no choice but to pick up the pieces and go on.

Chapter Five

Winds of Change

Estranged though the Academy and the National Gallery might be, like many divorced couples they were destined to endure years of continuing emotional backlash. Unhealed grievances, an almost paranoid sensitivity to one another's reactions, entanglement of practical affairs. It was definitely not a happy association on the administrative level. As might be anticipated the possibilities for misunderstanding were legion. For once established as a viable institution, the Gallery inevitably set about with missionary zeal to annex territory previously considered the traditional preserve of the Academy: senior advisor to the government on all manner of professional art matters, responsibility for international exhibitions, and in time even arbiters of excellence in Canadian art. Obviously the Academy was to lose much more than a voice in Gallery affairs, and warranted or not, the artists could hardly be expected to like it.

The bones of contention were not black and white. While no artists could possibly agree that their concerns were better shepherded without input from themselves, nevertheless the more rational Academicians recognized the revitalized National Gallery as a positive

support to Canadian art. What other source, after all, came regularly to exhibitions and purchased a dozen or so works? Such practical assistance was unprecedented, and the artists were very grateful.

But the situation was more complex. A fundamental shift in interpretation and approach to painting was sending fresh blasts of air through the entire system, and marked change always tends to polarize extremes. When it became suspect, after all the recent grounds for misgiving, that the National Gallery through its acquisitions policy was prejudiced towards the emerging school, a fuse began to sputter dangerously out from the midst of a handful of old Academy faithfuls. Their ire was all the more incendiary in that it was utterly sincere; Canadian art, the Academy, the National Gallery, all were going to the dogs. The status quo must be redeemed. And over a period of several years, through a combination of fluke circumstances, these diehards managed to entrench themselves at the core of Academy influence. As Arthur Lismer was to point out later on when the predictable fireworks were rocketing, the posture was a complete reversal of historical precedent. "It is usually the moderns, in the other countries, who have to assert their right to exhibit, protesting against the existing academic order and their old-fashioned tastes, but here, in a new democracy, it is the crusty academic painters who join hands with the raw amateurs against the modern painters."

Interestingly enough, after the strong generative and building years, the Academy was perfectly able to withstand pressures from both without and within.

As long as William Brymner was on hand there was every appearance of truce on all fronts. Sir Edmund Walker, having won the decisive bout over the National Gallery Act, reverted to his former cordial relations with his friends the artists, and as President of the Gallery and Chairman of the Board of Trustees, was very willing to work with them on matters that did not challenge Gallery sovereignty.

In fact by the autumn of 1913, in a highly credible move towards conciliation, Eric Brown was writing to Brymner to ask his advice on policy regarding an annual prize to be awarded to the most promising art student of the year for further study in Europe. The proposal was that the National Gallery would make a sum of $1,000 available annually for the project, while the Academy would draw up the rules and regulations and in the end adjudicate the competition. The Academy appointed Brymner and Robert Harris as the committee to work out the details, which they did with characteristic flair and know-how. Beginning from the premise that each winner should be under the age of thirty, should be a Canadian citizen, and should have shown by exhibited work that he or she would be likely to profit from the benefits of the scholarship, they hammered out the ways and means. By the Annual Meeting and exhibition in the autumn of 1914, they were ready with a slate of likely candidates. The jury was the assembled Academicians. They selected twenty-nine-year-old Emily Coonan of Montreal, a former star pupil of Brymner. However, due to the recent outbreak of the First World War, Miss Coonan as well as the three succeeding award winners was forced to mark time until 1920, before European travelling conditions were considered stable enough to justify releasing the funds.

Nevertheless, Emily Coonan had chosen perhaps the keynote Academy show of the decade to make her professional debut. It was held at the Toronto Reference Library on College Street and had, said the *Globe*, "... strength and variety and quality, but, above all, strength." The line-up of work was stunning. Paintings by Arthur Lismer, J.E.H. MacDonald, Lawren Harris, C.W. Jefferys, Maurice Cullen. A glowing "Winter Morning, Algonquin Park," by J.W. Beatty, forerunner of the already marshalling Group of Seven. A sweeping, dramatic "Fall Ploughing," by Herbert Palmer, sculpture by Emanuel Hahn and by newcomer Florence Wyle. And from newly elected Associate, A.Y. Jackson, "'Red Maple'... a dashing piece of impressionism, the blood red leaves of a small tree standing out against the blues and browns of a rushing stream."

Hector Charlesworth, of whom much more was to be heard, summed the exhibit up in his column in *Saturday Night*. "It is doubtful whether a better collection of Canadian pictures has ever been gathered together... not only a great variety of styles, but a genuinely vital impulse."

Whether he realized it or not, Charlesworth had underscored the core of Academy philosophy. This 1914 annual show was a synthesis, at its strongest, of the artists' recognition, with excellence and continuing personal quest as the common gauge. So young Jackson is blazing his own trail? Fine. That's what it's all about. What he's doing is excellent, exciting. He belongs in there with the Robert Harris's and the George Reids, the Maurice Cullens and the Suzor-Cotés, the Homer Watsons and the Horatio Walkers. For the key words were not "academic," or "modern," but creativity and growth. And it happened that Canadian artists as a whole had reached that vital stage in evolution where they felt enormous confidence in their own ability to interpret life around them. It was an exhilarating period in spite of gloomy world events.

The war did create great difficulties. Survival was tenuous for most artists in ordinary times. Now suddenly both they and their works were relegated to the ranks of the frivolous. The Academy countered by organizing the Patriotic Fund Exhibition to aid the country's war drive, and the effort was a raging success. Under their auspices, 83 works of art were donated from among their own ranks, and from members of the OSA as well as from the Canadian Art Club, a small but prestigious group of painters formed in 1908. The resulting collection toured nine cities, from Winnipeg to Montreal, and all the proceeds— the sale of pictures, entrance fees and net profit on sales of catalogues—went to the Fund. A competition for a poster to advertise the show was sponsored by the Academy, and was won by the gifted designer (and future member of the Group of Seven) J.E.H. MacDonald. The show proved immensely popular

J.E. H. MacDonald's winning design in RCA competition for a poster to advertise the Patriotic Fund Exhibition, 1914. Gift from RCA to the Ontario College of Art in 1953.

The R.C.A. Exhibition

By Hector Charlesworth.

MR. WILLIAM BRYMNER, of Montreal, President of the Royal Canadian Academy of Arts, could speak with a pride that was justified of the thirty-sixth annual exhibition of the institution when it was opened in Toronto last week. It is doubtful whether a better collection of Canadian pictures has ever been gathered together. At any rate it is quite evident that Canadian artists, young and old, have put their best feet forward this year. The pictures on display show not only a great variety of styles, but a genuinely vital impulse. There is much admirable performance, and a great deal of promise as well. The present exhibition sees the inaugura-

tion of a modest scheme to stimulate Canadian painting. The Academy has established a travelling scholarship, open to native painters (or those reared in Canada) of less than thirty years of age. The scholarship does not necessarily go to the competitor who exhibits the best work, but to the young painter who, in the judgment of the academicians, shows a talent that would be best benefited and developed by such a training and experience. Thus a young painter's work may be at present crude, but the committee may discern that in his or her work which promises well for the future.

Saturday Night, November 28, 1914. Review by Hector Charlesworth of the 36th RCA exhibition held at the Toronto Reference Library, College Street.

with the public. The method of purchase was such that anyone could make a bid on a work, and at the close of the final exhibition, the painting or sculpture went to the highest recorded bidder. The tour started in Toronto on December 30, 1914, and by July 13 the artists' gift to the fund was reported as $10,514.88. A great satisfaction, but a success to be taken in perspective. The Princess Patricia, on Vice-Regal duty in Ottawa with her father the Duke of Connaught, was accustomed, as had been the Princess Louise, to exhibit in RCA shows. She too had contributed a painting to the auction. The fact that it sold for appreciatively more than the work of such international Canadian luminaries as J.W. Morrice, or in fact any other artists in the show, pointed more to a display of purely patriotic rather than aesthetic fervour.

The thirty-eighth annual exhibition in 1916 opened in Montreal to a few discordant notes. Although the Academy's prestige had never been higher, the show met with mixed reviews. In actuality the out and out so-called radical works were limited to a few submissions from A.Y. Jackson, Arthur Lismer, J.E.H. MacDonald and Tom Thomson, although a number of interesting younger Montreal painters showed as well—Albert Robinson, Ozias Leduc, Edwin Holgate, Lilias Torrance, Emily Coonan. But Montreal at this stage was a fairly conservative bastion with the greater number of its established artists far from receptive to the new questing spirit. In sympathy, more than one columnist was deeply afronted by the few examples of what they termed "freak art" in an otherwise acceptable show, and complained bitterly over the use of outrageous colour in such works as MacDonald's now famous "Tangled Garden." Another correspondent, however, interpreted such licence as an indication of rising standards, noting that the younger artists were developing fast with the Toronto painters showing up strongly. Unperturbed by the querulous pens, the National Gallery purchased nineteen works for their collection, including several of the "freak" paintings.

Then early in 1917, unexpected tragedy that was to offer a first foothold to the diehards in assuming control of Academy affairs. Brymner suffered a severe stroke and was for a time completely incapacitated. Dyonnet, who occupied the top floor in the same building on Montreal's Bleury Street where Brymner lived and worked, called the next Council meeting in his own studio, a precedent that was to become a regular practice. With Brymner ill, although Homer Watson of Doon, Ontario, was Vice President, for convenience' sake Dyonnet assumed unusual secretarial responsibilities, and in effect assisted Brymner to run the Academy by remote control. At the same time Dyonnet, a man of personal generosity and kindness, patiently devoted himself to helping his colleague to walk sufficiently well again to resume his accustomed sketching trips. By late autumn Brymner was well enough to join the next meeting of Council, held again in Dyonnet's studio.

The gathering was particularly urgent. Reports were circulating that commissions had been given in England for pictures depicting war subjects, to be used for decoration in the new Parliament Buildings built to replace those that burned in Ottawa in 1916. Canadian artists were chagrined. Why English artists when qualified Canadians were available, some even fighting at the front? And so this special meeting had been called to consider how best to deal with the situation. A special delegation from the OSA attended, and between them they decided that the most productive route of action would be to approach the National Gallery for support in requesting the government to appoint Canadian artists to go overseas for the purpose of making artistic records. A committee, composed of architect W.S. Maxwell and painters Wyly Grier and J.W. Beatty, was delegated to undertake negotiations. Their overtures were well met by Eric Brown and Sir Edmund Walker who were able to influence Prime Minister Borden to approve the cause. But there was a catch. Funds for the project were being put up by Lord Beaverbrook in England, and his energy and enthusiasm were not always easy to divert. However, Academy painter William Hope was living in England at the time. Supplying copies of all relevant correspondence, the committee asked him to interview Beaverbrook in order to give him a first-hand account of the artists' concerns. He was able to do so, and when a vigorous petition arrived as well from Sir Edmund Walker the case was won. Hope himself was appointed a War Artist, as well as RCA members Maurice Cullen, Charles Simpson, J.W. Beatty and F.H. Varley, and they went to the continent to join A.Y. Jackson and Lionel Fosbery who had been previously fighting with Canadian troops in France. As

95

well, Eric Brown managed to convince the powers-that-be to devote a portion of the War Records funds to depicting war activities carried on at home in Canada. The move resulted directly in such commissions as those to sculptors Frances Loring and Florence Wyle, who created their notable group of bronze statuettes dramatizing women's work in the war.

Typical of the political edge that biased many of the National Gallery's undeniably supportive and beneficial actions, in later official references to the success of the War Records project, no mention was made of the Academy's considerable participation. Perhaps unintentional, perhaps unimportant, nevertheless the omission was exactly the kind of unilateral stance that helped to cast the Gallery as villain in some quarters as time moved on.

Despite the war, the annual shows continued with unabated vigour. In fact the war was actually a catalyst that smoothed over internal difficulties and sent them into temporary hibernation. And although Academy records list no exhibition and no Annual Meeting for the year 1917, the reasons were purely technical. The thirty-eighth exhibition had been scheduled to open in the new Art Gallery of Toronto in Grange Park. The fine new building, like most major cultural ventures of the era, was another of Sir Edmund Walker's triumphs (he had meanwhile been instrumental in founding the Royal Ontario Museum in 1914). The project had been languishing for lack of funds since the turn of the century. But Walker had been able to gently persuade Goldwin Smith to bequeath his

home, the Grange, for use as an art gallery. When the time came, Walker pried funds for reconstruction from various monied interests, and then worked closely with Academy architects Darling and Pearson to design the series of galleries that became so familiar to the Toronto public over the next fifty years. Unfortunately construction lagged behind schedule, and it was necessary to ask the Academy to postpone their opening until the spring of 1918. Since this coincided with the normal timing of the annual OSA show, the two Societies decided to combine forces once again in a gigantic joint exhibition.

Thus it happened that on April 4, 1918, the new Art Gallery of Toronto opened with a combined RCA and OSA exhibition, consisting of 305 works. The Toronto *Mail and Empire* was quick to praise the show: "... though the tones are quieter, the gallery contains plenty of the vigour and life that have made the work of our younger artists interesting, even when bordering on the extravagant."

At the General Assembly next day, William Brymner's resignation for obvious reasons of poor health was read. Homer Watson, the artist whose first major oil painting had been purchased for Queen Victoria from the inaugural exhibition of the Canadian Academy in 1880, was elected President. He was sixty-three years old at the time, a painter of international repute, a refined and gentle man of somewhat ingenuous nature, more comfortable in the studio than at the Council table.

The story of Homer Watson's development as a painter is yet another classic tale of the child who had to paint. He was born at mid-century into the comfortable home of a woollen mill owner at Doon, near Kitchener. Artists and art were not a part of the rural or his family's perception. The boy was only six years old when his father suddenly died leaving unresolved business debts and precipitating the family into very difficult circumstances. Young Homer's formal education was therefore limited and he went to work as a mill and factory hand when scarcely more than a boy. But unaccountably, much to the consternation of family and friends, he yearned to be an artist and wandered regularly out to the countryside to draw. His interest was so marked that a sympathetic aunt presented him with a set of oil paints. In time a portion of a small inheritance from his father was doled out to him with considerable misgivings by the family lawyer. With this stipend he set out for Toronto where he made contact with other artists and began a serious self-apprenticeship. Like so many others before him he supplemented his income by working as an assistant at Notman's photographic studio. Two years later he managed to move on to New York, always learning and sketching as he went. In 1878 he returned to Doon with the yearning stronger than ever in his blood, and he settled into depicting the countryside that he so loved with, in his own words, "faith, ignorance and delight."

The rest is the stuff of legends. The young man reading in the newspaper of the formation of the Academy and the coming exhibition. Diffidently packing up and sending off his painting, "The Pioneer Mill," on which he had worked so laboriously, fully expecting it to be turned down. Hearing that it was

accepted, then not only accepted but purchased for the Queen. It was far too late for the concerned importuning of his old guardian, the lawyer, who had advised him to "quit it and come into the office to become a businessman."

It was in 1882 that Watson first met Oscar Wilde, when that spectacular figure touched on Toronto while on an American tour. Wilde was very taken with the young painter's work, dubbed him the "Canadian Constable," asked to meet him, and commissioned a painting for his own collection. When Watson travelled to England with his wife later in the decade, both Wilde and Lord Lorne enthusiastically introduced him to London studio circles, and he very quickly found himself a decided success as an accepted painter in a competitive and demanding milieu. Yet after a time he came to feel that as an artist he must return to his rural roots, that he preferred to be a part of the fresher developments at home, and he left London in 1890.

By the time he was elected the sixth President of the Academy, Homer Watson had been back in Canada for nearly thirty years. Quietly, passionately, unceasingly he devoted himself to painting, with richly poetic instinct, the countryside around Doon that had spawned him. Part way along the route he had joined with a small group of fellow painters of no precise school to form the Canadian Art Club. They included several expatriates including J.W. Morrice and Horatio Walker. In general the Club was a high level attempt at exhibition for co-operative marketing. Watson was President for the first four of the Club's eight years, and the highly talented group stirred considerable public interest and admiration. But by 1915 the popular thirst for change was already becoming dominant, and the work of these artists who up until now had been looked upon as the top professionals in their field — Watson, Brymner, Suzor-Coté, Cullen, Gagnon and others — was considered in some circles to be behind the times. Their show that year, and it proved to be their final effort as a group, was reviewed by a patronising columnist who saw merit only in the new order. While admitting that the Club had been organized to break down traditions and foster vital things in Canadian art, he ended by gratuitously advising, "But if they wish to encourage Canadian art, let them follow the men who are painting the vital things in this country."

This then was the atmosphere building in the years immediately prior to Watson's election. Valid tensions were inevitable. The uneasiness was not helped by the strong impression that the National Gallery was downplaying the more traditional painters. The Gallery of course denied the charge, but as late as 1920 there were, for instance, only three Watsons in their collection. Of the other artists who had been members of the Canadian Art Club, Suzor-Coté had fared best. The Gallery had purchased five of his works — but none since 1913. And there was little doubt in anyone's mind that Eric Brown (who was given a fairly free hand by Walker) in his keen enthusiasm to make the National Gallery reflective of Canadian art, was interpreting his mandate through active promotion of those younger painters of the Ontario northlands who were soon to formalize themselves as the Group of Seven.

Yet, as Hector Charlesworth was to say with disconcerting rationalism in his column in *Saturday Night*, "Academic persons who speak

of a 'distinctively Canadian school of landscape,' as a development of the past five years are strongly ignorant of the work of such unmistakably native individualities as that of Homer Watson. . . . For is not the beautiful tract of Western Ontario which Watson interprets as much a part of Canada as Algonquin Park?"

The column was wonderful ammunition for the entrenched traditionalists who, for the most part dedicated but perhaps no longer inspired professionals, were becoming more and more deeply affronted by the success of work that looked to them like mere daubs of paint on canvas. The legitimate grievances of their more credible fellow realists such as Watson, over National Gallery policy were like a match to the wick of a Roman candle. And in the middle, covered in gunpowder, sat Edmund Dyonnet.

There was much to encourage the dissidents. Even Sir Edmund Walker, who was a man to fully appreciate the advantageous image of an institution moving step in step with a spontaneous, indigenous, highly visible local art movement, felt it necessary to temper Brown's open admiration. He wrote to him in 1921, "I approve of the purchase of five pictures from the Group of Seven show, but I remind you of the trouble we are likely to have if nothing is purchased from the recent OSA exhibition."

But by December, 1922, the situation began to get out of hand when Charlesworth, not an admirer of the "freak art" school and with the obvious backing of his publication, declared open war on the National Gallery. "National

98

Gallery a National Reproach," ran the column heading, and then proceeded in the following article to tear Gallery policy to shreds. His general theme was the "absence of aesthetic sensibility" in the curatorial selection of the Canadian collection, and he took particular umbrage at the "... glaring instances of over-representation by painters still in the experimental stage." Nonsense, of course, since at this stage the members of the Group were painting at the height of their power. But no more so than Sir Edmund Walker's reply which cited the modern Canadian school as being "something truly Canadian and does not depend for its style on a form of any other country or convention," while later scholars were to firmly pinpoint the strong influence on the Group of Seven by contemporary Scandinavian painters who were attempting to interpret similarly rugged terrain with a new and fervent brand of Impressionism.

To place the conflict in perspective it was, after all, a part of the great wheel of continuing evolution which, since the Group of Seven was highly vocal and welcomed controversy as a form of publicity, occasioned particularly audible raspings as the new order grated against the old. The Group had the advantage too of National Gallery backing which certainly did not endear them to less favoured colleagues. Twenty years later the wheel had gone full circle, and it was to be the turn of the now aging radicals to be dismissed as déclassé when the abstract expressionists ruled out landscape painting as beneath consideration. And so the course runs, leaving time to do the real sorting of the gems from the clods of earth.

Meanwhile, Homer Watson's elevation to the Presidency coincided with a period of full-scale escalation of such classic animosities. He was no match for the old academics who, despite the fact that four of the Group of Seven were already duly elected Associates of the Academy (MacDonald, Jackson, Lismer and Varley), conducted guerilla skirmishes in the background that were directly opposed to the more catholic views held by the general membership. Watson and others like him were probably slightly compromised in that although their own professionalism remained intact, they were ideologically caught in the middle of the fray, and were unable to wholeheartedly squelch the reactionary rumblings before they burgeoned out of all control.

The period between 1918 and 1922 was not marked by creative Academy activity, partly because Watson himself had been plunged into deepest grief by the recent death of his wife, his close companion of forty years, but particularly because of the demoralizing effect of covert dissension. There was a brief cessation of hostilities in 1919 when members paused to mourn the death of Robert Harris whom all considered to have "filled with honour and ability the highest position that can be gained by one of his profession in this country." And all cheered when in 1920 the four winners of the travelling scholarships — Emily Coonan, Dorothy Stevens, E.R. Glenn and Manly MacDonald — were finally able to set off for Europe. But Brymner's steadying influence was badly missed and in the absence of a unifying force, the administrative wheels turned automatically, with much discussion at meetings of petty expenditures, with earnest restating of principles mixed with careful recording of housekeeping details. Architect members were convinced the Academy's sluggishness could be remedied by a strong financial boost, and were all for approaching Ottawa with a petition to hike the annual grant from $2,500 to $25,000. Architects Percy Nobbs and Henry Sproatt (who was Vice President) actually interviewed the Minister of Finance in this regard, but were turned down. Then in 1922, with financial discussions much to the fore, G. Horne Russell from Montreal, a financially successful painter of competent portraits and landscapes, a close associate of Dyonnet's in the Pen and Pencil Club, came to the surface as the newly elected Treasurer.

Russell was apparently impressive in the new post because at the following year's Annual Meeting, bypassing the Vice President Henry Sproatt, he displaced the sincere and beleaguered Homer Watson as President. Of passing interest, six of that year's Council were fellow members of the Pen and Pencil Club. And a lamb among jackals, but fortunately with a hide like that of an elephant, recent Academician A.Y. Jackson was also elected to Council.

In spite of growing conflict, the annual exhibitions over this general period continued without missing a beat, and gave only oblique warning of the time bomb that was ticking away. Even in 1923 the tenor of the forty-fifth exhibition was noticeably catholic and vibrant,

with Augustus Bridle remarking in the Toronto *Star* that in its liberal interpretation of excellence the Academy conformed not to tradition, so much as to the spirit of the age. A timely, plucky and astute assessment, in view of the fact that for several months the Academy, along with the National Gallery, had been embroiled in the biggest three-ring circus ever to have hit Canadian art.

Chapter Six

The Wembley Controversy

The year 1923 began mildly enough. At the first Council meeting in January A.Y. Jackson put forward a very creative suggestion for a mural competition and it was supported by all concerned. The idea was to set up a hypothetical commission calling for designs for a decorative panel representing "The Settlement of Canada," supposedly meant for installation in a definite location at the Parliament Buildings in Ottawa. Size, shape and position were built in so that artists would be required to discipline themselves to work within specified conditions. Awards of $500 and $300 would go to the two top finalists, with the whole point of the exercise being to plant the idea of murals in the minds of those in a position to in fact commission such work. The project made for a good deal of professional enthusiasm, as did a further proposal from the architects that the Academy sponsor a scholarship to send a young architect to Europe to study the use of decoration in architecture.

Indeed the new President, Horne Russell, seemed determined to put the organization back on track with programs of practical significance to the members. Obviously a man of

action, he was sixty-one years old when he was so unexpectedly catapulted to the Presidency. But although he had been on the scene for many years, he had been a full Academician only since 1918. Born at Banff, Scotland, he had studied art in Aberdeen and then in London, before emigrating to Canada as a fully trained artist in 1900. He made Montreal his home and became widely accepted there as a painter of upper-class society. Summers were spent at St. Andrews, New Brunswick, a popular society resort, and he was often commissioned to paint the seaside estates of his wealthy clientele. His work was traditional and pleasing, although a painters' painter he was not. But he did have a well-established network of important contacts, and he doubtless expected to put both his energy and his contacts to the service of the Academy in an attempt to re-establish the organization's past unchallenged glory. Since he was one of those individuals who saw change as cardinal sin, he was the logical spokesman and standard bearer for the more reactionary of his colleagues.

Russell's election to the Presidency was unfortunate timing since the Academy was about to be asked to adapt even further to the shifting balance of the modern art world. The story tells itself very well. And as usual, there were mitigating elements that gave some justification or at least explanation for some of the more extravagant behaviour that erupted on both sides of the fence.

There is no denying that the Academy missed the first turn—and it was a fatal mistake. As early as May 1922, Council had reviewed a letter from the President of the Royal British Colonial Society of Artists, soliciting Homer Watson's opinion on the Exhibition of Fine Arts of the Empire to be held in London in 1924. Inexplicably the Council took a distinctly static view and instructed the President to reply offering the bureaucratic suggestion that in the event of such an exhibition it should be installed in a building expressly designed and lighted for the purpose. No further correspondence appeared to follow and the matter simply dropped. The initiative for the British Empire Exhibition might just as well have been handed to the National Gallery on a platter.

As it was, in 1823 Eric Brown got wind of the show, which was to take place at Wembley in northwest London in the following spring, and he immediately moved into action. Writing to friends in England he obtained the names of the two men in actual charge of the exhibition. He then composed a careful letter to them outlining the existing rift between the academic and rebel painters in Canada, pointing out that the management of the Canadian section should not be left to some self-centred and narrow-minded organization. His petition hit the mark. The Canadian government was approached by the manager of the British Empire Exhibition, suggesting that the Board of Trustees of the National Gallery was the appropriate authority to handle the Canadian exhibit.

Fortunately the Academy never did know the whole story. Brown wisely chose the tack that the invitation had appeared out of the blue, and that the exhibition authorities in London had through force of natural selection recommended the National Gallery as organizer of the Canadian section. The first inkling of developments to reach the Academy was the receipt by its members, on an individual basis, of entry forms and a circular for the show, which assured prospective exhibitors that "the Trustees and the Director of the National Gallery are to be assisted by a committee of representative artists." This was in May 1823, and at approximately the same time the Academy received a letter from Brown cancelling previous arrangements to hold their forty-fifth annual exhibition in Ottawa in November. The reason given was that since the National Gallery "has been entrusted by the Government to collect and ship works of art to the British Empire Exhibition in London in 1924," neither time nor space would now be available to accommodate the Academy's show.

Naturally the President and his advisors were furious. Had not all such previous invitations been directed to the Academy? Was not continuing responsibility for such exhibitions implicit, they reasoned rather shakily, in the clause of their Charter which pledged their

102

co-operation with the National Gallery in areas of mutual interest? But in any case had not the Academy, without exception, carried previous international efforts off with much honour?

There was no denying well-known history. Surely the matter needed only clarification. The Secretary immediately wrote back to Brown suggesting that the annual exhibition take place as planned, and following successful precedent, selection for Wembley, except for government-owned pictures, be made from the accepted entries. The cause was defeated before it began. Brown replied to the effect that such an approach was not possible due to practical circumstances. He did, however, invite the Academy to suggest names for the jury. This they flatly refused to do.

The gauntlet had now been thrown. The main event was about to begin. On the one hand fumed the outraged and outrageous Academy executive, and on the other stamped the pious and peremptory National Gallery administration. All further pronouncements from either corner were laced with acrimony and with intransigence to the point of outright manipulation of facts. Both sides believed themselves to be carrying the staff of Right, and it soon became evident that both were willing to fight to the death. From the beginning the National Gallery had the edge since in essence it held the bird in the hand and was offering an exhibition that was potentially important to Canadian artists. Their opponents on the other hand, not so much the

Eric Brown, first Director of the National Gallery from 1910 to 1939. Photo by John Vanderpant ca. 1928-1930. Courtesy National Gallery of Canada.

Academy membership in general as the small group of ultra conservatives who through a chain of circumstances happened to be at the Academy's helm, made the mistake of falling back on the murky and unimaginative grounds of demanding their traditional rights.

Eric Brown's role in the whole affair was a curious anomaly. All who knew him well regarded him as a man of great personal honour. No Director could have been more devoted to building the National Gallery — which was perhaps part of the trouble since he obviously came to regard it as the flagship of Canadian art and gradually became more and more defensive of its position as arbiter. In spite of frail health his energy and inventiveness in handling Gallery problems were remarkable. For instance, after the disastrous fire in the Parliament Buildings in 1916, the Victoria Museum was preempted for temporary government offices, leaving the National Gallery literally without walls. The collection was stored in the basement. Operating out of a small office, Brown conceived and initiated the Gallery's policy of circulating exhibitions. He continued to purchase from Academy exhibitions and from other sources, and he assembled a notable collection of both Canadian and European works. By the time the Gallery was able to re-open its doors in 1921, it had matured enormously and was prepared to widen its scope of activity.

Two years later the Wembley challenge presented itself. The exhibition was an obvious potential showcase for Canadian art. Brown was on recent record as declaring to friends that the time was ripe for a systematic move towards international exposure for the Group of Seven. And now here was the opportunity. There was no way that he was going to brook interference from the Academy, and he had the full support of his Board of Trustees.

How far the Wembley matter may have gone off track had not Brown, who was normally the soul of diplomacy, been conditioned since shortly after his arrival in Canada to regard the Academy as an enemy, is open for speculation. But it must be remembered that he had been only two years in the country when he was set, under the eye of his mentor Sir Edmund Walker, to draft the National Gallery Act. That document's main thesis was the total withdrawal of the Gallery from authority from any other body, namely the Academy. To in all conscience carry this policy through, it was necessary for those in charge to take a hard line — of us against them. When all was finished and done, Walker was able to relax his stand and to forgive and forget. But Brown, much younger and nervously disposed to start with, lacked Walker's depth of wisdom and understanding of the frailty of human nature, and knew little of the long struggle of the Academy to stimulate Canadian art and artists. He saw their protests as the unreasonable and unwarranted interference of a few hotheads, and appeared not to realize their grave alarm at the prospect of complete amputation of artists' insight from

Gallery policy. And beneath the surface this pre-conditioning coloured all his subsequent relations with the Academy.

By the time Wembley rolled around, on the administrative level there was certainly plenty of ammunition to fuel Brown's prejudice. But the administration was not the Academy and as the centre ring performance got underway, the members made it perfectly plain that they were not behind the summary pyrotechnics of their executive. Throughout Brown maintained his entrenched position. Artists he loved. But there were artists and there was the Academy. The fact that his artists were almost to a man members of the Academy, he found impossible to fit into his concept. The result was over-reaction to all the antics of the Academy diehards. This in turn simply served to spur the Academy diehards on to greater efforts.

The checklist of developments is pure slapstick.

The Academy kicked off on July 6, 1923, with a circular claimed to have been authorized by Council, but which was not. It was an in-house communication calling on members to show their loyalty by refusing to send works to the National Gallery in October for the Wembley jury. The facts thus far were outlined with considerable licence, stressing that "The Academy has thus been systematically ignored in the arrangements for the British Empire Exhibition." But the slightly hysterical tone of the appeal made the members wary. Most had in any case no strong objection to the National Gallery furthering artists' interests abroad, since because of the war it was some time since the Society had been able to do so. There matters might have rested.

However, after two months of gloomy rumination, both sides decided almost simultaneously to vindicate their position by taking their case to the public. On September 4 the Ottawa *Citizen* printed a reply from the National Gallery in response to the RCA circular. In a cool and calm point by point rebuttal, all accusations were negated with sanctimonious reason, with much made of the fact that after all, the Board of Trustees were only formally responsible for the selection of works of art. The actual jury was to be composed of representative Canadian artists who were *members or associate members of the Academy*. This was indeed good news, but definitely conveyed in a round-about way to the Academy.

Meanwhile, as it happened, Horne Russell had just despatched an open letter to the press addressed to Sir Edmund Walker, protesting the Gallery's handling of the exhibition. The style attempted to be dispassionate and the letter was fairly reasonable if a little long and dramatic. At the time of writing, Horne Russell had not yet read the Gallery's pronouncements in the *Citizen*. When he did he appeared to go berserk. One can picture him and his associate Dyonnet heatedly composing their reply, rashly jumping with all fours into the trap that would hereafter place them in the indefensible position of battling their own colleagues.

The press loved it. Every inflammatory statement that surfaced from here on was printed with impartial relish. Except that is by *Saturday Night*, and their editors were far from impartial. They happily printed Horne Rus-

The Wembley Jury, H. Hands, Ottawa. Courtesy Loring/Wyle Estate.

sell's extravagant statements and on the whole used the issue as a springboard to renew their bitter attack on the National Gallery, blithely stating in a lead article that "It was apparent that an effort would be made through the jury which the Trustees proposed to name, to make the younger and more freakish schools of landscape prominent in the display and eliminate the work of the elder and more accomplished craftsmen."

As the scene heated the National Gallery retired their Director from the front line and brought their big gun to the fore. Sir Edmund Walker wrote both to the Ottawa *Citizen* and to *Saturday Night*, and as in everything else to which he turned his hand, Sir Edmund was an excellent writer. In wise and measured tones, without a trace of recrimination, he deftly defended the Gallery's actions and masterfully obliterated any trace of Gallery indiscretion.

But it was impossible to check the conflagration. The press was too anxious to give space to any and every sensational statement, and the protagonists were only too willing to accommodate them. A juicy letter or interview would no sooner be printed in one journal than its substance would be taken up and reprinted in another. Even Homer Watson was persuaded to enter the fray. *Saturday Night* ruthlessly printed a letter from him in which he querulously invoked past conjecture, "Some members know that there was a spirit in the old advisory board of the National Gallery that was inimical, if not actually hostile to their work," and then completely pulled the rug from beneath him by printing an about-face addendum of their own:

Mr. Homer Watson's communication was written some days before the announcement of the names of the artists' jury selected by the Board of the National Gallery on September 25. The general character of the jury selected is so excellent and so representative of every point of view, that it tends to disarm criticism. The names are as follows: Horatio Walker, RCA; Franklin Brownell, RCA; E. Wyly Grier, RCA; Clarence Gagnon, RCA; Frederick S. Challener, RCA; R.S. Hewton, ARCA; Arthur Lismer, ARCA; Florence Wyle, ARCA.

Scarcely a one-sided jury after all, in fact irreproachable. Who could now protest? Following close on the heels of this announcement a letter was released simultaneously to a number of publications from another respected group of artists. With no histrionics, written with intelligent appraisal, it appealed to fellow members of the RCA to ignore the request for boycott, which they saw as destructive to the cause of Canadian art. The appeal was signed by seven painters, again representing a wide ideological perspective: F.H. Bridgen, E. Wyly Grier, Fred S. Haines, A.Y. Jackson, C.W. Jefferys, J.E.H. MacDonald, H.S. Palmer.

But the battle was not quite over yet. By now the diehards had lost all credibility. They were left standing at the centre of a handful of Montreal artists, well peppered with fellow members of the Pen and Pencil Club, whom they had been able to bully, cajole and regale into line with questionable facts. But they had not run out of steam. When the Toronto *Sunday World* referred to them as "old fogeys," they at once responded with a foolish letter in which they pretended to confound the signers of the earlier artists' letter with "the mystic number of seven" in a last-ditch attempt to intimate that the Group of Seven was behind all the trouble. And they proudly signed their names to the piece: G. Horne Russell, William Hope, E. Dyonnet.

An Appeal to Painters

Editor SATURDAY NIGHT,

Sir: With a desire to help, as far as lies in our power, the project of a British Empire Exhibition to be held in London in 1924, the undersigned give the following as their point of view of the situation as far as the Canadian Art Section is concerned.

The artists are already familiar with the statements that have been made by the Trustees of the National Gallery, on the one hand, and by a committee of the Royal Canadian Academy, on the other. Besides these statements (which the two institutions, respectively, set forth as a statement of fact) there have been comments in the Press.

It is not the purpose of the present writers to adjudicate on the respective merits of the arguments of the two bodies above mentioned. Each of these institutions will be held accountable for its actions by the Dominion Government, of which they are both beneficiaries, and by the Canadian public whose funds they spend, and whom, therefore, they are expected to serve. But it is our purpose to point out certain salient features in the situation: and, in doing so, we address not only the members of the Royal Canadian Academy but all professional artists of Canada.

A circular issued to its members by the Royal Canadian Academy on July 6th, 1923, signed by Messrs. Horne Russell (Present), Wm. Hope and E. Dyonnet, purports to be a summary of an interchange of correspondence between the Academy and the National Gallery. Paragraph 3 relates that the Royal Canadian Academy asked for the "right" to appoint a jury of selection. Paragraph 6 is virtually an effort to induce members to abstain from sending works to the British Empire Exhibition; and members of the Academy are urged to be "loyal to that institution and to uphold its dignity."

Looking at the matter in the large it seems to us that about as "dignified" a method as could be devised in the effort to rehabilitate the commercial and industrial condition of the war-scarred British Empire is that of holding such an exhibition as the one to which artists are invited (not wholly without advantage to themselves) to contribute. And we are of the opinion that our highest loyalty is owed to that Empire.

In the Constitution of the Royal Canadian Academy we find that "The objects of the Academy are......to continue to aid in the advancement of the National Gallery (the institution of which was one of the chief objects set forth in the original Act of Incorporation of the Academy) and to enjoy such privileges in connection with it as the Academy may now have or be hereafter granted." And it is interesting to note that the late President, Mr. Homer Watson, in his last annual report, says "moreover it will be our duty to carry Canada's name to foreign countries and to apprise them of the fact that besides its forests, its mines, its wheat fields, our country possesses a civilizing factor in its painters, sculptors, architects, designers, etc."

The document signed by Messrs. Russell, Hope and Dyonnet no doubt will be dealt with by the assembled membership of the Academy at a later date; but, meanwhile, we feel that loyalty to the Empire and to the Throne (whose Heir is Chairman of the Board of Directors) will be best expressed by the artists of Canada by sending their most important work to the Empire Exhibition; and that in the final issue, such action will be clearly seen to have been true loyalty to the Royal Canadian Academy.

F. H. BRIGDEN
E. WYLY GRIER
FRED S. HAINES
A. Y. JACKSON
C. W. JEFFERYS
J. E. H. MACDONALD
H. S. PALMER

Toronto, Sept. 25, 1923.

An open letter published in several Canadian newspapers in September of 1923, signed by seven painters, and appealing to Canadian artists to ignore the Academy Executives' call for a boycott of the British Empire Exhibition to be held at Wembley, England, in 1924.

The *Sunday World* dubbed them "The Dauntless Three." They came back with the incredible pronouncement that, "...the enforcement of rights and privileges shows strength, not weakness." And finally in an exclusive interview given by The Dauntless Three to the thirsting Montreal correspondent of the *Sunday World*, they surpassed themselves. Horne Russell in the closing statement proclaimed that it was indeed a battle between the loyal artists in Montreal and their disloyal brethren in Toronto, "And we are going to win."

With this, the issue passed far into the realm of blind hysteria, with the original grievance lost completely from sight. Not even the press could stomach more. They quickly let the whole chorus die. Eric Brown was at last allowed to get on with the business of organization, which he did with a thoroughness worthy of Robert Harris in earlier times. The jury met and from 500 entries chose 125 richly varied works, including a fine representation of Group of Seven. Brown, who was definitely a persuasive man under congenial circumstances, managed to convince the Wembley authorities that the Canadian exhibit warranted the best available space, and Canada was actually assigned galleries twice the size of any other British Dominion. Differences appeared to heal over with temporary scar tissue.

And the Academy? Incredibly, throughout the whole fiasco business had gone on as usual. Far from being left in bloody tatters the structure of the organization was almost unscathed. Murderous battles there may have been, but they had not been waged across the sacred Council table. After all, important projects and responsibilities were in the works and must be carried through, and to do so it was necessary to speak to one another. With Russell calmly in the chair the mural competition developed, passed through semi-final stage, with in the end first and second prize actually going to two of the radicals, J.E.H. MacDonald and F.H. Varley respectively. A committee was set up to research candidates for the architectural scholarship, and the annual exhibition was re-routed most successfully to the Art Gallery of Toronto. At the Annual Meeting in November the conflict was not even officially mentioned. For it was one thing for a faction to attempt from time to time to fly dirty linen from the masthead, but quite another to openly violate the inner sanctum.

Then dramatically, in the lee of the controversy, Sir Edmund Walker fell ill with pneumonia and died very suddenly on March 27, 1924. The newspapers were full of his eulogies and indeed as far as Canadian art was concerned, his passing was like a great and stable ship going down. He did not live to see the gratifying success of the Canadian show at Wembley.

The actual exhibition was almost anticlimactic, but at last, in May of 1924, the British Empire Exhibition opened in the Fine Arts Building at Wembley Park. No sooner had the first reviews appeared when it became apparent that the Canadians were the stars of the show. In a generally top calibre display, the British critics particularly noted the work of those painters who were at last interpreting the qualities of the land that their predecessors had always wanted to see, and the praise was unqualified. "We feel, as we look at these pictures, the rush of the mighty winds as they sweep the prairies, the swirl and roar of the swollen river torrents, and the awful silent majesty of her snows," wrote J.M. Millman. And from J. Lewis Hind: "These Canadian landscapes, I think, are the most vital group of paintings produced since the war—indeed this century." There was praise also for the National Gallery's preparations, which were superior to those of any other country and included a beautifully printed catalogue and a fine portfolio of reproductions of Canadian work which attempted to convey its range and general character. Also, the Canadians were ready on time in contrast to other exhibitors. In all it was a major victory both for Canadian artists and for Eric Brown.

Back at home it was a case of the prophet being not without honour except in his own own land. *Saturday Night* railed at the praise in the British press, implying that it was the result of some kind of devilish lobby by the "group of painters which elects to present in exaggerated terms the crudest and most sinister aspects of the Canadian wilds."

"Canada is developing a school of landscape painters who are strongly racy of the soil," enthused the London *Times*.

"Flub-dub!" responded *Saturday Night*.

Horne Russell certainly agreed. He swooped down on London for a zero hour attempt to sabotage the exhibit en situ. "G. Horne Russell Says Exhibit Poor," ran a headline at home, an excerpt from an interview he had given to the London *Daily News*.

But Russell's attack was like the buzzing of a gnat. He assailed officials in charge of the show with the accusation that the Canadian exhibit was not representative of Canadian art (it was, and to the fullest degree—almost every respected name in Canadian art of the day was included except for those few who had refused to submit work). The officials quietly dismissed the confrontation as a domestic quarrel. Nevertheless the National Gallery was again very upset, with neurotic telegrams flying back and forth from Ottawa to London on the subject of firing or not firing the young Ottawa painter, Harold Beament, who was on duty in the Canadian section as information officer, and who had been incorrectly quoted in the press as having pronounced Russell's accusations ill advised when in fact it was National Gallery policy to maintain a diplomatic silence. In the end Eric Brown's sense of fair play prevailed and Beament, who had been largely responsible for encouraging the generally magnificent press coverage, was left to continue with his duties.

Beament and Brown were both there when the Royal Family came to see the exhibit. The entire building was closed to the public for the occasion and the King (George V) and Queen with their two sons, the Prince of Wales and the Duke of York, moved in progession from gallery to gallery. It was a trying experience for those in attendance since an alcoholic fog accompanied the royal party, with one royal temper on edge and an appreciation of modern art thought in very slight evidence. The King, however, expressed himself with warm sincerity as wishing to have the wilder Canadian works explained, a challenge which Eric Brown met with considerable finesse.

But the final word on the Wembley exhibit was personified by a young South African artist, Will Ogilvie, who had recently arrived in London for further study. So positively did he respond to the fresh vigour and very personal expression of the Canadians, that he set aside plans for staying in London in favour of seeking out the painting atmosphere in the country that had nurtured such vivid works. And so Canada, and later the Academy, acquired another distinguished artist.

Ironically, the triumph of the Wembley exhibition did not endear Eric Brown to his enemies at home. Quite the opposite. They simply pulled their necks back into their shells and waited for a suitable opportunity to attack him again.

Robert Harris
The Countess of Minto
Oil on canvas 52″ x 38″
Exhibited RCA 1903
Montreal Museum of Fine Arts

Philippe Hébert
L'Inspiration
Bronze 22½″ high
RCA Diploma sculpture, deposited 1907
National Gallery of Canada

Aurèle de Foy Suzor-Coté
Settlement on the Hillside
Oil on canvas 23″ x 28¾″
Exhibited RCA 1909
National Gallery of Canada

Laura Muntz Lyall
A Daffodil
Oil on canvas 25¼″ x 18½″
Exhibited RCA 1910
National Gallery of Canada

Horatio Walker
Evening, Ile d'Orléans
Oil on canvas 28¼″ x 36″
Exhibited RCA 1909, Wembley 1924
Art Gallery of Ontario

Maurice Cullen
The Old Ferry, Louise Basin, Quebec
Oil on canvas 23³/₄″ x 28³/₄″
Exhibited RCA, Liverpool, 1910
National Gallery of Canada

A.Y. Jackson
The Edge of the Maple Wood
Oil on canvas 22½″ x 26″
Exhibited RCA 1910, Liverpool 1910
National Gallery of Canada

A. Dickson Patterson
Portrait of Homer Watson
Oil on canvas 24″ x 30″
Exhibited RCA 1910 and 1922
National Gallery of Canada
(Gift of RCA, 1930)

F.M. Bell-Smith
Mists and Glaciers of the Selkirks
Oil on canvas 33¼″ x 49½″
Exhibited RCA 1911, Wembley 1924
National Gallery of Canada

J. W. Morrice
Dieppe, The Beach, Grey Effect
Oil on canvas 23¹/₄″ x 31¹/₂″
Exhibited RCA 1912, Wembley 1924
National Gallery of Canada

J.E.H. MacDonald
Tracks and Traffic
Oil on canvas 28″ x 40″
Exhibited RCA, Winnipeg 1912
Art Gallery of Ontario

E. Wyly Grier
The Master of Northcote
Oil on canvas 28¼″ x 23″
Exhibited RCA 1913
National Gallery of Canada

Homer Watson
Evening After Rain
Oil on canvas 31⁵/₈″ x 40¹/₂″
Exhibited RCA 1913
Art Gallery of Ontario

Mary Heister Reid
A Study in Greys
Oil on canvas 25³/₁₆″ x 30¹/₈″
Exhibited RCA 1913
Art Gallery of Ontario

A.Y. Jackson
The Red Maple
Oil on canvas 34$\frac{1}{2}$″ x 38$\frac{1}{4}$″
Exhibited RCA 1914
National Gallery of Canada

Herbert S. Palmer
Fall Ploughing
Oil on canvas 43½″ x 47½″
Exhibited RCA 1914
National Gallery of Canada

Arthur Lismer
The Guide's Home, Algonquin
Oil on canvas 39½″ x 44½″
Exhibited RCA 1914 and 1915
National Gallery of Canada

Henry Sproatt
Design for Burwash Hall,
Victoria College, Toronto
Drawing, water colour 18¾″ x 52″
RCA Diploma work, deposited 1915
National Gallery of Canada

J.W. Beatty
Morning, Algonquin Park
Oil on canvas 30″ x 36″
Exhibited RCA 1914, 1915, Wembley 1924
National Gallery of Canada

J.E.H. MacDonald
The Tangled Garden
Oil on board 48″ x 60″
Exhibited RCA 1916
National Gallery of Canada

Ozias Leduc
Neige dorée
Oil on canvas 54″ x 30″
Exhibited RCA 1916, Wembley 1924
National Gallery of Canada

A. Curtis Williamson
Portrait of Dr. J.M. MacCallum ('A Cynic')
Oil on canvas 26½″ x 21½″
Exhibited RCA 1918 and 1919
National Gallery of Canada

G. Horne Russell
Carting Seaweed
Oil on canvas 32″ x 47″
Exhibited RCA 1918
Art Gallery of Ontario

F. H. Varley
Self Portrait
Oil on canvas 24″ x 20″
Exhibited RCA 1920
National Gallery of Canada

Walter Allward
The Storm
Bronze 13¼″ high
RCA Diploma sculpture,
deposited 1921
National Gallery of Canada

Henri Hébert
Evangeline
Bronze
Exhibited RCA 1921
National Gallery of Canada

E. Wyly Grier
Portrait of Sir Edmund Walker
Oil on canvas 50³/₈″ x 40¹/₈″
Exhibited RCA 1922
Art Gallery of Ontario

Ernest Fosbery
**Portrait of Affy, Daughter
of the Artist**
Oil on canvas 30″ x 25″
Exhibited RCA 1922, Wembley 1924
National Gallery of Canada

Walter J. Phillips
Lake of the Woods
Water colour on canvas
19⅝″ x 15⅝″
Exhibited RCA 1922
Art Gallery of Ontario

Florence Wyle
Bust of F. H. Varley
Bronze 15″ high
Exhibited RCA 1922
National Gallery of Canada

A. H. Robinson
Returning from Easter Mass
Oil on canvas 27¹/₂″ x 33¹/₂″
Exhibited RCA 1923
Art Gallery of Ontario

R. F. Gagen
Late Afternoon
Oil on canvas 27¼″ x 36¼″
Exhibited RCA 1923
National Gallery of Canada

Arthur Lismer
A September Gale, Georgian Bay
Oil on canvas 48″ x 64″
Exhibited RCA 1922, Wembley 1924
National Gallery of Canada

Horatio Walker
Oxen Drinking
Oil on canvas 47$^{1}/_{2}$″ x 35$^{1}/_{2}$″
Exhibited Wembley 1924,
RCA Horatio Walker Retrospect 1959
National Gallery of Canada

Edwin H. Holgate
Suzy
Oil on canvas 23¼″ x 28¼″
Exhibited RCA 1922, Wembley 1924
National Gallery of Canada

Clarence Gagnon
A Laurentian Homestead, Winter
Oil on canvas 20¼" x 26¼"
Exhibited RCA 1919 and 1925,
Wembley 1924
National Gallery of Canada

Randolph S. Hewton
Portrait of Audrey Buller
Oil on canvas 39½″ x 30″
Exhibited Wembley 1924
National Gallery of Canada

Lilias Torrance Newton
Anna
Oil on canvas 29$^1/_2''$ x 23$^1/_2''$
Exhibited Wembley 1924
National Gallery of Canada

F. H. Varley
Stormy Weather, Georgian Bay
Oil on canvas 52″ x 64″
Exhibited Wembley 1924
National Gallery of Canada

A. J. Casson
Clearing
Oil on canvas $36^1/2''$ x $45^1/4''$
Exhibited Wembley 1924
National Gallery of Canada

J. E. H. MacDonald
The Beaver Dam
Oil on canvas 32⅛″ x 34⅛″
Exhibited RCA 1919, Wembley 1924
Art Gallery of Ontario

A.Y. Jackson
The Entrance to Halifax Harbour
Exhibited Wembley 1924, and purchased
by the Tate Gallery, London

Chapter Seven

Renegades in Cry

PAINTERS DEMAND THE HEAD OF THE ART DICTATOR OF CANADA.

Dramatic copy. No wonder that after a quiet year or two the Toronto *Star* was amenable to fuelling the old controversy. In November of 1926 a reporter interviewed several members of the Academy and printed a long diatribe against Eric Brown and his support of the Group of Seven. "Mr. Eric Brown, the curator of the National Gallery at Ottawa, is acting as the art dictator of Canada. Some of us demand his head. Some will be satisfied if his wings are clipped. All of us are determined to assert our rights as the supreme art authority of Canada."

Although the protagonists were not identified, the flavour was surely vintage Horne Russell. In any case as one of his first official acts of office the new Academy President, architect Henry Sproatt was called upon to disclaim the interview in a letter to the *Star*, as having nothing to do with RCA policy.

The contest was hardly new, but simply an addendum to the issues surrounding the Wembley exhibition, which from their beginning in 1923 were to drag on for a full decade.

Incredibly, Horne Russell lasted as President for two years following the Wembley confrontation, which was an indication of the potency of his limited base of support. To his enduring credit he carried on as though nothing had happened and managed to push ahead with several positive programs. The architectural competition was resolved resulting in young Montreal architect Leslie A. Perry setting off for six months' work in Europe. A poster competition was held and drew in forty-eight entries from across the country. The subject, chosen by the artists, was to be approached as an advertisement for Canada, and the winning entry was that of Robertson Mulholland of Toronto, with O. Leger of Montreal awarded second prize. And in 1926 another original and highly successful mural competition was staged. This time the Academy managed to put up $2,000, and arranged for the final works to be carried out in suitable public buildings. In this way George Reid decorated walls in Earlscourt Library in Toronto, Charles W. Simpson a strip of wall above the large doors of the lecture hall of the Art Association of Montreal, Hal Ross Perrigard a mural in the ladies' waiting room in Montreal's Windsor Station, Robert W. Pilot a portion of a wall in Montreal High School (which he had once attended), and Donald Hill an area in Strathcarn School, Montreal.

RCA Associate Membership Diploma for Charles
Comfort, ARCA 1936, RCA 1945. Designed in 1907 by
A.H. Howard.

But the time of comparative regeneration
was short. The minute Russell was out of
office the acceleration of guerilla tactics was
obvious, and this time it was with active input
of a few disaffected individuals in Ontario. A
blessing in a sense, Brymner, who had earlier
worked so hard to forestall such destructive
behaviour, had been spared by his protracted
illness from direct exposure to the immodera-
tion of his old comrades in arms in Montreal,
and he had died in 1925 while on a visit to
England with his wife. For all in all Henry
Sproatt, the eminent architect who had
designed the recently completed Hart House
at the University of Toronto, took over a hor-
net's nest when he followed Russell as President of the Academy.

He was of course the first Academy President who was not a painter. O'Brien, Jacobi,
Harris, Reid, Brymner, Russell. It will be
remembered too that he had been Vice President when Russell was elected President, and
so had had a ringside seat throughout the
Wembley performance. He must surely have
hesitated before agreeing to stand at the helm.

He was, however, an excellent choice at the
time since he was by predilection a man with a
foot in the past and therefore acceptable to
the renegades, but he had also a strong sense
of responsibility to the arts in general and
would take only so much disruptive nonsense
before putting his foot down. His background
too fitted him admirably for riding calmly
against the storm. Born in Toronto in 1886,
with his family he had followed in the wake of
his father's postings throughout rural Ontario
as a railway construction engineer. Mt. Forest,

Orangeville, Caledon. It was an interesting, solid, unflappable kind of childhood. At sixteen he was articled to the Toronto architect Arthur R. Dennison, and subsequently studied further in New York and eventually in Europe. By 1893 he was back in Toronto, and after progressing through several architectural partnerships, he finally formed the firm of Sproatt and Rolph and quickly began to make a reputation as an authority on Gothic architecture, which indeed he built. Bishop Strachan School, Toronto; Victoria College Library and Burwash Hall, Victoria College, University of Toronto; and his masterpiece, Hart House. In an era where startling new architectural concepts were beginning to change the look of the western world, Sproatt, who has been referred to in all respect as a medieval man, serenely followed his own dictum, albeit six or seven hundred years out of date. "Each style has its own place, but Gothic collegiate architecture is one architecture developed for scholastic work. It has proved a success and a joy. Why throw it away?"

Balancing this philosophy, architecture was the dominating force in Sproatt's life, and in contrast to many architects of his time he approached it as a profession and an art, rather than as a business, which gave him insight into the obscure world of painters and sculptors. During his term as Academy President, he unfortunately laboured under the crippling drawbacks of a recent severe cutback of the annual grant due to government economies, and from the continuing threat of right-wing explosion.

The first major volleys were not long in coming. Early in the new year of 1927 Ernest Fosbery, an Associate of the Academy who for many years had been in charge of the Academy Life Classes in Ottawa, wrote a letter to the press in which he took issue with a newly published book which extolled the Group of Seven, *A Canadian Art Movement*, by F.B. Housser. He used the book as a springboard to reopen the attack on the National Gallery purchasing policy, and particularly on Eric Brown. Fosbery, along with Academician John Hammond of Sackville, Nova Scotia — both highly traditional painters of long experience — then interviewed the Prime Minister and attempted to convince him of Brown's biased policy.

When the Prime Minister did not act, Fosbery repeated the charges in the press, at which time the Gallery's Board of Directors entered the ring to issue a denial of the accusation. Undeterred, Fosbery attacked again, ignoring the rebuttal of his earlier indictment.

Meanwhile Brown, the object of so much concerted interest, was out of the immediate line of fire in France, where he was arranging for the installation of an upcoming Canadian exhibit. The French government had invited Canada to send the second British Empire Exhibition (1925) from London on to Paris, with the addition of works by the late painters Morrice and Thomson to complete the Canadian survey. The invitation was of course prestigious, and another feather in Brown's cap.

No matter, back at home some of his own Board of Trustees began to squirm uncomfortably as the new attack was pressed. Shades of the first Wembley exhibit were conjured up by Fosbery who claimed that Horne Russell, at the time in question President of the Academy, had not been invited to submit.

Sheer absurdity, as the Trustees might have been expected to remember. And to Fosbery's charge that Brown's art lectures given across the country extolled only the virtues of the Group of Seven, the worthy gentlemen began to react with distinct unease: "...this may be indiscreet for an official of the National Gallery." Poor Brown, besieged on all sides. Fortunately his position was very ably defended by his lieutenant at the Gallery, H.O. McCurry, a man with both feet firmly on the ground, and well able to walk the fine line between obviously disgruntled artists and nervous members of the Board.

McCurry after all maneuvered from a position of some strength. There is every evidence that while the National Gallery may have in the past outdistanced discretion with its seeming infatuation with the Group, there were no longer grounds for such a charge. Their purchasing policy now centred around an annual exhibit gathered together in Ottawa, and which consisted of the cream of the crop skimmed mainly from the regular juried exhibitions of the RCA, the OSA and the AAM, held throughout that year. The Societies in each case appointed a jury to work with Eric Brown in choosing work from their respective exhibits, and from these assembled paintings and sculptures the National Gallery made its yearly purchases. The system was widely applauded by Canadian artists, and when Fosbery showed no signs of running down, a respected group organized themselves to make their position clear. By the end of March three informal petitions had arrived in Ottawa from artists including many Academy members in Montreal, Toronto and Ottawa, all emphatically supporting Eric Brown. And at the Annual Assembly the following autumn the Academy broke its longstanding unofficial policy of non-alignment in ideological disputes:

It was moved by Percy E. Nobbs, seconded by C.W. Simpson, that with a view to securing better discipline within the ranks of the Academy the President be requested to circularize members pointing out in such terms as his expression may suggest that it is not in the interest of the Academy that members should give public, individual expression to their views on the conduct and capacity of Government officials.

But although the combined censure of both their peers and of the Academy slowed the momentum of the renegades, it was more in the sense of closing a sequence rather than of ending the issue. The worst was yet to come.

In the interim, there were definitely one or two factors contributing to discontent with the Gallery.

Typical fodder for the cannon was the peremptory response from the National Gallery to a very serious, if naive Academy petition in 1928. In February of that year Henry Sproatt headed a deputation consisting of the Vice President Wyly Grier, and the Secretary Edmund Dyonnet, to meet with the Trustees of the National Gallery. Dyonnet aside, the other two men were highly credible pros, enormously respected within their own disciplines—Grier was later knighted—and both had unblemished records in previous brushes with Gallery officials. In fact Grier had signed the famous letter from the seven artists supporting the National Gallery at the height of the Wembley furor, and had also been one of the jurors.

However, their brief was of a highly distasteful nature to the Trustees, requesting once again as it did the representation on their Board of the President of the Academy. Further, the brief asked that responsibility for selection of pictures representative of Canada for both foreign and at home exhibitions revert again to the Academy. The only point to which the Gallery was able to respond was that of asking friendly co-operation in the restoration of the Academy's $7,500 annual government grant of recent years, which had suddenly been cut back to $2,500. And while polite language was used to the delegates on the spot, ensuing correspondence between the Director and his Board lacked the same moderation. The tenor of the written response being drafted was so officious that it roused the heated objection of one Board member, Dr. Newton McTavish, who was appalled by the high-toned reasons being spelled out to justify adamant rejection of the President of the Academy as a representative on the Board.

McTavish's voice would probably not have carried much weight on its own. He was a maverick and his past actions as a somewhat irascible defender of the artists' point of view had earned him a reputation as a discordant influence on the Board. But this time there was one other Trustee who recognized, although he didn't agree with it, that the Academy was presenting a petition based on sincere conviction, and as such it was neither necessary nor fitting to treat their brief as the work of naughty children. Vincent Massey readily acceded to McTavish's demand that a particularly offending paragraph be deleted from the Gallery's reply. In face of such

respected opinion the remaining officials agreed, although the end result remained unchanged. The Academy's requests were flatly denied.

Another incident in that same year underlined the growing impatience of the National Gallery in the face of critical challenge. Mortimer Lamb, a west coast writer and art critic, strongly suggested in an article in the Vancouver *Province*, that both the Academy and the National Gallery should give more attention to the development and encouragement of art in the West, which he claimed was neglected. For, he pointed out, "It's difficult for art to blossom in an uncongenial and uncultivated soil."

Lamb minced no words in outlining his theme, but he did so with informed intelligence and his approach was highly constructive. The Academy for instance he felt might, without lowering its standards, confer Associate status on a selected number of western artists, and he cited Victoria artist Emily Carr as a case in point. And while he recognized that it was probably not practical for the Academy to mount its full exhibitions out west, he suggested that they might arrange for the most representative paintings hung at the annual exhibitions to tour the principal western cities. Both highly sensible and feasible possibilities.

But then he went on to the crux of his unease and took the National Gallery to task for not dealing adequately with western needs. "The national collections of paintings and other works should not be hoarded in Ottawa." It seems that while the West was receiving travelling shows, they encompassed only Canadian work, and not the best at that.

155

Examples from the Gallery's European collection and the more valuable and important Canadian works were never sent, and impoverished local centres had to pay expenses and insurance to get the works at all. Lamb urged the National Gallery to foster development of a series of local galleries in co-operation with local governments, which would be suitable for receiving the more interesting and vital works.

Obviously a man ahead of his time (all his points were eventually to be realized at least in modified form), Lamb's blueprint for a more equitable distribution of cultural resources did not strike Eric Brown as at all plausible. His reactions were made plain in a reply to the Vancouver *Province*. "There was never any intention of making the National Gallery into a permanent national supply for art. . . ." Railing on about the negative effects of such "destructive and irresponsible criticism," he ended with an outright threat. "The effect of such untempered criticism will be that in future efforts [the National Gallery] will very naturally take the line of least resistance and gravitate towards appreciation and away from its opposite."

It was language worthy only of the most intransigent of the Academy diehards, and would never have issued from the National Gallery in the days of Sir Edmund Walker. Undoubtedly Brown, who had given so much of himself and so successfully to the cause of Canadian art, was justified in feeling that Lamb was unacquainted with the full facts of the Gallery's unstinting efforts. But as Lamb so nicely put his reply, ". . .as a wise man and public servant his role was to presume (even if

he did not believe) that I was actuated by disinterested public-spirited motives; and if it was necessary for him to disagree with a point of view, a courteous and sympathetic dissent would have preserved the amenities."

This then was part of the temper of the times when in 1929 Henry Sproatt, who had been struggling under tremendous negative pressures, offered his resignation to the Annual Assembly and was replaced as President by E. Wyly Grier. Relevant too was the situation reflected that year in the election of Ernest Fosbery as a full Academician. Only two years earlier Fosbery had been chastized by his fellow artists as a renegade. How then could he have bypassed such competition as Group of Seven member J.E.H. MacDonald when this vacancy for an Academician painter occurred? The two men had been elected Associates in 1912. MacDonald, on the merits of his professional performance, should have been accorded full membership years earlier. He had won two Academy competitions, had over and over again submitted his most superb landscapes to Academy shows, and he was the much loved principal of the Ontario College of Art. The fact that at this time he was left behind by a less inspired painter of traditional portraits, merely pointed up renewed signs of life in the renegade ranks and showed clearly their ability to play for support among the now largely ageing and increasingly conservative body of Academicians. For of course as time went by, with the number of full Academicians set by the Constitution, gradually the average age of members had increased, leaving the younger artists in a holding pattern as Associates, with no legal say in the society's business. All in all, time was ripening for a final showdown.

On the surface, as so often before, matters appeared to be moving well enough. Of the annual exhibition in 1928, art critic Augustus Bridle had written in the *Star*, "Almost monotonously fine.... Excellence by the square yard." Arrangements were made to supply sixteen pictures for an exhibit at the Imperial Gallery of Art in London, England, and as if in response to Lamb's eloquent plea, an Academy show was organized by Winnipeg member W.J. Phillips, and successfully toured Calgary, Vancouver and Edmonton. Most important, former President George Reid, himself almost seventy years old, called at a Council meeting in May of 1929 for fundamental alterations to the Constitution to make it more democratic—the first crack in the dyke that would eventually give voice and voting privileges to the Associates.

Wyly Grier, aside from O.R. Jacobi, was at sixty-seven years of age the oldest man to be elected President of the Academy. His association with the Society had already spanned nearly half a century. It was in 1883, at the opening of the Academy's fourth exhibition in Toronto, that the Princess Louise had been struck by a painting "The Connoisseur," and had asked to have the artist presented to her. Grier was that artist, a youth of twenty-one whose work was making its first appearance on Academy walls. The presentation uncannily presaged a career that would bring him, as a distinguished portrait painter, into contact with many wealthy and influential patrons.

Unlike many of his predecessors, Grier's artistic leanings had been encouraged at home from earliest childhood. Born in Melbourne, Australia, he had moved with his peripatetic family to Canada (he attended Upper Canada College in 1877), then back and forth to England twice before finally settling in Toronto in 1891. The intriguing story is told of how in England he was apprenticed to a surveying engineer, in a mistaken attempt on the part of his parents to fit their son's artistic ability into practical channels. The youth very soon fell violently ill, and did not recover until his doctor father recognized the psychological source of the disorder, and immediately reversed his attitude to now back his son in his painting without reservation. Study followed in London, Rome and Paris and was attended by remarkable success. Not only was his work noted en route in the Academy show in provincial Toronto, it was also soon accepted in exhibitions of the Royal Academy in London, and in 1890 he won a gold medal at the prestigious Paris Salon. By the mid-nineties, back in Toronto for good, he was already successful as a genre and portrait painter, and his good fortune appeared to continue without pause throughout the length of his career.

A man of enormous exuberance for life, Grier excelled at many things—riding, hunting, fishing, canoeing, and not the least as family man. He was an accomplished drawing room baritone, a fine raconteur who could entertain restive sitters with a stream of amusing anecdotes, and a public speaker of almost professional calibre. Past President of the OSA (1908-1913), founding member of the Arts and Letters Club (Toronto's more sophisticated answer to Montreal's Pen and Pencil Club, founded in 1908), an artist of voluminous output and solid attainment, it is difficult to reconcile a professional of his wide experience as aligning himself with the renegades.

And yet he did, and at a time when they were gearing into their least credible phase. In retrospect one can only assume that as a traditional painter he empathized with the root cause of the disenchantment with the National Gallery, that he despaired of its improving, and once involved was ethically committed out of loyalty to his immediate associates to see the whole thing through to its conclusion.

The year was 1932.

On January 15, Arthur Hemming, a Toronto artist, wrote to H.S. Southam who was publisher of the Ottawa *Citizen*, and currently Chairman of the Board of Trustees at the National Gallery. Like an old saw the tune of the letter was over-familiar. It asked for the dismissal of Eric Brown on the grounds of his allowing personal and distorted judgement of art to colour his selections of Gallery purchases.

In essence Hemming, who was essentially an illustrator only recently adapting to a fully colour palette for his exhibition paintings, had been offended when his painting had not been chosen from the 1931 RCA show in Montreal for inclusion in the next National Gallery annual exhibition. Following a convoluted logic, he claimed discrimination in that although the National Gallery already owned two of his works, they were both from a set of illustrations for a book, and therefore as such did not represent his painting.

Scarcely cause for war. Most artists who chanced to hear of the episode at all merely yawned and thought, surely not again!

But the issue was not to be so easily dismissed. Ernest Fosbery, sincere but querulous man that he was, still brooding over his earlier thwarted quarrel with the National Gallery, saw circumstances propitious to strike again. As Hemming continued on one front with a letter to the Prime Minister, R.B. Bennett, Fosbery moved to engage a lawyer to organize a formal petition of protest against the common enemy. During the spring sixty-five names were gathered which included a number of well-known academic painters together with many totally unknown names of purported painters. The petition was addressed to the Governor General in Council, with a summary of related facts forwarded to the Prime Minister. In face of all that had gone before it was obviously not a very convincing case, and the authorities tended to ignore the petition as far as possible. Most artists knew little or nothing about it and no more was heard of the business until June, when the National Gallery received a letter of apology from the British Columbia Society of Fine Arts, who had just realized that their name had been used as a sponsor on the petition without their consent.

As late as October the President of the OSA, L.A.C. Panton was writing to H.O. McCurry at the National Gallery for confirmation of the rumours of Fosbery's subversive activity. "Yes," answered McCurry, "a lawyer has been 'working' on the 'case' for nearly six months. What he will accomplish except to spend his client's money and make some Canadian artists more ridiculous, I cannot imagine."

Throughout, the National Gallery played it cool. McCurry, who was on truly friendly terms with a number of artists, kept lines of communication open to them and maintained a realistic perspective on the diversion. Brown, who had been most unfairly accused, kept a low profile and left the public relations in McCurry's less nervous hands. At this point there was actually nothing to connect the incipient trouble with the Academy, other than the fact that one of the ringleaders was a member. In November the Academy show took place as usual, and Eric Brown met with members Wyly Grier, Emanuel Hahn and J.E.H. MacDonald (who had finally been elected a member the previous year, and who was to die within a month) to choose works for the National Gallery exhibit. Grier expressed himself, in word and by following letter, as being extremely pleased with the results of the jurying.

It was therefore a severe shock to all but the protagonists when, on December 8, the Ottawa *Journal* flew a column head and article proclaiming:
ARTISTS BOYCOTT NATIONAL GALLERY UNTIL RADICAL REFORM TAKES PLACE.

"More than 100 artists from coast to coast [for more signatures had been collected] many of whose names are household words, have signed an agreement... 'to refuse to send any of their work to the National Gallery or to any exhibition initiated by it.'" Almost simultaneously similar material appeared in newspapers across the country with Wyly Grier, as President of the Royal Canadian Academy of Arts, quoted as asking for a "searching investigation" of National Gallery policy.

Reaction was swift and by the time all was said and done, no artist in the country remained untouched.

Toronto sculptor and Academy Associate Florence Wyle, herself a traditionalist as far as her own work was concerned, was the first to be interviewed by the Canadian Press for her reaction. She advised, "If our artists, including the 118, would leave amateur politics alone and paint, they might have less cause for complaint." And she went on, "Mr. Eric Brown, the curator, and the trustees of the National Gallery have a thankless task. In my opinion they have done much for Canadian art, all that has been within their power."

By December 12 rumours were circulating that A.Y. Jackson had resigned from the Academy in protest of the actions of the President and others, which had placed the Academy in the position of being unfriendly to the National Gallery, and the rumour was later confirmed.

Meanwhile, although this time around the National Gallery was very careful to make no piously inflammatory remarks in their own defence, nevertheless behind the scenes the usual hysteria unleashed itself like the tendrils of an old nightmare. Memoranda placed sinister interpretation on developments. "The present riot has been staged with no other purpose than to gain control of the National Institution by the Royal Canadian Academy, such as was contemplated by the individual who inserted the objectional clause in the Bill introduced in 1913."

Yet it was to be from the ranks of the Academy that Brown's strength of support was to come. Arthur Lismer ARCA, who at the time was contributing a byline to the Ottawa *Citizen* wrote, "...the artist's business is to paint, while the Gallery's business is to hold exhibitions and to circulate pictures, sculptures and educational material. The Gallery's duty is primarily to the public and not to the artist." At the same time in Toronto rousing meetings were being held night after night in either the old church studio of Frances Loring and Florence Wyle on Glenrose Avenue, or in the Studio Building on Severn Street, as artists of both the Academy and the OSA attempted to contrive a way to defuse once and for all their fanatic and indefatiguable colleagues. Finally a manifesto in support of Eric Brown and the National Gallery was satisfactorily hammered out and sculptors Frances Loring ARCA and Elizabeth Wyn Wood ARCA undertook the complex task of circulating it in the form of a petition to professional artists throughout the entire country. The result, for the times, was a massive demonstration of unanimity in support of Brown and the National Gallery.

Even an unaffiliated artist such as the reclusive David Milne of Palgrave, Ontario, was roused to respond. Certainly his letter to H.O. McCurry at the height of the furor shows him for the lone wolf that he was. "So far as the RCA and the OSA, and even the Group of Seven are concerned I am not a bit worried. They may shoot their heads off and welcome if it pleases them." But he was all for the National Gallery and when the time came his name was on the petition prepared by the members of precisely those groups.

On January 30, 1933, the completed petition was delivered to the National Gallery. It contained the signatures of nearly three hundred professional artists from nearly every province in the country:

We, the undersigned artists, believe that the policy of the National Gallery of Canada to be fair to all Canadian artists and all phases of Canadian art, and we have full confidence in the Trustees and the Director, Mr. Eric Brown, and in their administration of the Gallery.

And at last, after ten long years there was the silence of defeat in the renegade camp.

Chapter Eight

Towards Democracy

When Arthur Lismer was elected a full Academician in 1946, fellow member Harold Beament telephoned to congratulate him. "Well Harold, it's about time," Lismer responded. "Do you know how long I've waited as an Associate? Twenty-seven bloody years!"

And it was true that in this area the Constitution had remained unchanged since 1880. A specified number of Academicians in each discipline (22 painters, 5 sculptors, 9 architects, 4 designers, etchers and engravers) made up a total of forty. An unlimited number of Associates (there were 65 in 1946) was allowed however, and as a vacancy occurred through death or retirement among the Academicians, it was filled by voting an Associate up from the ranks. In the early years the system had worked well and had posed no particular problem. There were far fewer artists in general, and a rigorously controlled membership was a means of building standards where none before had existed. But by the time fifty years had passed, inevitably it was a different world. Obviously there were a great many more artists working, standards had re-aligned, and problems had become more complex. Yet with no compulsory retirement age for Academicians, the average age of full members had gradually become older, and older, and older, with a surprising number tracing their Academy connections back to the very earliest years. They were on the whole a hardy lot, and vacancies were at a premium with the numbers of highly eligible Associates far exceeding the possibilities for elevation.

Some of course never made it at all, had even died before their turn came around. Other fine talents sometimes became disillusioned and gave up and resigned after years of waiting on the shelf. By the mid thirties, with no vote and thus no real participation in Academy affairs, these men and women who represented the younger and more vigorous elements in Canadian art found themselves in an increasingly frustrating position. New blood was needed to combat the internal demoralization that resulted from the years of infighting. And yet the changes that would allow this were continually blocked by the older Academicians who in spite of their very real devotion to the organization, had for the most part long since ceased to be aware of altered priorities.

Paradoxically, it is in this period of apparent atrophy that the great strength of the Academy becomes most evident. For although reform was slow in coming, come it did, from within, and was the major preoccupation of a growing number of both Associates and Academicians throughout the late thirties and the forties. And despite the debilitating activities of the previous decade, the enormous value placed by artists on Academy membership should not be underestimated. Most members belonged as well to other organizations, to one or several of the special interest groups that had splintered off over the years to promote specific areas in the arts: the Canadian Society of Painters-Etchers, the Graphic Art Society, the Canadian Society of Painters in Water Colour, the Sculptors' Society of Canada, the Canadian Group of Painters. But as far as the artists, or for that matter the public were concerned, Academy membership carried very special significance. Charles Comfort, who was an emerging painter in the thirties, later described it in terms of an accumulative and coveted honour in which membership in the OSA could be equated to an artist receiving his BA degree, with ARCA and finally RCA parallel to an MA and then a PhD in the scale of professional achievement. The source of this prestige and of the self-renewing qualities of the organization, was the artistic excellence of its members — Academicians and Associates — who with very few oversights or holdouts (Emily Carr, David Milne, Lawren Harris) represented the best there was at the time in Canadian art. On this level, no matter what the borders of ideological reserve, certain bonds of artistic empathy were impervious to storms. Lismer, that most quotable of painters, had written earlier, "...art is not a professional practice

Sir Wyly Grier, President RCA 1929-1939. Photo courtesy National Gallery of Canada.

but a way of life." And there was not a man among the most hidebound traditionalists who in common with the ultra moderns did not understand, first hand, the implications of commitment implicit in that statement. Nor were there many who did not look to the Academy as the chief hope for defence of this truth in a materially oriented society.

On this basis it was therefore quite possible for Wyly Grier to continue after 1932 as an effective President, and the thirties were surprisingly lively years for the Academy. Accustomed as they were to recurring periods of stark difficulty the artists were troubled less than most people by the lack of opportunity in the Great Depression. Fortunate, since in 1932 no works of art whatsoever sold from the Academy show in Toronto. It was little better in the following year when only two small landscapes sold, but the opening in Montreal was festive because of the presence of the new Governor General and his wife, the Earl and Countess of Bessborough. Stealing the scene however was portrait painter Marion Long, who at the Annual Assembly that day had been elected an Academician, the first woman to achieve full membership since Charlotte Schreiber was named a Charter member over fifty years earlier. Painter Fred Haines was also elevated and was shortly to surface in his new position as a quiet but unrelenting advocate for change in Associate status.

George Reid's bid several years earlier to move towards a more democratic structure had not met with a very lively response, but of course attention had been rivetted elsewhere in the intervening period. In 1934, with the Associates becoming restive, Fred Haines made the first concrete move to activate momentum by proposing that "The Associates shall at the Annual Assembly elect one of their number to act as a member of Council with full voting privileges." This was however a strong first dose for the Academicians to swallow, and they compromised by passing a motion endorsing the principle of election of an Associate as an "advisory" member of Council.

At least it was a step in the right direction and there appeared to be reasonable hope for restructure. But the reformers had figured without the immutability of Mr. Dyonnet, who at seventy-five was still entrenched at the core of Academy affairs. Charming old curmudgeon, he was passionately loyal in his own fashion to the Academy. And when it came to organizing the yearly exhibitions, no one could touch him for efficiency. Alas, his devotion was exceeded only by his implacable resistance to and active manipulation against all moves for reform. As time passed it was to become increasingly evident that no matter what the makeup of Council and no matter who was President, long-practised political strategist Mr. Dyonnet would find means of circumventing all change. Yet because of his strong image as devoted and irreplaceable servant, only those close to the centre of activity realized the full extent of his interference — and none dared to confront him. In the end it was to be Fred Haines who was called upon to bell the cat.

Well before that time the continuous embarrassment caused to the Academy by the Secretary's unlicenced prejudices was underlined in a letter from Percy E. Nobbs to H.O. McCurry at the National Gallery. Nobbs was Dean of Architecture at McGill University,

and was serving at the time on the Academy Council. It seemed that McCurry had been receiving offensive missiles from Dyonnet, and Nobbs was writing an indulgent apology. "Treat them as pathological," he advised. "The dear old fellow is getting 'difficult.' No amount of reason or fact can dislodge an idea that has once got into his head."

Otherwise relations with the National Gallery had taken a new and positive turn. McCurry appeared to have assumed all liaison with the artists, with Eric Brown whose nerves and health had suffered in the recent and final public skirmish with the diehards, retreating to the more theoretic realms of directorship at which he so excelled. In a welcome change of policy, unheard of for many years, the National Gallery invited the Academy to select seventy-five pictures for a Gallery-sponsored travelling exhibit. The show was to open in Ottawa early in 1934, and then to travel extensively throughout the West. The resulting tour was a great success and marked the beginning of a series of similar ventures over a number of years.

The truce while sincere was somewhat uneasy. That same year an Academy History had appeared, written by architect member Hugh Jones of Montreal. It was a fine, if somewhat dry account of the highlights of the Academy's first fifty years. But since Dyonnet had acted as Jones' chief source of information, there were necessarily interpretations that did not strike the National Gallery as factual. When a mimeographed copy reached McCurry he wrote, again to Nobbs, suggesting that if such inaccuracies were printed, the National Gallery would have no recourse but to respond, which might prove embarrassing for senior Academy members including the

President, who had been deeply involved in the 1932 dispute. Fortunately it was possible to contain the differences by alerting only Jones. And as Jones was to point out, the edition of 200 mimeographed copies had been printed, bound, and even mailed to members out of his own pocket, with only a few extra copies later issued by the Academy. The book had been written essentially for the information of Academy members, and Jones could not conceive of the kind of public interest that would warrant official publication. As for the controversies, as a relative newcomer (ARCA 1925, RCA 1926), he felt that having approached them from a previously uninformed bias, it appeared clear to him that all concerned "said and did things that they should now be heartily ashamed of."

McCurry, doubtless swallowing hard, very wisely allowed the matter to drop, with no resulting negative reverberations. And the new co-operative if wary relationship between the Academy and the National Gallery continued unimpaired.

The exhibition and concurrent annual assembly of 1936 were important in that they showed very clearly the pulse of new life surging through the Academy at the grass roots level. Staid, dignified, saddled with a stuffy public image that was the residue of so many foolish individual statements in the past, underneath the Academy was seething with healthy ferment. The exhibition brought attention to a number of less familiar names. Charles Comfort, Franklin Arbuckle, Jack Bush, John Alfsen, L.A.C. Panton, all painters who at the time were moving back towards figure interpretations, away from the swarms

Frances Loring, Sculptor, ARCA 1920, RCA 1947. Photo Ashley and Crippen.

of imitators who were following closely in the wake of the now disbanded Group of Seven. Indeed the exhibition was described in an article in *Saturday Night* as "chaotic" and "undignified," which surely disqualified the popular reactionary image.

Elected among that year's batch of new Associates were three future Presidents of the Academy. Again, Charles Comfort and Franklin Arbuckle, as well as Harold Beament. Conversely, at that same meeting the death was announced of Homer Watson, who, following the deaths of Horne Russell in 1933 and of Henry Sproatt in 1934, was the third President to die in three years.

At the time however the meeting was chiefly marked by the strong challenge presented by the Associates as a group. Led by sculptor Frances Loring, painter L.A.C. Panton and architect William Somerville, the Associates made it plain that while they appreciated Council's expressed desire to hear their point of view, it was in fact something more tangible that they had in mind. Politely but firmly, both in written and verbal report, they recommended that Associates be given full voting rights and be eligible for election to Council and for jury duty. Finally they asked for what at the time would have been regarded as extremist reform, that "...the RCA title be awarded by election of the whole body and that there be no limit to the number of honours thus given." Associates to be actually given a vote? A flood of young pups elected to full membership? Unheard of. The line-up of older Academicians must have sat and blinked like owls.

None of the Associates' demands carried at the time although the first two were to be realized in the foreseeable future. However the concept of unlimited Academicians would not become palatable for almost another four decades. For the time the Associates had to compromise with only a toehold in the door — they were at last officially authorized to elect two of their number, one from Toronto and one from Montreal, to act as advisory members of Council, and retirement age for Academicians was set at seventy, thereby making room for a slight increase of Associates into the upper echelons of the Society.

Academy Dinners meanwhile were often vicariously entertaining affairs. Under Grier's Presidency they were, by all reports, characterized by potentially dull formality. At one gathering at Toronto's York Club in the days before "the ladies" were invited (which was not until 1934), Grier proceeded as was his custom after dinner with a long, dignified, beautifully phrased speech that had the well-fed group dozing in their chairs. But the mood was mellow and indulgent since although prohibition was in force, someone had managed to smuggle in a few bottles. Grier droned on making noble points. A waiter moved about discreetly offering cigars. Suddenly a thumping from one of the tables cut into Grier's monologue. John Gordon, a feisty member from Hamilton who had obviously managed to appropriate more than his share of the whiskey, was demanding that the entire box of cigars be left beside him on the table. Order was restored and Grier resumed only to see Gordon get up after a time and make his way towards the door. Reaching his goal he turned around to point at the President. "Grier," he flung back, "you're a damned liar." With that he lurched on his heel out into the hallway, where conveniently there happened to be a couch. Stretching himself out, Gordon immediately fell sound asleep.

Every time the unfortunate President paused for breath the silence was filled by a loud snore.

At another dinner later in the thirties, after Grier had become "Sir Wyly," as President he was again delivering his accustomed oration. This time he was developing a favourite theme, his view that a chain of office should be designed for the President of the Academy. In the past he had spoken of this several times, and there was considerable support for the proposal. Now he cited the case of the Lord Mayor of London who sported just such a chain when greeting important visitors, or on special occasions, "such as this one." As Grier waxed more and more eloquent on the subject, Clarence Gagnon was seen to beckon to a waiter and to whisper something in his ear. Hurrying off, the waiter returned shortly and handed something to Gagnon who immediately crouched down, his chin just above the table. With the President still pressing his topic, Gagnon suddenly rose with great clatter. Around his neck was a chain of knives, forks and spoons, tied together with string. The whole assembly roared with laughter and nothing more was heard of the chain of office.

Concern with design did figure largely in other contexts. In 1937 the stock of Membership Diplomas had again been depleted and a competition for a new design was called. This time it was most successful and was won by member A. Scott Carter, a heraldic artist and illuminator. His presentation, which incorporated the original "Art et labore" inscription used by William Revell in 1880, remained in use until 1973.

The sculptors meanwhile, although still not flourishing, had gained considerable ground since the days when sculpture in Canada had meant, in effect, monuments and portraits by two or three artists. The field of opportunity was still not welcoming, with not nearly enough commissioned work to go around, and the number of professional sculptors (i.e., those totally committed but who did not necessarily earn their bread and butter solely from their work) remained few more than a handful. Still, they were a dedicated, enduring group of individuals who laboured away to blaze a trail that others would follow in greater numbers later in the century. In fact very soon after 1900 a number of new talents had begun to assert themselves. Walter S. Allward, largely self-taught and perhaps the one Canadian with a true sense of the monumental in sculpture. George Hill, Alfred Laliberté and Henri Hébert (son of Louis Philippe), all from Quebec and much involved with the sculpting of public monuments. R. Tait MacKenzie, the sculptor-physician who gained a wide reputation for his studies of the human body in motion. Emanuel Hahn (preceded in the Academy by his elder brother Gustav, a designer) who for years headed the sculpture department at the Ontario College of Art. All of these men were solid contributors to the general development of Canadian sculpture, with Allward soaring above to become a major talent of international stature.

And then there were the women. Florence Wyle, Frances Loring, Elizabeth Wyn Wood. Three highly motivated and gifted Toronto sculptors, very vocal and active in Academy affairs from their position as Associates (Loring and Wyle were both elected in 1920, Wyn Wood, who was younger, in 1929). Florence Wyle served as the only woman on the famous Wembley jury, and in 1938 she became the fourth woman and first woman sculptor to reach full Academician status. Wyn Wood and Loring were the team that organized the artists' petition of support for Eric Brown in 1932. Collectively their work was in a way more interesting than that of the men in that, commissions or not, they tended to sail ahead full steam with smaller, more intimate and thoughtful studio works that presaged the approach to sculpture taken by later generations. But interestingly, although the three were progressive thinkers, only Wyn Wood's early work reflected the new thought that had so affected the direction of the painters. Influenced by the sparks flying out from the Group of Seven, she developed highly original sculptures that were actually very successful three-dimensional interpretations of landscape. Typical of the sculptural philosophy of their day, Loring and Wyle expressed themselves through a romanticized version of the old neo-classical precepts that had been pouring out of both European and American art schools for generations. In their case honest, idealized, often very beautiful, but lagging several decades behind the work of their very close friends who had formed the Group. And they explained, "We had settled into our point of view before we came in contact with the Group."

Sculpture of any style however was certainly not a primary Academy concern. In principle it was an important component of the organization, but in practice the painters, who dominated the Society through sheer force of superior numbers, quite frankly did not see beyond their own discipline. "The sculpture?" A.Y. Jackson was reported responding to hos-

Elizabeth Wyn Wood, Sculptor, ARCA 1929, RCA 1948. Photo courtesy Public Archives of Canada.

tess Florence Wyle who had interrupted his enthusiastic account of an Academy exhibition currently on view in Montreal. "I didn't notice the sculpture." Scarcely surprising that although they did not pull away as individual Academy members (and for that matter the OSA was just as guilty of placing the sculpture in the darker corners in deference to the painting), in 1928 a core group (Loring, Wyle, Wyn Wood, Hahn, Laliberté, Hébert) struck out to form the Sculptors' Society of Canada.

On the other hand it was in the area of design that the Academy had least fulfilled its mandate over the years, and this was a reflection of a general attitude prevalent in the local art world. Painting, sculpture, architecture, and to a lesser extent etching and engraving, although not necessarily well supported were at least recognized as legitimate mediums of aesthetic expression. Design as such was not only misunderstood as "craft" or even "trade," but it was almost totally ignored. As far as the Academy's original intent to encourage "the production of beautiful and excellent work in manufactures," it had been lost by the wayside long ago. Bauhaus philosophy which had spread out from Germany in the 1920s, integrating art with all facets of practical design, had yet to make any impact on the Canadian art consciousness. It was time to do something about it and a handful of Academicians took the challenge seriously.

The idea of organizing an art in industry exhibition had first been broached by Hugh Jones in 1934, in emulation of a similar venture being sponsored by the Royal Academy in England. Tentative approval was given by the Council at the time but lack of informed interest in the undertaking slowed progress until 1936 when Fred Haines took over as con-

venor. Well known for his qualities of energy, humour and patience, and with a deep personal conviction that it was the responsibility of the Academy to sponsor excellence in art beyond the traditional disciplines, he was able to move the hierarchy to some enthusiasm. Two thousand dollars was voted to finance the venture from the now dwindling fund remaining from the sale of the Academy lot early in the century. Working with able committees in Montreal and Toronto, manufacturers and individuals were contacted whose goods or objects depended strongly on design content. Birks-Ellis-Ryrie, Bridgens Limited, Canadian Industries Limited, T. Eaton Company, Findlays Limited, General Steel Wares, Ltd., Ridpath's Limited. Douglas Duncan, Eric Aldwinkle, Albert Cloutier, Thoreau MacDonald. Rowley Murphy, Philippe Beaudoin. Salada Tea, The Ryerson Press, Sampson Matthews Limited, Dominion Textile Co. Ltd. Furniture, silverware, bookbinding, appliances, illustration, graphic design. The list was long and comprehensive. In April of 1938 the Canadian Industrial Arts Exhibition, unique in Canadian history, opened at the Art Gallery of Toronto with a total of 379 exhibits on display. Again, it presaged by decades developments that were to become very important within the Academy and to the art scene as a whole.

Not surprisingly, the success of the exhibition combined with other unique qualifications to place Fred Haines in direct line to inherit the Presidency when Sir Wyly Grier announced in 1938 that he was entering his tenth and final year in office. At the General

Florence Wyle, Sculptor, ARCA 1920, RCA 1938. Photo Ashley and Crippen.

Assembly in 1939 Haines received nine nominations and was elected President by acclamation.

Fred Haines was not young when he was so honoured by the Academy. He was sixty years old and brought with him enormous experience in traditional arts administration. Nor had he been a striker of new paths in relation to his own painting, serene, pastoral landscapes in which he interpreted nature with breadth, simplicity and quiet colourful composure. But as Pearl McCarthy was to describe him in the *Globe and Mail* only a short time later, ". . . he has old tradition in his ways, but new vision in his mind."

An Ontario boy, born in Meaford on Georgian Bay, like so many of his colleagues he decided at an early age that he must become an artist. As a mature painter he liked to tell the remarkable story of leaving home at seventeen years of age for the great art metropolis of Toronto, with three dollars in his pocket, and of earning his living at some form of art for the rest of his life. He managed to finance study at the Ontario School of Art and Design under George Reid and William Cruikshank, and by the time he was twenty-two was exhibiting with the OSA, of which he became a member five years later. It was while living in the village of Meadowvale, north of Toronto, that he decided in 1913 that he needed further art education. Selling everything he owned to finance the venture, he set off with his wife and young daughter for Belgium and the Académie Royale de Beaux Arts in Antwerp. While there he was awarded a gold medal for figure painting, the Académie's highest recognition for a non-Belgian. Returning home he threw himself into his work and by 1919 was elected as Associate of the Academy in good

time to witness the Wembley sideshow — and like Grier before him had been one of the signers of the letter of protest from the seven artists. As the years passed, although his painting remained his primary vocation, step by step he also became perhaps the most respected arts administrator and educator of his generation. In 1924 he was appointed Commissioner of Fine Arts for the CNE, where he introduced important contemporary works — by Picasso and Dali — to an unwary public. From 1924-27 he served as President of the OSA, from 1927-32 as Curator of the Art Gallery of Toronto, and in 1932 he was appointed Principal of the Ontario College of Art, a position which he held until 1951.

For a painter who has been described as quiet, retiring, with little taste for personal publicity, Fred Haines' early life and later achievements would appear to suggest other qualities of firmer tenor — of reserves of initiative and of personal courage. He was to need them as he faced perhaps the most trying term of office of any Academy President. For as a man of unqualified liberal outlook he was to be placed cheek by jowl in the nest of implacable conservative opposition. Further compromising his position, the outbreak of the Second World War in 1939 not only diverted the concern of the artists from the struggle for Academy principles, but actually physically removed for several years many artists who would normally have offered Haines a base of liberal support.

The first tremor was felt at the Council meeting immediately following his election. It was now several years since the reform bylaw had passed requiring Academicians at seventy years of age to move to the new category of Senior Academician, which meant in effect retirement, without voting privileges or right to hold office. Edmund Dyonnet appeared however to be exempt, and was elected year after year without opposition not only as Secretary, but also as a member of Council. This time, now age eighty, he had been reaffirmed once again. Sensing the danger of a new broom, in a superb political maneuvre he handed his resignation to the new President at the beginning of the first meeting. "For some time past I have felt that the duties of Secretary of the Academy were those of a man younger than I am."

Haines could not, as his first act as President, summarily accept the generous resignation of the faithful servant of the Academy. It was tabled until the following meeting some months later. At that time, with Dyonnet absent but with Council loaded with long-standing colleagues in arms, and with the rest still naively regarding him as "the poor old dear," a letter was written to him asking him to withdraw his resignation. The old war horse was now reinstated in an almost impregnable position.

Theoretically Haines, long a supporter of measures that would bring new life to the Academy, was at last in a position to open the doors. Younger men and women of marked talent and innovative ideas were standing in the wings and should be brought into the Society. The creative concept should be enlarged to include visual artists from all media — textiles, stained glass, graphic design.

He was of course whistling in the wind. With many of the comparatively younger members now away in the armed forces, some as official war artists, every move to broaden the Academy's base was nipped in the bud by the aging membership whose representative, Dyonnet, reigned behind the scenes with unflagging zeal. The annual exhibitions continued with their usual air of excellence. A special benefit exhibit and sale of work was held at the gallery of the T. Eaton Company, resulting in a donation of $1,200 from the Academy to the Red Cross. But innovative programming for the arts was beginning to come from outside the Academy. The Kingston Conference was announced in 1941 by André Biéler, and the following year artists from across Canada converged on Kingston to discuss problems of art and artists in general. The consensus of the Conference called for an alliance of artists and related professions to promote the arts in Canada, and the mood of ferment resulted in the formation of the Federation of Canadian Artists which for a time appeared to be the great white hope for artists who felt they must work together to help themselves towards a more equitable place in society. The Academy core meanwhile steadfastly refused to listen to its own Associates, who repeatedly called for reform — and who although powerless were certainly never silent.

The climax came at the Annual Assembly in 1942. Fred Haines had been President for only three years, with two more years in office normally ahead of him. But it was now clear to him that under the existing circumstances no President could effect the slightest change in the Society. He was aware that Edmund Dyonnet and Hugh Jones had recently sent circulars out to the membership, promoting their own election (Jones, himself ill, was running for Treasurer in place of C.W. Simpson who had recently died) on the grounds of erroneous information. Mr. Dyonnet was now eighty-four years of age, Mr. Jones seventy.

When the results of the election were tabulated Dyonnet had been re-elected as Secretary and to Council. Hugh Jones was Treasurer. Fred Haines, obviously not surprised, rose to address the meeting and handed his resignation as President to the Secretary. He made it clear that his move was made "in view of the action of the General Assembly in re-electing the Secretary." He went on to outline the role expected of a Secretary in a modern art society, and pointed out that the present Secretary was fourteen years over the retirement age. In conclusion he read the bylaw governing the retirement age for Academicians.

A later press interview left Haines' position abundantly clear. "It is part of an uphill fight for democracy," he told the reporters mildly. "The Society has a privileged class. There are eighty Associates but they have practically no say in its affairs, which are run by a small group of about a dozen, appointed by Council. It is an outmoded institution. Changes are needed. The Secretary is 84 years of age. The Treasurer has been confined to his room through illness, and is now in hospital. I believe the Academy needs a young Secretary." And he concluded, "You cannot attack privilege without suffering. So I am out."

It would be pleasant to report that the Academy hierarchy now stopped, took stock of itself, and began to pull up its socks. But it did not. It was mired in a curious labyrinth of its own design and was impervious to reality. Dyonnet stayed on for another six years, until after the war ended. Immediately following Fred Haines' resignation, Percy Nobbs as Vice President was called upon to take over until the end of the year as acting President. An uneasy situation since he had openly supported Haines in his stand for a new Secretary. In retaliation Dyonnet refused to speak directly to him throughout his year in office, resorting instead to notes and telegrams when communication was unavoidable. Then in a final exhibition of inflexibility, when the office of President was again at stake, the diehards elected Ernest Fosbery, the former spearhead of two slapstick public controversies. Ill-fated man, even he had trouble with the Secretary who no longer found him firm enough in enforcing traditional policies. In protest, whenever Fosbery who had a faint and gentle voice attempted to address a meeting, inevitably Dyonnet would get up and go over to the small trunk, famous as the travelling residuary of all his papers and documents, and rattle through them noisily until the President had finished.

But it was finally to come to an end. At age eighty-nine Edmund Dyonnet at last retired. Irascible, fanatic, irrepressible, he had defended his convictions to the end. And now it was as though a door had swung shut on the past.

At the Assembly of 1948 A.J. Casson, youngest member of the Group of Seven, was elected President of the Academy. Robert Pilot, born in Newfoundland, bred in Montreal, painter of evocative twilight views of Quebec land and cityscapes, stepson of the renowned Maurice Cullen, was his Vice President. The Academy was ready to rejoin the modern world.

Chapter Nine

Reform at Last

Mercifully, the years of Academy histrionics were finally over and presumably professional concerns would now assume new priority. Which they did. But in retrospect there were uneasy times ahead in which reform was late, indeed almost too late to bring the Academy back into the mainstream of swiftly developing changes in the art world. For after all the years of recalcitrance the Society had lost more ground than anyone had been able to perceive.

Inevitably some of the old touchstones had gone. The year 1949 for instance had seen the end of the RCA Life Classes, but the field of art education had long been adequately served by full-time institutions. Toronto had been the first to give way to the times and Life Classes had been discontinued there as early as 1933. Montreal had followed suit in 1940, while the less well-served centres of Ottawa and Hamiton continued until 1949, when the funds were directed instead to a student scholarship which was won by Gustav Weisman of Toronto for his painting "Firefighters." But the real stirring at the roots of things had very

little to do with solutions, however salutary, to Academy housekeeping problems. For the western art world — only recently come to partial terms with post-Impressionist concepts such as Cubism and Surrealism — was about to be inundated by the tidal wave of abstraction. It was to prove difficult for most Academy members to adjust, especially since the new creed appeared to demand total subjugation of all past traditions.

The early signs as the swell approached Canada were tentative enough but they were to grow by leaps and bounds. Actually, a small group of French-speaking artists in Quebec, with Borduas as their guiding star, had been responding to European-based surrealism since the late thirties almost unnoticed by their fellow Canadians. But men and women from other parts of the country had also come back from the war with a feeling of dislocation with the past and found themselves reacting with excitement to reverberations emanating from New York, where vigorous, compelling Abstract Expressionist painting had been important for some years. This questing mood was to be reflected in Ontario by the formation of Painters Eleven in 1954, a loosely knit group of committed abstractionists of varying ages who for a time found it advantageous to challenge the public from the strength of a collective base. The same instinct for exploration of new fields was nourished on the Prairies by the Emma Lake workshops, a series of summer art seminars at a camp north of Saskatoon to which pivotal American painters were invited to act as yeasting agents to a receptive circle of young artists. A similar smouldering of new creative expression was taking place on the west coast, although not formalized as in other areas by an allied common front. In the new perception gone was landscape painting per se, gone was figure painting, and in a complete turnabout from earlier conviction, gone was the undercurrent of nationalism from Canadian art.

However, viewed without the benefit of foresight, in 1949 the public prestige of the Academy was still such that a move towards reform was considered important news in the local art world. "Steps towards a new ideal for the Academy were taken at the annual meeting [seventieth], making it probably a milestone in Canadian art," wrote the Toronto *Star's* current art critic Pearl McCarthy in November of that year. "It was agreed that the constitution and bylaws be brought more in line with the needs of the present day."

As it happened, A.J. Casson had not been a week in office before he got together with painter L.A.C. Panton to discuss the future of the Academy. Both men had passed through the earlier controversies firmly on the liberal side and both had supported Fred Haines in his stand for reform. And now finally with

A. J. Casson, President RCA 1948-1952. Photo courtesy National Gallery of Canada.

Dyonnet's retirement (in which he was contenting himself by sending scurrilous letters off to the Director of the Montreal Museum of Fine Arts in defence of colleagues whose work had not made it past the jury for the spring show), the seal on resistance to change had been broken. If the Constitution was ever to be stripped of its antiquated dictums, now was the time.

Casson's nature and background fitted him supremely for seeing such changes past the predictable opposition. As latter-day Presidents went, at fifty years of age he was a young man when he took office, the youngest since George Reid's election over forty years earlier. His introduction into the Academy had been most unusual in that in the 1920s he had been taken under the wing of the Group of Seven, at that time hardly popular patronage in the eyes of the Academy hierarchy. "Look, young man," he was cautioned one day by two older Academicians as he was leaving the Arts and Letters Club where he had lunched at the traditional Group table. "We've been watching your work for some time and we think you'd be a good prospect for the Academy." But, they implied, he was keeping bad company.

The fact that he became a member of the Group and an Associate of the Academy in the same year, 1926, immediately tells something of his open nature and innate sense of diplomacy. Indeed he was a man of such natural goodwill toward his fellow man that even the most hidebound diehards could forgive him his tendency toward reform.

His method of dealing with the den of reactionary opposition in Montreal, where the largely English-speaking membership were still fuming and sputtering like a bonfire soused with a pail of water, was an early indication of his style. Realizing that these feisty diehards could still play havoc with the necessary changes, he had his Vice President, Pilot, who was in full accord with him, call a meeting at the Montreal Arts Club. No minutes were taken and the meeting was short. Facing a large turnout, the new President laid his cards on the table and asked for complaints and grievances to be brought forward once and for all. Obviously confounded by such ingenuousness, scarcely a word was mustered in response. The old bickering, if it was there, was not heard openly again.

With the way now relatively clear for moving ahead, Casson with Pilot, and especially with L.A.C. Panton, set about ploughing through the convolutions of the old Constitution, crisscrossing back and forth through a maze of conflicting amendments, and amendments to amendments. By 1949 the draft of the central issues was ready and presented to the General Assembly by Panton. Casson, wearing his hat as diplomat, had carefully prepared the stage. The normal business of the meeting was dispatched as quickly as possible and then Casson as President announced that the final matter was extremely important and the vote would have to be counted very carefully. For this reason he requested the Academicians to sit in the front two rows, leaving two rows between themselves and the Associates who were seated behind. It was perfect. The unsuspecting Academicians were isolated in full view of their junior colleagues.

Clause by clause the items were read by Panton and then voted upon. "Associates shall be eligible for membership on Council, and for such other offices as the Council may deem necessary." What could the reluctant Academicians do? They were preconditioned to accept the inevitability of some sort of change, and with fifty or so pairs of eyes boring into them from behind there was no escape. Every clause passed. Essentially, Associates were given limited voting privileges, the total number of Academicians was raised to forty-five, a firmly enforced retirement age was set at seventy and the Secretary (member Herbert Palmer had taken over from Dyonnet) from here on was to be appointed by and responsible to Council. Not earthshaking, but certainly the acceptable limit in 1949. The problem was, it was a case of shutting the barn door after the horse was gone. By the time the Constitution and all the nuts and bolts of the bylaws had been smoothed out, then ushered safely past the Senate and the House of Commons in 1952, new waves of thought were already overtaking the Academy just as it most needed to catch its breath and regenerate.

The finances of the organizatoin continued to be a source of great anxiety and the Treasurer, architect W. L. Somerville, reported serious doubts that they could continue. It was one thing for his lawyer son to have gladly donated his services in drafting the legislation for the new Constitution, but quite another for the Society to survive, let alone move ahead in the fifties on a pre-Depression annual grant of $2,025. Fortunately Casson with the backing of H.O. McCurry (who had

New Policy Approved By Academy

By PEARL McCARTHY

A. J. Casson has been elected president of the Royal Canadian Academy. Steps toward a new ideal for the academy were taken at the annual meeting, making it probably a milestone in Canadian art. It was agreed that the constitution and by-laws be brought more into line with the needs of the present day. When asked whether membership or exhibitions might be affected, Mr. Casson said: "Both." His own ideal for academy exhibitions, he said, was that they might supply a display of the best work done by artists during the year, something which would indicate the standard to which Canadian art had attained, an exhibition in which each exhibitor would make his supreme try for quality and excellence; not a mere representation of names nor a display geared to sales. Academicians would deliberately paint for such an exhibition, not just send in a sample of their work. Mr. Casson was next asked whether the academy might take steps to embrace a broader field of the arts, including industrial design. He answered that he hoped so. In all fields, he would like to see a bringing up to date, he said.

Officers elected included: Vice-president, Robert W. Pilot of Montreal; treasurer, Wm. L. Somerville; secretary, Herbert S. Palmer; elected to council for two years A. Barnes, C. F. Comfort, H. L. Fetherstonhaugh, F. S. Haines, H. S. Palmer; representative to Art Gallery of Toronto, Florence Wyle; to CNE Association, F. H. Brigden.

Academicians elected were: Manly MacDonald, R. York Wilson, painters; Elizabeth Wyn Wood, sculptor, Associates elected were: Adrian Dingle, B. Cogill Haworth (Toronto), Frances-Anne Johnston, Frederick B. Taylor (Montreal), painters; Sing Hoo, sculptor; Charles Davis, David Shennan, John Roxburgh Smith (Montreal), architects.

Toronto **Star**, November 27, 1948, by Pearl McCarthy.

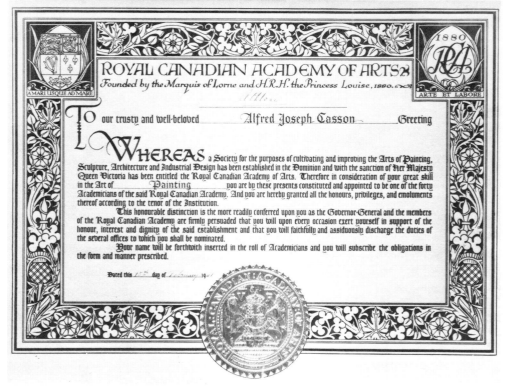

RCA Membership Diploma for A. J. Casson.
Designed by A. Scott Carter in 1937.

succeeded Eric Brown as Director of the National Gallery) was finally able in 1952 to persuade the Treasury Board to up the ante by $2,000. And although this made it plausible during Robert Pilot's term as President (1952-1954) to develop a modest RCA scholarship award for students, there was little to spare for other new programs. When an invitation came from the National Academy of Design in New York to hold a major exhibition on their premises, it was impossible for financial reasons to take advantage of the opportunity.

But these were mechanical problems of a kind that had always been with the Academy. Yet unlike the days when the Group of Seven were bursting onto the scene, Academy exhibitions now evidenced only the subtlest reflection of the new fertile period pressing in from the wings. A few individuals like Panton, York Wilson, or in the earlier less alarming stages of his development, Jack Bush, managed to insinuate exploratory work into Academy shows, but juries were definitely wary of experimental forms and young radicals, unwilling to subject themselves to the probability of rejection, began to consider alternative venues for their work. Concurrently, exhibition catalogues of the fifties reflect a highly competent conservatism spiced here and there with token glimpses of the growing guerilla movement. In 1951 even the jury had reported themselves discouraged by the less than exciting work that had been submitted by members, yet at this early stage it did not really seem to occur to anyone that the Academy might be in danger of being left in a backwash.

Publicity for that year's show at the Art Gallery of Toronto was generated by an as yet traditional work of a young artist who was soon to develop as one of the country's major abstract painters. Harold Town had entered an oil, "Two Nudes," a rather poetic, pensive study of two young men. Some wit had managed to evade the eye of Gallery security long enough to scratch a suggestive arcing line down from the front posed figure, causing outraged reaction from some viewers, which was picked up with relish by the press. "...the display of this ugly thing in a public gallery, where respectable old ladies and innocent school children are daily visitors, is an affront to decency," ran a column in the tabloid *Flash*. "If you have a young daughter keep her out of the Toronto Art Gallery." It was a marvellous spotlight for a young artist, but hardly an indication of a vital show.

Interestingly, some of the revolutionaries from those earlier times were still on hand and involved in Academy affairs. A.Y. Jackson had rejoined in 1953 and Lismer served more than one term on Council over this general period — and no wool was allowed to gather when he was around. Still noted for his acerbic, witty tongue, he was never a man to suffer pretentiousness without a rise. Familiars could always tell when he was coming up with something as a peculiar look would come over his face and his mouth would begin to pucker as he formed his dart. At one meeting he was mumbling away with asides to the business on the table when the President asked him to speak more clearly. Taking a split second to prepare he retorted, "I was just saying that people who are hard of hearing are mentally deficient."

There was certainly effort made. Under Robert Pilot (who served only two years as President) the Academy was able to co-operate in two instances as art advisors in mural competitions. Pilot managed to persuade McGill University to place the organization and adjudication of a competition for a mural for the new library in the hands of the Academy, and in an open contest it was won by R. York Wilson of Toronto. In 1954 another opportunity developed when architect Hugh Allward was able to direct a competition for murals for the new Veterans' Affairs Building in Ottawa to the Academy under similar conditions. This time three works were to be involved and the project was announced at that year's Annual Assembly, and the news undoubtedly had inadvertent influence over one of the most dramatic presidential elections in the Academy's history.

The seventy-fifth, the Jubilee Exhibition, which opened the evening before was a grand success, although perhaps more for social reasons than otherwise. It was held at the Montreal Museum of Fine Arts and the show itself was impressive in the currently conservative tradition of RCA shows, and was buttressed by a special exhibit of the Diploma collection borrowed from the National Gallery for the special occasion. However, it was the accompanying ball that was lauded as magnificent and brought press coverage unprecedented since the days of the Marquis of Lorne.

But at the Assembly the following day an unusual situation developed; a contest arose over the nomination of the new President. The year before Hugh Allward, architect son of the famous sculptor of the Vimy Ridge Memorial, had been elected Vice President in place of the incumbent L.A.C. Panton, who had then taken over in the lesser position as Treasurer. But although in the past the succession of the Presidency had created few waves since it was traditionally uncontested, when Pilot vacated the office both the Vice President and the Treasurer were nominated to take his place. By all normal sense of progression the honour might have been expected to go to Panton, who had earned it by virtue of many years of active devotion to the Academy and to the concerns of his fellow artists. He was an enormously capable man and although he was deeply involved in art education and was currently Principal of the Ontario College of Art, he had always managed ongoing exploration and growth in his own painting.

But he was not an easy man. Those who were close to him knew him as a human being and as an artist of deep integrity. He was, however, outwardly austere and uncompromising, and one not hesitant to take and follow an indicated course no matter what the consequences in terms of injured egos. Naturally not everyone regarded him with warmth. Allward on the other hand was a charming man of great social grace, and no one had a reason in the world to have anything against

Arthur Lismer at RCA Council Meeting, Harold Beament, pencil on paper. Collection of artist.

him. And he was definitely the more conservative of the two at a time when many artists were feeling threatened by the unknown. Add to that the appealing fact that he had just landed a juicy commitment for the Academy. When the ballots were counted, he had won by one or two votes.

No one could have foreseen the consequences or understood the depth of emotion that lurked unseen behind Panton's severe facade. Following the meeting he and A.J. Casson travelled back together to Toronto on the train and after parting, spoke briefly again over the telephone about the result of the election. At midnight Casson's telephone rang again. It was Panton's wife. Her husband had gone to bed to read, had suffered a severe heart attack, and died. Obviously in the eyes of an artist, the Presidency of the Academy was still a position of great honour.

By 1956 the organization's defences were beginning to show definite signs of siege. Robert Ayre wrote in the Montreal *Star* of that year's exhibition, "You don't go the Academy looking for innovations and other excitements, but even in established tradition, you expect a stronger pulse." The members were naturally indignant, but privately there was a great deal of concern over lack of top level submissions to the shows even from among their own ranks, and it was acknowledged over the Council table that they had picked up considerable deadwood over the years. At the same time when Associate sculptor Jean Horne, who had not been active in her work for several years and therefore had not supported recent exhibitions, handed in her resignation the following year on a point of prin-

176

ciple to make room for active talent, no others in her position followed her example. And when the President, after following his Council's advice to write to members urging participation received some pithy replies in return, official reaction ducked the issue. "It was the opinion of Council that there was nothing in the complaints made." Further, in 1958 the nominations committee was forced to report that for the first time they had encountered reluctance on the part of the artists to joining the Academy, and that several nominees had declined to stand.

Serious frustrations were obviously building for the Academy and they were to focus more and more around the exhibitions which had always been the Society's major raison d'être and source of strength. Essentially, quite apart from the question of whether they were or were not falling behind the times, a new element was making itself strongly felt. The introduction into the heart of the scene of credible commercial art galleries was suddenly pulling the plug on the monopoly of the art societies as the principal, literally the only showcases for Canadian artists. Council began to question aloud whether the Academy was without purpose. Compounding these troubles, like an impending death knell in 1956, the Art Gallery of Toronto announced a change in exhibition policy which in effect would seriously curtail exhibition privileges of the Academy and of other art societies. Accustomed as the Academy was to unlimited space being made available in Toronto every other year, now they were to be cut back to a much smaller show every three years. The Gallery's expressed rationale was that it wished to devote more space to its permanent collection, and in fairness there were by now a number of art societies who expected regular accommodation for their shows, boxing the Gallery into a repetitive schedule over which it had no control. The move was certainly unpopular with artists and did nothing for their existing lack of affection for the Director, Martin Baldwin, long felt to be unduly influenced by directives from sister art institutions in the United States. The policy change was to come into effect by the following year and indeed Baldwin underscored his move by writing to the Academy making it clear that the number of rooms available for their coming exhibition was contingent on the importance of the person officiating at the opening.

The Academy artists, seasoned pros that they were, did not panic over this new state of affairs. They did however recognize that if their organization and other art societies did not fight to keep their independence, a trend was developing that would eventually see museum and gallery directors exercising an unbalanced control over Canadian artists and art. Much soul searching was precipitated and it was admitted that the exhibitions needed upgrading and that those members who may have become apathetic needed new reason to put their support behind the Society. On the whole they accepted the blow as a challenge and while it would be facile to suggest that many of the established artists who were members of the Academy, who had developed within and felt great loyalty to the Society system, did not find it wounding when signs began to indicate that times were bypassing them, there was more to their resistance than mere protectionism. It was their sincere conviction that an artist must not be stampeded into conformity with current fashion if his muse led him elsewhere, and that it was one of the responsibilities of the Society to defend this basic precept. After all, although the Academy was not the avant-garde, the membership still represented many of the country's most renowned artists, who surely were not to be swept under the rug in a complete sell-out to change. Moreover, although it had certainly not been the case in the early days of the Academy, it had come to be the belief of most Academicians that it was not the role of the Academy to search out new talent or to identify new art movements, but rather to acknowledge achievement where and when it occurred. Justified or not, it was an attitude that was to place the RCA in a defensive position, vulnerable in face of the all-inclusive permutations that lay ahead in the coming decade.

Homer Watson
The Flood Gate
Oil on canvas 32$\frac{1}{2}$″ x 46$\frac{3}{4}$″
Exhibited RCA 1924
National Gallery of Canada

Aurèle de Foy Suzor-Côté
Indiennes de Caughnawaga
Bronze 17¼″ x 22″
Exhibited RCA 1924
National Gallery of Canada

A. Y. Jackson
Barns
Oil on canvas 32$\frac{1}{8}$″ x 40$\frac{3}{16}$″
Exhibited RCA 1926 and 1927
Art Gallery of Ontario

Clarence A. Gagnon
Horse Racing in Winter, Quebec
Oil on canvas 40³/₄″ x 51¹/₂″
Exhibited RCA 1927 and 1928
Art Gallery of Ontario

Charles W. Jefferys
Willow Creek, May
Water colour 19″ x 25¾″
RCA Diploma work, deposited 1928
National Gallery of Canada

Randolph Hewton
Sleeping Woman
Oil on canvas 40″ x 60″
Exhibited RCA 1929
National Gallery of Canada

Edwin H. Holgate
Totem Poles, Gitsegluklas
Oil on canvas 32″ x 32″
Exhibited RCA 1929
National Gallery of Canada

Emanuel Hahn
Head of Vilhjalmur Stefansson
Bronze 18″ high
Exhibited RCA 1931
National Gallery of Canada

Charles Comfort
Louise
Oil on canvas
Exhibited RCA 1932
Collection of artist
Photograph: VIDA/Saltmarche, Toronto

Dorothy Stevens
Coloured Nude
Oil on canvas 34″ x 30″
Exhibited RCA 1932
Art Gallery of Ontario

Fred Haines
A Muskoka Farm
Oil on canvas 28″ x 34″
RCA Diploma work, deposited 1934
National Gallery of Canada

L.A.C. Panton
Sullen Earth
Oil on canvas 33⁷/₈″ x 40³/₁₆″
Exhibited RCA 1933
Art Gallery of Ontario

Carl Schaefer
Before Rain, Parry Sound
Water colour on paper 15¹/₂″ x 22″
Exhibited RCA 1935
Art Gallery of Ontario

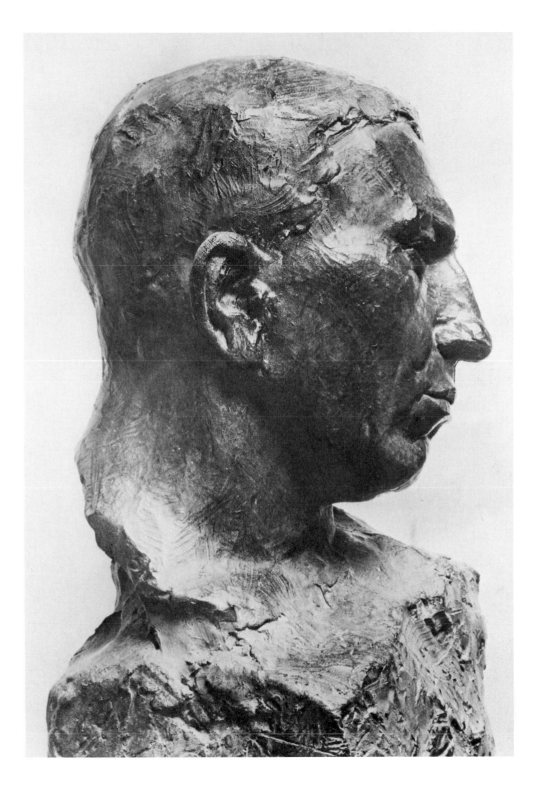

Frances Loring
Head of Sir Frederick Banting
Bronze 24″ high
Exhibited RCA 1934
National Gallery of Canada

191

Marion Long
Evan Macdonald
Oil on canvas 42″ x 36″
Exhibited RCA 1934 and 1935
Collection London Regional
Art Gallery

Robert W. Pilot
Twilight, Lévis
Oil on canvas 30″ x 40″
RCA Diploma work, deposited 1935
National Gallery of Canada

Elizabeth Wyn Wood
Reef and Rainbow
Cast tin on black marble base
9³/₄″ x 37³/₄″
Exhibited RCA 1935
Art Gallery of Ontario

Edmund Dyonnet
Self Portrait
Oil on canvas 29″ x 24″
Similar version exhibited RCA 1938
Montreal Museum of Fine Arts

Lilias Torrance Newton
Portrait of Louis Muhlstock
Oil on canvas 24″ x 25¼″
RCA Diploma work, deposited 1940
National Gallery of Canada

Franklin Carmichael
Snow Clouds
Oil on canvas 37³/₄″ x 47³/₄″
RCA Diploma work, deposited 1940
National Gallery of Canada

L.A.C. Panton
Morning, Little Cove, Grand Manan
Oil on canvas 28″ x 32″
RCA Diploma work, deposited 1944
National Gallery of Canada

John Alfsen
Self Portrait
Pencil on paper 13¹⁄₈″ x 9¹⁄₂″
Exhibited RCA 1946, travelling
show 1947 and 1948
Art Gallery of Ontario

Charles Comfort
Flight Lieut. Carl Schaefer R.C.A.F.
Water colour on paper
32³/₈″ x 30³/₈″
Exhibited RCA 1948
Art Gallery of Ontario

R. York Wilson
Toluca Market
Pyroxalin 48″ x 84″
Exhibited RCA 1952
Collection Mrs. John Goba, Toronto

Kay Daly
Eskimo Children, Labrador
Oil on canvas
Exhibited RCA 1951
Collection Mr. Roland Daly, Toronto
Photograph: VIDA/Saltmarche, Toronto

Yvonne McKague Housser
The Little Clearing
Oil on board 24¾" x 32"
RCA Diploma work, deposited 1952
National Gallery of Canada

Cleeve Horne
Portrait of Howard Dunington-Grubb Esq.
Oil on canvas
Exhibited RCA 1952
Collection of artist

Dorothy Stevens
Frank Erichsen-Brown
Oil on canvas 38″ x 28″
Exhibited RCA 1953
Art Gallery of Ontario

A.J. Casson
Calm after Storm
Oil on canvas 37″ x 45″
Exhibited RCA 1952
Montreal Museum of Fine Arts

Jacobine Jones
Circus Pony
Bronze 11″ high
RCA Diploma sculpture, deposited 1954
National Gallery of Canada

Franklin Arbuckle
St. Lawrence River Barn
Oil on canvas 30$\frac{1}{8}$″ x 40$\frac{1}{16}$″
Exhibited RCA 1954
Art Gallery of Ontario

Louis Archambault
Femme se coiffant
Bronze 15¹/₄″ high
Exhibited RCA 1955
National Gallery of Canada

Peter Haworth
Driftwood
Water colour 19¹/₂″ x 25¹/₄″
Exhibited RCA 1953
RCA Diploma work, deposited 1955
National Gallery of Canada

Alan C. Collier
**Ore Car on the 2975 Foot Level,
Delnite Mine**
Oil on masonite 28″ x 36″
Exhibited RCA 1954
National Gallery of Canada

André Biéler
Tout en cherchant
Oil on canvas
Exhibited RCA 1955
Collection Queen's University, Kingston
Photograph: VIDA/Saltmarche, Toronto

Carl Schaefer
Still Life, Yellow
Water colour 15″ x 22″
Exhibited RCA 1955
Art Gallery of Ontario

Dora dePedery-Hunt
Artist (a portrait of Frances Loring)
Artificial stone 16½″ high
Exhibited RCA 1956
National Gallery of Canada

Sydney H. Watson
The Music Shop
Oil on canvas 28″ x 36″
RCA Diploma work, deposited 1956
National Gallery of Canada

George D. Pepper
Spanish Village
Oil on canvas 31″ x 37″
RCA Diploma work, deposited 1958
National Gallery of Canada

Goodridge Roberts
Laurentian Landscape
Oil on canvas 32″ x 48¹/₂″
RCA Diploma work, deposited 1958
National Gallery of Canada

Ghitta Caiserman-Roth
Still Life with Lovers
Oil on canvas
Exhibited RCA 1959
London Regional Art Gallery
Photograph: VIDA/Saltmarche, Toronto

Chapter Ten

Beleaguered

Twists of rusty industrial piping in the sculpture court of the Art Gallery of Ontario? Piles of dingy undercarpeting to be re-arranged at will by the public at the National Gallery? Giant hamburgers, beds wrapped in fabric and sprayed with aluminum paint? The great modern British sculptor Henry Moore dismissed as old fashioned? Op art, Pop art, hard edge. Minimalists, conceptualists, constructivists, and finally heading ninety degrees in the opposite direction, magic realists. These were the sixties, and if the era was confusing for the artists, it was a complete enigma to the public. There were many muttered allusions to the fable of the emperor and his non-existent new clothes.

Not change, but anarchy. Or so it seemed. And when one considers the tale of a prominent public gallery director awarding a prize to what he categorized as a brilliant piece of collage—composed of empty toothpaste tubes and bottle caps among other materials—but which in fact was shortly revealed as having been submitted as an outright joke by a college student, one can see there was indeed room for caprice. Or the story of a noted landscape painter who alone among his colleagues made it past one vaunted international jury. He had

meticulously painted a canvas to resemble a painting wrapped in brown paper and tied with twine. Again, a joke, but apparently not distinguishable by the panel of avant-garde judges from the serious works. So there were legitimate grounds for much unease which offended many artists and prevented them from recognizing the resounding vitality at the core of the new movements.

The dilemma of the Academy in adjusting to recognition of the authenticity of the revolution without compromising deeply felt evolutionary principles was reflected in the frequent turnover of its presiding officer. During the period 1950-1970 the Society passed through a succession of eight Presidents: A.J. Casson, Robert W. Pilot, Hugh Allward, Charles Comfort, Franklin Arbuckle, Harold Beament, Clare Bice and finally John C. Parkin. Each tried with fresh energy and varying degrees of success to counteract the trends that were undermining the position of the Academy, and as they thought, the position of the artists in an altered and questionable milieu. But for the better part of two decades the main current, no matter what measures they took, was to be against them.

In a move to revitalize the exhibitions it was decided to explore the possibility of reshaping the whole exhibition concept around more selective shows that could be sent on circuit to smaller galleries in widely scattered centres across the country, an imaginative and sound response to the shifting emphasis of the times. In 1958 Charles Comfort, who had served since 1954 as Allward's second-in-command, was elected President and his immediate mandate was to implement the new policy. This he did with energy and finesse. Halifax, Vancouver, Quebec City, Winnipeg. The strategy worked in that it provided a credible new focus in the eyes of the members themselves, and was perhaps the first concrete step in the process of the Society's self-renewal. Unfortunately (for the organization) Comfort's administrative capabilities and stature in the art world were such that in early 1960 he was appointed Director of the National Gallery, replacing Alan Jarvis who had followed H.O. McCurry in that post. His Vice President, Franklin Arbuckle, took over the remainder of the year and was confirmed in office at the next General Assembly.

Arbuckle's position was unique at the time in that he had been just twenty-six years old and a recent graduate of the Ontario Art College when he was elected an Associate of the Academy in 1936. Only three others, Paul Peel, George Reid and Homer Watson had been younger at the time of election. So that although he was just over fifty when he became President, he had been a member for nearly a quarter of a century and had the advantage of long association with Academy tradition, yet was close enough to new developments to recognize their serious impact. His term of office therefore was a period of most determined effort to address the current problems of the Society's artists.

In spite of growing accusations from younger artists that the Academy had become an exclusive private club, from 1960 onwards there is every evidence of tremendous effort to support programs of benefit to the general art community. In 1960 Council worked with the Ontario Society of Artists to win an important decision over the Decorators and Paperhangers Union who were claiming jurisdiction over the painting of a large mural in Toronto's O'Keefe Centre. The Union tried to force artist R. York Wilson and his two assistants to take out union cards authorizing them to work on the mural. Wilson insisted that as a creative artist the union had nothing to offer him and would only impede his work. The union was militant, and without the backing of the two major art societies the artists' position would have been in jeopardy. As well, at the urging of design member Marius Plamondon (descendant of Antoine Plamondon) of Quebec City, the Academy pioneered in efforts to persuade government to establish a percentage of total cost of public buildings to be spent on the arts.

The year 1961 was very active for the Academy on several counts. Plans were afoot to develop an Academy Medal, to be presented to individuals outside the membership who had made an outstanding contribution to artistic development in Canada. Sydney Watson and Cleeve Horne undertook the design and production of the medal and its completion was seen as an opportunity to broaden the Academy's base. But overshadowing all other projects was the timely offer of Toronto art collectors Sam and Ayala Zacks to donate a substantial sum each year for three years, to be awarded to a work in the RCA exhibition. The prize-winning picture would be chosen in each case by the Director of a famous public gallery in Europe, and donated to their collection at the end of the show. In addition a cash award would go the runner-up. All expenses of the invited adjudicators would be met by Mr. and Mrs. Zacks. It was a long while since the Academy had been associated with such glamour and even the Art Gallery of Toronto unbent and waived its three-year RCA exhibition schedule in order to accommodate the first presentation of the Samuel and Ayala Zacks Purchase and Gift Award, planned for the autumn of 1962, but postponed until January of 1963 to fit the Gallery's line-up.

Word was sent out to artists across the country, resulting in a massive response to the show. In the painting category alone 521 works were submitted of which 77 were accepted. Sir John Rothenstein was invited to come from the Tate Gallery in London to select the winning works. Attendance on opening night was thought to be the largest ever on record for an Academy opening. The purchase award went to Toni Onley of Vancouver for his painting "Polar #1," with Harold Town's "Tyranny of the Corner, Persian Set" selected for the second prize. In the end the Zacks decided to purchase Town's work as well, and both works were sent to the Tate. Topping off the excitement was the presentation of the first RCA medals to two artists whose disciplines were not as yet included in Academy membership—Carl Dair, typographer, and Norman McLaren, film designer—as well as a third to Finnish architect Viljo Revell, designer of the new Toronto City Hall.

The same keen interest repeated itself the following year when the eighty-fourth exhibi-

RCA Medal, bronze, designed by Cleeve Horne and Sydney Watson, 1962.

tion was held in Ottawa. The location itself was enough to create considerable stir, since there had not been an RCA exhibition at the National Gallery since the bitter days back in 1924. But the deep freeze had gradually thawed and then, of course, Charles Comfort was by this time the Director. Again there was a rich flood of submissions, which gave an off-key ring to a petulant review in the Montreal *Star* claiming, "The prevailing face of society exhibitions today has assumed the greyness of anonymity." For a curious side effect to the recent phenomenon of the trend to one-man shows at commercial galleries, was the development of a popular disdain for the old-style Society shows, which had prevailed as spectrums of a wide range of aesthetic interpretation. In this sense the eighty-fourth typified old Academy tradition, for along with long familiar names was a rich mix of newer talent that was far from anonymous: Dennis Burton, Harold Town, Kenneth Lockhead, David Partridge, Christine Pflugg, John Gould, Graham Coughtry, Rita Letendre, Jean McEwen, Richard Gorman, Kazuo Nakamura, Jack Reppen, Michael Snow, Gordon A. Smith. A young sculptor, Ron Baird, entered a great metal "Raven," and its acceptance and display alongside the work of long-established artists gave him (and the significance was still a vivid impression fifteen years later) the same sense of tremendous encouragement and personal achievement as it had to young artists in the old days.

Dr. William Sanberg of the Stedelijk Museum in Amsterdam chose the prize-winning works that year, and top award went to Marcel Barbeau of Montreal, an early follower of Borduas, for his painting "Tonquilene." Runner-up was Mashel Teitelbaum

for "White Jazz." And extending the display, for the first time in years the architects had come up with a stunning section. Usually a limited collection of rather lacklustre photographs, this time it had been taken in hand by Gordon S. Adamson with such striking improvement in scope and display that it was later toured on its own by the Gallery.

The final Zacks Award was made at the eighty-fifth annual exhibition held in Montreal and this time the honours were carried out by D. Franz Meyer of the Kunstmuseum in Basel, Switzerland. His choice for the purchase prize was "Rouge Asymétrique" by the young Montreal Op artist, Guido Molinari, with second prize going to Réal Arsenault for "Andoise," and honorable mention to York Wilson for "Endymion." Furthering the success of the previous year, the architects came up with a comparative tour-de-force. Working with colleagues Eric Arthur and John C. Parkin, Adamson (now Vice President) rounded up an exhibit of ninety-eight entries which for the first time brought to the public a comprehensive view of the best of modern Canadian architecture.

Yet in spite of the Academy's evident responsible acceptance of the necessity to meet the challenge of conflicting times with sane, positive and professional programs, it was soon to become clear that they were no longer able to compete for the younger artists' support in face of the double lure of sales supposedly offered through exhibitions in the successful commercial art galleries, and of the grants now available through the newly developed government funding agencies to the arts. Loyalty to the Academy which, undeniably, had ignored them only a few years earlier? Again, unlike the Group of Seven in their avant-garde days—who developed within the system and retained a sense of responsibility to the arts in common with their more traditional peers—the rebels of the more prosperous ego-tripping sixties felt no such compunction. Art societies? Who needed them? With the termination of the Zacks Awards, many of the bright young men and women of Canadian art abruptly ceased submitting to Academy shows and attached their loyalty, perhaps understandably, to the newer, more hopeful sources of income.

Supposedly old-fashioned then, concerned with such outmoded precepts as standards and protection of an artist's right to follow his own route, with preserving an independent voice as they saw their world increasingly overwhelmed by a new breed of non-creative administrators and by curators speculating on winning trends with which they could associate themselves with honour, the Academy categorically refused to abdicate its traditional responsibilities.

True, it became increasingly difficult to fund programs on the small and static annual grant. Although since 1960 the Canada Council (formed in 1958) had defrayed exhibition expenses with a supplement for a grand total of $7,025, it was not nearly enough to operate effectively in the present times. Montreal painter Harold Beament took over the Presidency from Franklin Arbuckle in 1964, and was immediately plunged into steering the Academy through perhaps its most beleaguered period, a metaphor particularly apt since he had served as a Commander in the Canadian navy during the Second World War before taking over as Senior Naval War Artist. Beament will be remembered as the young Ottawa artist who had first come into public view as the National Gallery's information officer at the Wembley exhibition. Since that time, as a regular exhibitor, then as an Associate in 1936 and a full member ten years later, he had never been far removed from Academy affairs.

Travelling exhibitions were still high on the list of priorities in the mid sixties, and during Beament's term they surfaced in Sarnia, Hamilton, Winnipeg, Saskatoon and Victoria. On special invitation from Moncrieff Williamson of the Confederation Art Centre in Charlottetown, a particularly fine show was put together in 1966 in the form of a recent RCA retrospect. But year by year there were recurring signs of a deepening alienation between the art societies and the public galleries in the major centres which, counteracting the old institutional image that shied away from change, were identifying themselves with the new trends and were more intolerant in their favour than the Academy had ever been against them. Obviously it was only to be a matter of time before the more catholic art societies were barred from these traditional venues altogether.

Curiously enough the most immediate threat to the Academy's viability was to come from the recent substantial increase of government funding to the arts. Whereas in the past the Society's problems of financial survival had been a matter of prying marginal support from a succession of culturally underdeveloped governments, suddenly the situation

221

was much more complex. Through a combination of circumstances the encouragement of Canadian art was finally perceived as the mining of a natural resource, and funding to the arts on various levels became politically astute. As funding increased, more hands materialized and were reaching into the pie for the same plums, and naturally the Secretary of State (now the overseer for the arts) became concerned that these plums be distributed for maximum impact. The Academy? The organization that since 1880 had time and again fought for artists and defended their right to create in face of the most dispiriting apathy? In the flux of change, in the eyes of new young turks all artists' societies were self-perpetuating and exclusive and quite definitely in the way — and were welcome to go the way of the albatross.

The Academy was well aware of this categorization and that as senior art organization they were first in line for criticism which their recent record did not warrant. But memory was shortlived in the confusion of the sixties and when Clare Bice was elected President in 1967 it was to a situation that required immediate action to convince the Secretary of State that the Academy was indeed alive and well and deserving of support. Great effort was put into preparing a brief stressing recent achievements — the record of reorganization (the membership had again been expanded), initiative in defending the artist's position in society — and asking for a heightened grant without which the Society could not continue to operate on its present level. Bice, a painter from London, Ontario, for many years the artist-oriented Curator of the London Library and Art Museum, was a man not unfamiliar with the intricacies of bureaucracy, and he

was fortunately assisted by a particularly able Vice President, architect John C. Parkin. Between them they managed to present a strong enough case that by 1969 a grant came through for $11,000 to cover current expenses, with a further $2,500 to go towards a bilingual catalogue for the coming exhibition. At the same time it was stressed that this was not to be considered a permanent grant and indeed part way through the year word came from the Secretary of State advising that with the whole grant process under review, yet another more detailed brief was required from the Academy if they wished to be considered for any further support. In effect it meant that the Academy, now in its ninetieth year, after weathering endless financial crises with a truly astounding record of good managership, for the first time in its history found itself without an assured annual grant. A very careful brief was prepared under the direction of the Vice President and dispatched to Ottawa.

Months passed and no word came back to confirm the Academy's fate one way or another. Plans went ahead for the ninetieth exhibition which was to feature a special section on the graphic and industrial arts, and it duly opened in Ottawa in January of 1970. At the General Assembly the following day the President reported inadequate funds to carry through to the legal year end on March 31, and announced plans to borrow on the remaining Academy bonds (the residue from the old Academy lot) in the likelihood that assistance would eventually materialize.

And on that note Clare Bice, who had not been well, handed over his office to the newly elected President, John C. Parkin.

Chapter Eleven

The Academy in Transition

If creativity in the sixties was characterized by compulsive change, the seventies were marked by an officially sponsored move toward the democratization of the arts. Funding, through the Canada Council, the recently formed National Museums Corporation, and through parallel provincial bodies was unprecedented in Canadian experience. Ballet, opera, symphony, theatre, art galleries, museums, and of course the individual artists were beneficiaries of the new largesse and the arts mushroomed across the country with resulting new public awareness. This desirable phenomenon was not without negative implications, at least in the visual arts. Following the pattern of government funding, the tendency was to back the apparent front runners and then to infuse the general field by means of democratic embrace that did not readily distinguish between the committed artist and the dilettante. "I don't believe much in 'encouraging' art," A.Y. Jackson had cautioned back in 1929. "Too much encouragement would induce people to go in for art because they believed themselves assured of making a good living at it. We need the adventurous soul to go into art for the love of it." In an age that included grantsmanship as part of visual arts curricula, an old-fashioned sentiment indeed.

Obviously the Academy was to have new problems. For an organization that in the past had been the peer-appointed dispensers of the equivalent of PhD degrees for professional excellence in the arts, it was difficult to condone the new fine arts mandarins who from the isolation of their growing bureaucratic machines increasingly saw artists as the base unit in a massive cultural superstructure, and who showed every evidence of an assumption that Canadian art had begun with their own recent involvement. "The Royal Canadian Academy of Arts? Never heard of it!" was a standard official reaction in the early seventies. So much for over ninety years of contribution.

Obviously too, if the Academy was prepared to take a stand to protect the integrity of the artist's right to speak on his own behalf, to defend his right to stand in the sun with or without either government or curatorial sanction, it would have to do so within the context of a changed and more competitive world. In this sense the past experience of the new President was a godsend.

"The architect-urbanist," John Parkin had been quoted by an interviewer in the year before his election, "must have political instincts, the sense of survival, the will to prevail." And because those qualities were personified in himself and were backed by both a towering professional stature and a social conscience towards the arts and their place in the living world, he was possibly one of the few Academicians since Lucius O'Brien capable of seeing the Academy through the coming period of transition.

Born in 1922, the elder son of a Winnipeg chartered accountant, he grew up under privileged circumstances where his childhood interest in architecture was actively encouraged at home. By the time he was twenty-four years old he was not only an honours graduate of both the University of Winnipeg and of Harvard, but was already in architectural partnership in Toronto with a chance namesake, John B. Parkin. Four years later, as design partner he had five coveted Massey Medals (the country's highest architectural awards) to his credit. "No one has influenced Canadian architecture more," Eric Arthur, revered Professor Emeritus of Architecture from the University of Toronto was to observe, although Parkin was by no means a non-controversial figure. In 1963 *MacLean's* magazine had pointed out the price of spectacular success. "Critics view his zeal as ambition, his principles as prejudices, his poise as arrogance, and his confidence as conceit." But if the uninitiated were known to sometimes equate his starkly disciplined, contemporary buildings with shoeboxes or sewage plants, he himself saw the new architecture as an environmental art form. "Beauty is built in — by proportion. An extension of function is beauty. We are not fine artists but social art-

John C. Parkin, President RCA 1970-1980. Photo Ashley and Crippen.

ists." His design for Toronto International Airport, Terminal 1, was a prime example of his philosophy — and the fact that by 1970 his firm was the largest in the country is as much a tribute to his persuasive powers as to his acknowledged vision. Small wonder that he was to take his place, along with perhaps O'Brien and Harris, as one of the great Academy Presidents.

Elected ARCA in 1954 and RCA ten years later, he was by no means an Academy new boy when at the age of forty-seven he became the Academy's third youngest President. Neither was he new to creative directorship in the arts, having served as Chairman of the Canadian Conference of the Arts and of the National Design Council during policy setting periods in the development of both those organizations. His interest in the applied arts, which he saw as artificially separated from the fine arts, was to have timely influence on the grassroots realignment of the modern Academy.

The organization that John Parkin inherited in 1970 was already in a state of hesitant metamorphosis. In 1964 a bylaw had been passed opening the membership to allow for sixty full Academicians, and by the late sixties new names began to appear on the list that were reflective of the effervescence of the period. For as the decade waned the honeymoon with commercial galleries, which after all were of necessity motivated by commercial instincts that were not necessarily in the artists' interests, began to go sour. Many artists who had been anti-Society were once again aware of the value of collective support. And very tentatively, signs began to appear within the Academy itself that indicated a crumbling of the old resistance that delegated painting, sculpture and architecture to one exclusive camp, and the general design disciplines to another. In 1967 a textile design, "Landscape," by European-born and trained Helen Frances Gregor, made its way past an Academy jury on its own merits as a work of art. And although by no means the first in Canada to explore this field — Micheline Beauchemin and Mariette Rousseau-Vermette, both from Quebec, had already acquired international reputations — Gregor was the first to teach and to press successfully for recognition of textile arts in what had traditionally been a closed shop reserved for the fine arts here at home. In 1969, as Vice President, John Parkin was urging the widest possible interpretation of the design category in recognition of those by now highly sophisticated areas of applied and visual arts that had become very much a part of the Canadian cultural mainstream. His colleagues agreed and the following year Allan Fleming (famous for the CN logo) and Christopher Chapman (the film "A Place to Stand," Expo '67), both earlier recipients of the Academy Medal on the grounds of outstanding contribution to the arts in disciplines not considered eligible for actual membership, were elected to the Academy. It was a lifting of a corner of the curtain, and throughout the seventies the trend was to develop as an integral part of the new Academy.

Meanwhile there were practical problems to overcome. The story of the reinstatement of the annual grant is one of the classic adventures of the Academy, a tale of faith, mettle, and in final desperation, of cool political brinksmanship.

RCA Membership Diploma for John Reeves RCA 1975. Designed by Allan Fleming in 1972.

The basics were harsh. After approval of the long-delayed grant in 1969, the Academy received no further funds for four years. The brief prepared and sent to Ottawa on the directive from the Secretary of State may as well have been dropped down a well. A year after it was dispatched, no acknowledgement had yet come back. Repeated attempts to gain an interview with the Secretary were invariably deflected. Council began to be distinctly uneasy but in the age-old tradition of impoverished nobility, took it for granted that business must go on as usual. A decision was taken to proceed with arrangements for the 1971 exhibition, and plans were approved for a new logo and bilingual Membership Diploma (designed by Allan Fleming) in keeping with the recent change giving legal bilingual status to the Academy's name.

The exhibition came and went. For one last time the Montreal Museum of Fine Arts gave space for a "small" show. Accordingly from close to 700 entries, 46 paintings and 8 sculptures were chosen for exhibition along with representative sections of graphic and industrial design, and for the first time, film. As in the good old days the show was highly controversial. "This year a real battle developed and it ended as a struggle for endurance in which the avant-gardists won," explained Vice President and Chairman of the painting jury Jean McEwen to a titillated press. In their zeal to "project an image of a dynamic new Academy," it seemed that some of the jury members had found themselves carried away and pressed the inclusion of what they took to

be a large conceptual work, but which in time revealed itself as simply a painting still wrapped in its packing. The press were delighted, although some of the older members were not amused.

In a way the vitality of the event was a fitting finale to ninety-one years of annual Academy exhibitions — for it was indeed the last. At the show's end the Academy was in debt for expenses to the tune of nearly $14,000, with still no word from Ottawa. The treasury was almost empty. In fact for some time the part-time Secretary (no longer a member since the death of Fred Finley three year earlier) had been paid through money borrowed on the personal guarantee of certain members. For the first time in the Academy's history the question surfaced of the legal ownership of the Diploma Collection. It had certainly always been in the possession of the National Gallery, but was the Academy the real owner? Could it possibly be sold, perhaps to the National Gallery, to put the Society back on its feet?

The fleeting consideration was soon discarded as unlikely and besides such a proposition was basically distasteful in that it smacked of selling their own birthright. They discussed instead forming a Foundation to build up an investment fund which would provide a permanent solution to their future financial problems. But the present still threatened to annihilate them. Inquiries were made and it was confirmed that the Public Archives in Ottawa would be interested in purchasing the Academy archives for the sum of $5,000. Before taking up the offer another attempt was made to interview the Secretary of State. This time a date was set. John Parkin and Guido Molinari travelled to Ottawa to keep

226

the appointment only to find it cancelled when the Secretary was delayed out of town. A further meeting was arranged for two weeks later, but it too had to be cancelled at the last moment. By March 26, 1971, the Treasurer, Alan Collier, reported that the Academy had borrowed to the limit of its resources.

Again the question of the Diploma Collection loomed. The Gallery was sounded and advice sought. It appeared that in legal terms the question of ownership was murky, and Dr. Jean Boggs, the current Director of the Gallery, did not take kindly to talk of Academy claims. Friendly legal advice to the Academy suggested the futility of an attempt to take on the Government of Canada in a legal battle. But the more the members talked, and because in their desperate position so much was now at stake, the more they were able to convince themselves that yes, they probably were the rightful owners of this unique record in the development of Canadian art. The case was pressed with some heat.

Finally the National Gallery suggested a compromise solution. They offered to buy selected Diploma pieces over a period of ten years at the rate of $10,000 per year. The remaining pieces would then be the responsibility of the Academy to house and insure. In other words the Gallery would retain the masterpieces and allow the Academy to take the lesser works off their hands. But aside from the doubtful aesthetics of such a division, members were unanimous in their unwillingness to consider a situation in which the historic collection would not remain intact. It was

RCA Centennial Medal, designed by Dora de Pedery-Hunt, 1979. Bronze 3⅜" diameter. Obverse: artist's hand outlining current RCA emblem. Reverse: RCA monogram designed in 1937.

to be all or nothing. With no immediately apparent solution the matter was left to simmer on a back burner.

Meanwhile, in September of 1971 the President had finally been able to see the Secretary of State, but after a pleasant discussion had come away empty-handed. The Academy, the Secretary had pointed out in the spirit of the day, was not democratic enough to fit the current grid, and he could not predict when or if assistance would be forthcoming.

By all rights and expectations the Academy should now have looped up its trailing grey beard and quietly melted into the shadows of the past. This convenient disposition did not appear to occur to the President and Council. Aside from their lack of means of support, they were healthier and more reflective of Canadian artists and art than they had been for many years. And problems of survival, both physical and psychological, were scarcely new to artists. On a one-to-one basis it has been, is and will continue to be a recurring confrontation throughout most artists' careers. After all they offer a service which although history shows to have been integral to the development of man, has never readily been perceived by the general public as useful to life on a daily basis. A painting that allows a brief glimpse through the veil of the spirit? A building that provides extension to human endeavour as opposed to simple shelter? A design for a household utensil that offers beauty with utility? Their effect most often makes its mark through a process of osmosis. Survival, flexibility in the most positive sense

are bywords of the men and women who insist on this creative stand. The Academy was made up of these individuals.

Amazingly, due to sale of the Academy archives to Ottawa along with receipt of further fees, and most significantly through cash donations from members amounting to over $6,000, at the next General Assembly the Treasurer was able to announce that the huge exhibition deficit had been reduced to $3,250. Further exhibition programs had of course, most reluctantly, to be cancelled, and one of the last remaining Academy bonds was cashed to pay the back wages of the Secretary.

In the midst of all these complications another interesting development rose to the surface. During Arbuckle's Presidency in the early sixties, sculptors Frances Loring and Florence Wyle had arranged to bequeath their studio to the Academy. They had hoped that it would be used for a meeting-place for artists but were generous-souled enough to realize that this might prove impractical and they left its disposal to the discretion of the Academy. They did however express the wish that proceeds from a possible sale be used "for the particular development and encouragement of, and education in, Canadian sculpture."

Loring and Wyle both died in 1968, and eventually the studio came to the Academy as arranged. Unfortunately the timing was not good and with the building in considerable state of disrepair, there was no possibility of the Academy's restoring and maintaining it as the sculptors would have preferred. Finally in 1972 it was advantageously sold, and when later that year another small bequest was received from the estate of the late Hugh Allward, in his and his famous father's name, the two together made a very respectable sum.

Although legally the Academy was not bound to restrictions in use of the money, and at this juncture they might well have seen it as a justifiable means of escape from their difficult position, morally they were committed to respect the spirit in which it had been given. In this light it was decided to create a separate Trust which could not be tapped for administrative purposes. Under member Cleeve Horne's expert guidance, except for a small portion used to clear the books of debt, the balance was invested with the interest to be used each year for the encouragement of Canadian art. Once the interest began to accumulate on a regular basis it was immediately put to work in the form of grants to sculpture students attending the Ontario College of Art's off-campus school in Florence, Italy; as the basis for a sculpture competition; and as grants to emerging public galleries across Canada for the acquisition of works of art for their permanent collections. Exactly the kind of ongoing program that the Academy through its earlier intermittent scholarship efforts had always hoped to establish.

The domestic troubles however continued to appear insoluble. Negotiations had opened again with the National Gallery and resulted in the Gallery upping the price offer for the key pieces from the Diploma Collection, a proposition still not of interest to the Academy. "Get tough," Council finally advised the President and he pressed further. The mythology of the story retains rumours of threats to send up Brink's trucks to cart away the Academy's rightful property. Whatever the impetus, a light began to appear in the distance. In April of 1972 the President read a letter to Council from Dr. Boggs in which she graciously agreed to apply to Treasury Board on the Academy's behalf for subvention of $20,000, to be administered through the National Gallery as part of their funding, "provided there will be no question of the title of the Diploma Works."

Shortly over a year later Dr. Boggs wrote that the Academy grant had been approved by Treasury Board, and on June 27, 1973, the cheque was actually in their hands. At last they were back in business.

For that matter, although they had certainly been out of funds, they had never really been out of business. In the year before the grant was assured there had already been enormous effort put into strengthening the base of the membership. Forty-five years earlier the old disenfranchised Associates had recommended that there be no limit to the numbers of Academicians, and now after long and thoughtful discussions it was seen as the only plausible means for the Academy to catch up with their commitment to the applied arts, let alone to the ebullience of the art scene in general. In fact there must be a new Constitution that would end the old stratification of membership and provide for only one category: Academician. The qualifications would remain as before: excellence within one's own discipline. Accordingly, new bylaws were prepared and the whole concept passed easily through the General Assembly in November of 1973. And at last the new Membership Diplomas, hanging fire since 1970 for lack of funds, were sent off to be printed and presented to all Academicians, new and old.

The comparative financial security that came with the grant (its continuity was never to be taken as a matter of course) changed life completely for the Academy. A full-time secretariat was established in permanent office space and the various programs on the books put into motion. Work began on preparing a standard artist-client agreement for use and support of artists involved in commissioned work. Plans were put into motion to hold a large open-juried exhibition in conjunction with the Montreal Olympics in 1976 — and here a paradox presented itself. By 1974 the Treasurer was forced to point out that the budget was almost completely taken up with operating expenses, leaving no provision for exhibition funds. The fact that the 1971 show had accumulated nearly $14,000 in expenses which in a period of spiralling costs would five years later come close to devouring the entire resources of the Academy, underlined the existence of a new vicious circle. In order to move ahead with competitive strength a full-time base was needed. But when even a modest base was maintained, there was no money left for traditional programs. Add to this other relative ingredients: the long-foreseen barring by major public galleries of exhibitions not initiated and selected by themselves; the now literally hundreds of young hopefuls being churned out yearly from art schools and university art courses, looking for places to exhibit and ready to swamp any open-juried show of stature; and

the impossibility of handling and providing services for such numbers without very substantial alternative funding. The concept of Society exhibitions as forums to encourage the young and to bring mature excellence before the public was fast becoming an anachronism.

The Academy's Spectrum Canada show was a prime example of the inherent weaknesses. The concept was very exciting. A top-level exhibit that would show Olympics visitors the full range of Canadian talent in the visual arts. But hamstrung by unworkable guidelines imposed by Museums Canada who provided the balance of the funding, tripped up by unfulfilled assurances from the Olympic organization, enmeshed in unprecedented administrative detail, it was doomed almost from the beginning. The quality of the flood of 1,500 submissions was generally low and the allotted space in Montreal was shamefully inadequate. The result was an exhibition that was infinitely more expensive, more time-consuming to produce and, with the exception of a few exciting and beautiful pieces, more mediocre than any with which the Academy had ever been associated. It was time to begin to explore new avenues of service.

It was at this juncture that an unparalleled opportunity was opened to the Academy. Talks had been proceeding for some time between John Parkin, industrialist E.P. Taylor, and the Borough of North York. Mr. Taylor had some time earlier proposed bequesting his estate, Windfields, to the Borough in which it was situated, but no clear plan for the specific use of the property had materialized. It was immediately apparent enough to John Parkin. A fine stone mansion with a number of outbuildings, set in twenty acres of prime parkland. An ideal national headquarters for the Academy. Exhibition space, lecture areas, outdoor sculpture gardens, a retreat for visiting artists. The possibilities boggled the mind. Mr. Taylor was approached with the concept of the Academy as central to the development of a national arts centre at Windfields, run by artists themselves. He and his wife were keen and by 1976 an agreement had been hammered out between Taylor, the Academy and the Borough of North York, in which the Academy would provide the creative implementation of the centre while North York would own and maintain the property. It had the earmarks of being one of the most exhilarating developments to have hit Canadian art in a long time.

The problem of funding would of course be crucial to success. Once underway such an undertaking would qualify on several levels for both federal and provincial assistance. But by now the Academy was more than fully aware of the pitfalls embedded in the route to public funding, and it seemed obvious that if they were to have any hope for success either at Windfields or on any other front, a contingency fund of their own was integral to stability and retention of control over their own destiny. They decided to push ahead with a fund-raising drive and to build towards their second century when, at least partly supported by interest from the new Trust, they could once again rely on the strength of their own well-honed professional judgement in creating programs relevant to artists' aspira-

tions. They could easily see Windfields as the core of a vortex capable of reaching out to encourage art and artists across the country, that might foster excellence in art through the creation of commissions in co-operation with industry, that might interpret the many new disciplines to the public through smaller definitive exhibitions, that would be in a position to offer facilities to sister societies. That might, and this was the most exciting idea of all, extend the boundaries of Canadian cultural life through the development of an artists' colony on the grounds, to which artists might come from other parts of the world for limited periods of sanctuary and cross-pollination conducive to creativity.

Quite apart from developing plans for Windfields and kicking off the fund-raising drive, there was a good deal of internal building during the latter part of the seventies, with a concerted attempt to enlarge the membership on a national, interdisciplinary basis. At the close of 1979 the membership list read like a who's who in Canadian art and counted close to 600 artists of varying ages, from painters to silversmiths to photographers to yacht designers.

With this enlarged membership has come a new potential. There is no doubt that for many years Academy activity radiated out from the two major centres of Canadian art activity—Montreal and Toronto. But the picture has very much altered. In several provinces there are now sufficient numbers of members to constitute informal regional social and political bases for the artists. British Columbia, Alberta, Manitoba, and of course Ontario and Quebec. It is probable that in the near future the Atlantic Provinces as a unit will find themselves in the same position.

Communication is extremely important to artists, whose work often by its very nature isolates them in studios and workshops. Yet stimulation to other parts of the country from headquarters in Toronto is a rather bloodless link, not sufficiently sensitive to local needs. The obvious solution is heightened regional activity that can depend on national backing when major issues develop. The creative confrontation of the Manitoba members with the Winnipeg Art Gallery in the autumn of 1979 was in effect a test case.

Alone among all other public galleries in Canada, the Winnipeg Art Gallery was the one institution to plan a contemporary exhibition in recognition of the Academy's coming centennial. Although the National Gallery had earlier spoken of a show that would include works of Academy members representative of the ten decades of its existence, in the end they opted for a very beautiful historical presentation of works by selected early members from 1880 to 1913, when formal ties between the Gallery and the Academy had ceased. Were it not for the Winnipeg Gallery, which in less bounteous times in the past had more than welcomed Academy travelling shows, the contemporary artists would have been completely ignored. Even so the Winnipeg show did not develop without discord. The Gallery's first impulse in planning a Manitoba RCA members' show was to follow current curatorial practice which dictates thematic selection, presumably on the grounds that varying styles diminish one another's impact. Works on paper must hang with works on paper, hard-edge with hard-edge, conceptual with conceptual, or the show will lack the all-important unity.

Now to a point thematic shows are an interesting and effective tool in presenting art to the public, but considered as a universal policy they face a danger not only of becoming censored interpretations out of context with their milieu but of being downright misleading. Life itself is diversified, and public sensibilities are quite capable of assimilating a richer diet from time to time. In the case of the RCA show, fourteen of the fifteen Manitoba members agreed that the time had come to press this point. Only "works on paper" by a selected few to represent the Academy in its 100th year? The artists rebelled. Either use the work of all the members (and they ranged from architects to painters and printmakers to a sculptor and a photographer), or not even the annointed would take part. It was a fine example of artistic solidarity on a point of principle. In the end the Gallery saw their point of view and chose a catholic show more in keeping with the historic spirit of the RCA, a victory to the artists and a tribute to a public gallery not apprehensive of intelligent dialogue with the local art community.

And if Winnipeg was lively as the Academy began its second century (and the show which was hung in late January of 1980 was alternately scathingly criticized or praised to the skies by local pundits), let it not be said that Academy Annual Dinners had lost the colourful zest of earlier years. The ninety-eighth Dinner, which was to be the last before the centennial celebrations, had been unexpectedly set in a class by itself. It was held in Toronto at the Park Plaza Hotel where some two hundred members and guests dined ele-

232

gantly at tables lit by great candelabra. During a pause in the program two young men appeared in the doorway of the dining room wearing chefs' uniforms and bearing what was purported to be a surprise cake. The treat as it later became clear had been commissioned by a disgruntled artist (not an Academician!) with an old peeve against one of the head-table guests. His agents paused long enough to identify their quarry, then one of them strode confidently up and pushed the creamy cake adroitly in his face. In the ensuing pandemonium the culprits decamped with the speed of athletes through the emergency door. "Well," another head-table guest was overheard to remark with some enthusiasm as she wiped splashes of whipped cream from the skirt of her evening dress, "I had no idea that Academy dinners were so interesting!"

Meanwhile, a grand plan begins to unfold for the coming decade. The Windfields era should bring the Academy finally into its own. "Let us dream of a future Academy," Hugh Jones had written in his History in 1934, and then had gone on to fantasize about the day when endowment funds would be available for disinterested public service—and in a small way this is already happening. The earliest members dreamed of a time when the Academy would have a permanent home with facilities to enlarge the artists' window on the world—and this is approaching realization. O'Brien, Bourassa, Harris, Reid, Brymner, Dyonnet, Jackson, Watson, Grier, Loring, Wyle, Wyn Wood, Haines, Casson, Panton— all fought for what they understood to be the

integrity of the artists' position in society. It is scarcely likely that in the shangri-la of Windfields the artists of the future will necessarily fight with more heart or more conviction. But at least they will have advantages unheard of by their predecessors and will be in a position as never before to adapt with changing times to artists', and by extension, public needs.

Yet the fact of Windfields will never be viable unless two uneasy elements can be reconciled: the visual artist's native reluctance to involve himself, except spasmodically, outside his own studio; and the bureaucratic misgivings when indeed he does.

But throughout history, and in all cultures that have achieved artistic greatness—whether in China, India, Egypt, Greece, Europe, Mexico, Peru, the North American West Coast, the Arctic—the true value of art has never been in its material contribution to the mundane world, nor necessarily in its decorative beauty. Rather it has been in its intrinsic role as a restless spirit, a cry from the heart, as a breath from the fringes of human consciousness, that it has justified itself as a lasting contributor to society. And if in this young country only several generations removed from the raw, materialistic pioneer struggle for survival, the impending danger to art in the eighties would seem to be the cautious official perception and sanction of the arts as a form of public service, why then it is time for the artist to venture down from his ivory tower or forever hold his peace. And in no other profession, either law, or medicine, or space technology—or fishing or farming—would he as initiator not be invited, welcomed to act as interpreter at the door of his own house.

Public art galleries? There are many now across the country providing a fine, if sometimes saran-wrapped service to the public. Funding agencies? They are securely in place, going about their business with admirable, if sometimes overbearing thoroughness. The Academy should not be concerned with disputing their jurisdiction unless it is willing to expend energy in bloody, self-destructive battles, or to become itself an administrative body for the arts. But to assume responsibility as sentinel, interpreter reminding the world at large that art is more than the baking of a sophisticated cultural cake, to be divided judiciously in democratic slabs as a sort of recreational enrichment? Now there is a challenge worthy of the organization that during its first hundred years, despite turbulent periods, has been dedicated to clearing not only a place for artists and art, but for professional excellence in the arts in an only recently receptive milieu.

It is, after all, the artist's self-generated search for understanding of the limits of his universe that builds the art heritage of a country. And at its highest level it is the function of an organization of professional artists to defend, to speak for, and to maintain the ethical balance of the artist's individual requirements within the context of his responsibility to society. The Academy's strength has always been the vital force of its members, with their instinct to regroup to support the precious evolutionary aesthetic core, like defending a treasure ship in stormy seas. In an increasingly impersonal world, if they can now rouse themselves once again to counteract the present levelling drift towards a politically motivated mediocrity in the arts, with creative, enlightening, alternate tacks in programming, and *through new vigilance in all levels of artists' affairs*, this may well prove to be the Academy's century.

Frances Gage
Portrait of a Person
Bronze 19″ high
Exhibited RCA 1961
RCA Diploma sculpture, deposited 1977
Royal Canadian Academy of Arts
Photograph: VIDA/Saltmarche, Toronto

Elza Mayhew
Cerberus
Bronze 36″ x 14″ x 14″
Exhibited RCA 1963
Collection the artist

Grant Macdonald
Embarkation
24″ x 53″
Exhibited RCA 1963
Collection Mr. and Mrs. J. R. Beattie,
Mountain, Ontario
Photograph: VIDA/Saltmarche, Toronto

Toni Onley
Polar #1
Exhibited RCA 1963
Winner of Zacks Purchase Award
Collection the Tate Gallery, London

Harold Town
Tyranny of the Corner, Persian Set
Exhibited RCA 1963
Collection the Tate Gallery, London

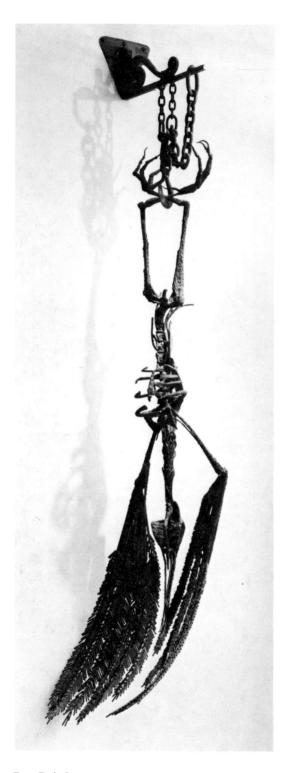

Ron Baird
Raven
Welded metal
Exhibited RCA 1964
Collection Mr. George Farrow,
Oakville, Ontario
Photograph: VIDA/Saltmarche, Toronto

Guido Molinari
Rouge asymétrique
Exhibited RCA 1964
Winner of Zacks Purchase Award
Collection the Kunstmuseum,
Basel, Switzerland

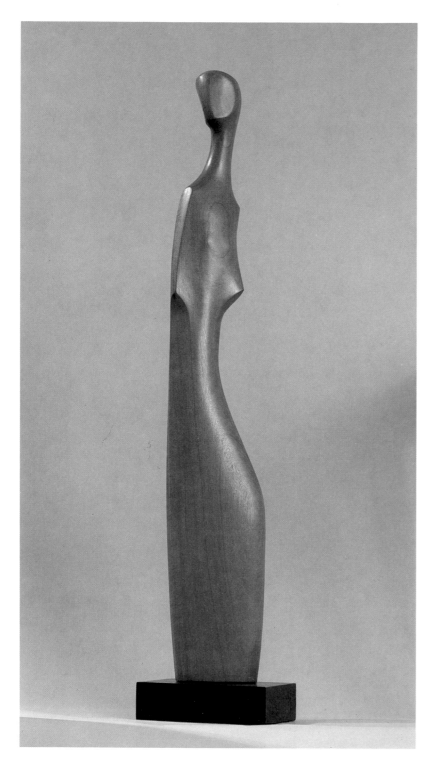

Sylvia Daoust
Femme debout
Mahogany 36″ high
Exhibited RCA 1964
Private collection, Montreal
Photograph: VIDA/Saltmarche, Toronto

John Ivor Smith
Patrician Head
Bronze 23″ high
Exhibited RCA 1964
Courtesy the Isaacs Gallery, Toronto

242

John Gould
The Ancestors
Oil turpentine wash 30″ x 40″
Exhibited RCA 1964
Collection Concordia University
Photograph: VIDA/Saltmarche, Toronto

Harold Beament
Lava Forms, Night, Tenerife
Oil on canvas 48″ x 60″
Exhibited RCA 1964, RCA in Retrospect 1966
Collection of artist
Photograph: VIDA/Saltmarche, Toronto

B. Cogill Haworth
Gros Morn
Exhibited RCA in Retrospect, 1966
Collection McCarthy & McCarthy,
Toronto-Dominion Centre
Photograph: VIDA/Saltmarche, Toronto

John C. Parkin
Ottawa Union Station, Ottawa, Ontario
Exhibited RCA 1967
Photograph: Fiona Spalding-Smith

S.V. Gersovitz
Sidewalk Artist
Etching
Exhibited RCA 1967
Collection Concordia University and others
Photograph: VIDA/Saltmarche, Toronto

R.T. Affleck
**Stephen Leacock Building,
McGill University, Montreal**
Exhibited RCA 1967

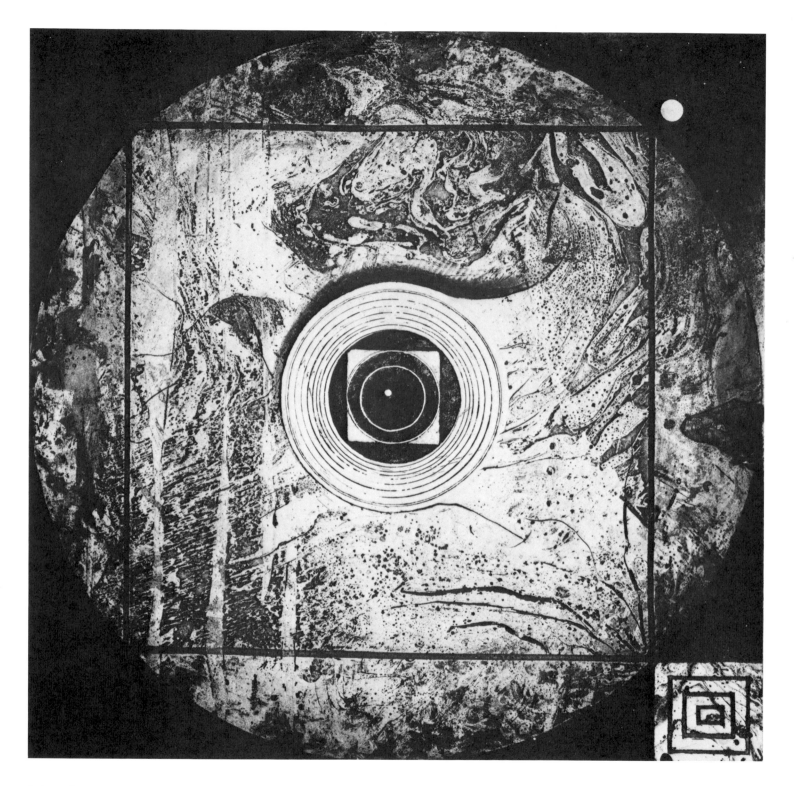

John Esler
Distant Light, Diary of a Lost Hunter
Black and white etching, edition of 100
Exhibited RCA 1968
Collection Miriam Waddington and others
Photograph: VIDA/Saltmarche, Toronto

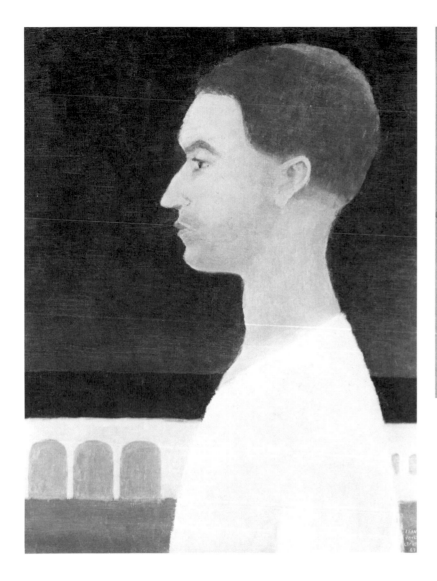

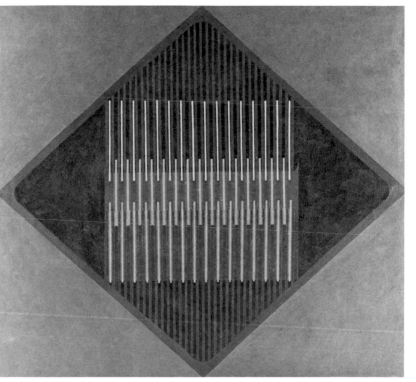

Jean Paul Lemieux
Portrait of Claude Ives
Oil on canvas 24″ x 19″
RCA Diploma work, deposited 1968
National Gallery of Canada

Gordon A. Smith
Black Diamond
Oil on canvas 50″ x 55″
RCA Diploma work, deposited 1968
National Gallery of Canada

D. MacKay Houston
Molecular Assemblage
60″ x 50″
Exhibited RCA 1968
Collection Mississauga Central Library
Photograph: VIDA/Saltmarche, Toronto

Jean McEwen
Le Feu des Signes
Liquitex on canvas 78″ x 68″
Exhibited RCA 1968
RCA Diploma work, deposited 1968
National Gallery of Canada

E. J. Hughes
Kaslo on Kootenay Lake
Oil on canvas 32¹/₈″ x 25″
RCA Diploma work, deposited 1969
National Gallery of Canada

David Blackwood
**Captain Ned Bishop with officers
on the bridge of the S.S. Eagle**
Lost Party Series
Lithograph 20″ x 30″
Exhibited RCA 1970
Collection Memorial University,
St. John's, Newfoundland and others

Eric Freifeld
Self Portrait
Carbon pencil over wash, on paper 20″ x 15¹/₈″
Exhibited RCA 1970
Art Gallery of Ontario

Clare Bice
On the Terrace
Oil and lucite 40″ x 49⅞″
Exhibited RCA 1970
RCA Diploma work, deposited 1970
National Gallery of Canada

Maxwell Bates
View in Grasse, South of France
Oil on canvas 24″ x 30″
Exhibited RCA 1971
RCA Diploma work, deposited 1973
National Gallery of Canada

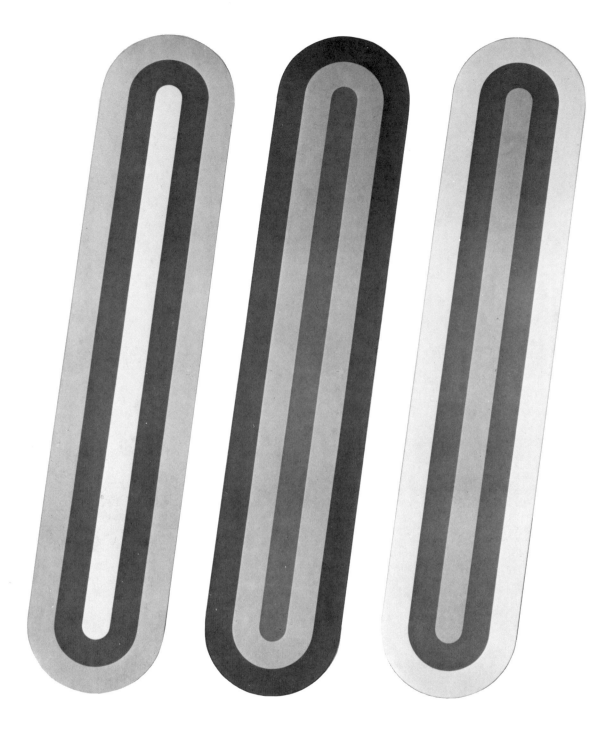

Claude Tousignant
Tryptique, 3 Elements
24″ x 120″
Exhibited RCA 1971

Louis Archambault
Modulation No. 111
Plywood prototype 13′ long
Exhibited RCA 1970
Collection of artist

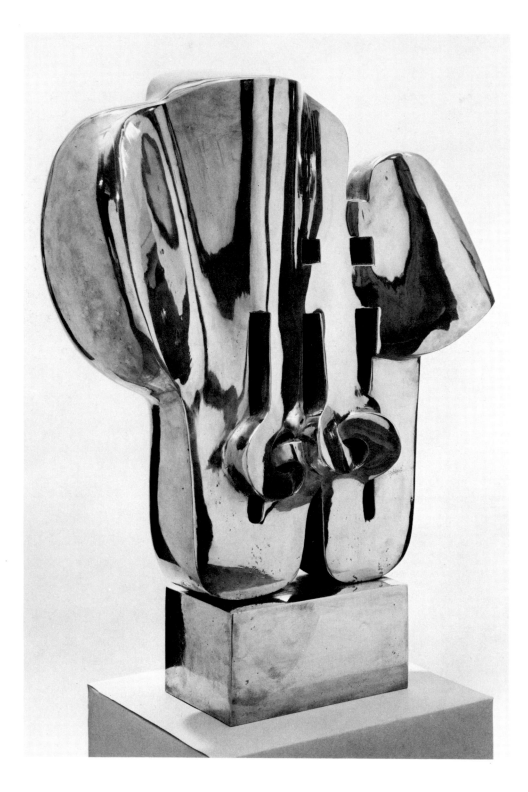

Sorel Etrog
Prophet II
Bronze 30″ high
Exhibited RCA 1970
Collection the Tate Gallery, London

Clifford Wiens
Silton Chapel, Silton, Saskatchewan
Exhibited RCA 1971

Tony Tascona
Sonar Device
Acrylic on canvas 48″ x 72″
Exhibited RCA 1971
Collection Mr. and Mrs. J. Orzechowski,
St. Vital, Manitoba

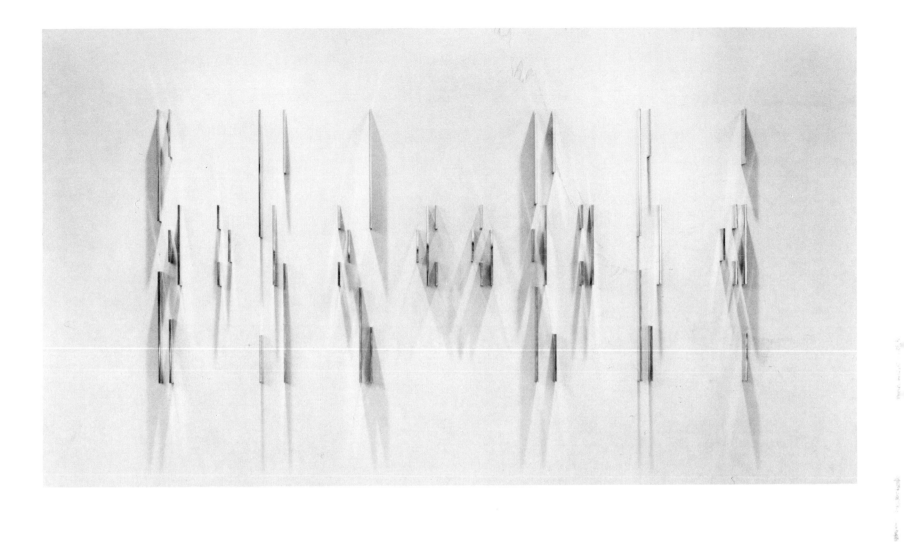

Gino Lorcini
Theta Magna
46″ x 78″
Exhibited RCA 1971
Collection *London Free Press*,
London, Ontario
Photograph: VIDA/Saltmarche, Toronto

Ron Thom
Thomas J. Bata Library,
Trent University, Peterborough, Ontario
Exhibited RCA 1971

Douglas Cardinal
Grande Prairie College,
Grande Prairie, Alberta
Exhibited RCA 1976

Ann MacIntosh Duff
Evening View, North Channel
Water colour 22^1/$_4$″ x 29^7/$_8$″
RCA Diploma work, deposited 1976
National Gallery of Canada

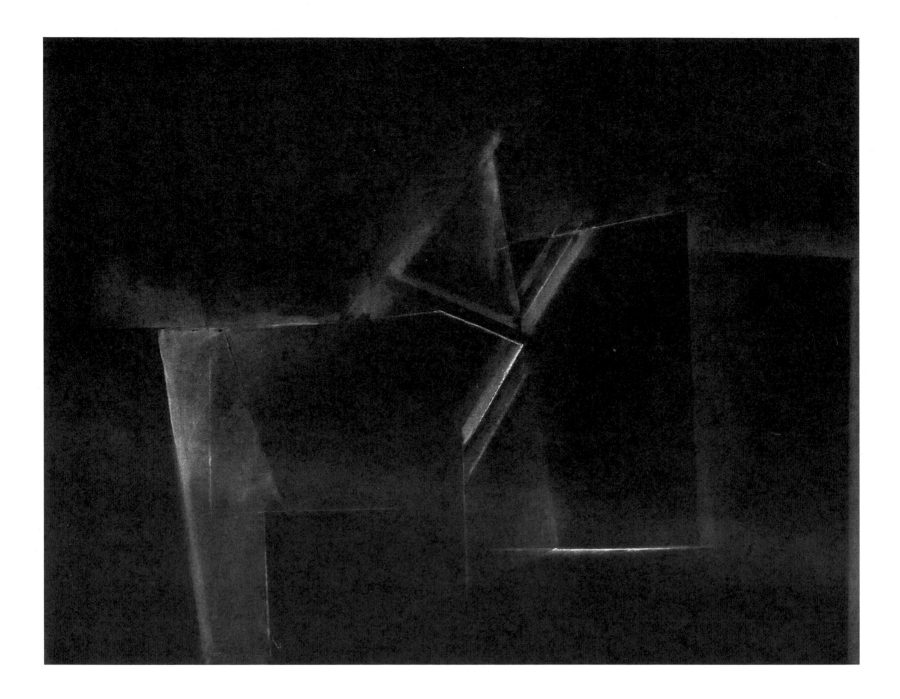

Fleming Jorgensen
White Island No. 2
Acrylic 42″ x 54″
Exhibited RCA 1976
Collection of artist

Victor Tolgesy
Acrobat's Horse
Laminated plywood 7′ x 7′ x 2′
Exhibited RCA 1976

K.J. Butler
Shaman
Gouache 30″ x 31″
Exhibited RCA 1976
Collection Mrs. Faye Settler, Winnipeg

Arthur Erickson
Museum of Anthropology,
University of British Columbia
Vancouver, B.C.
Exhibited RCA 1976
Photograph: Eberhard Otto,
cover of "Architecture as Cultural Expression,"
artscanada, October/November 1976

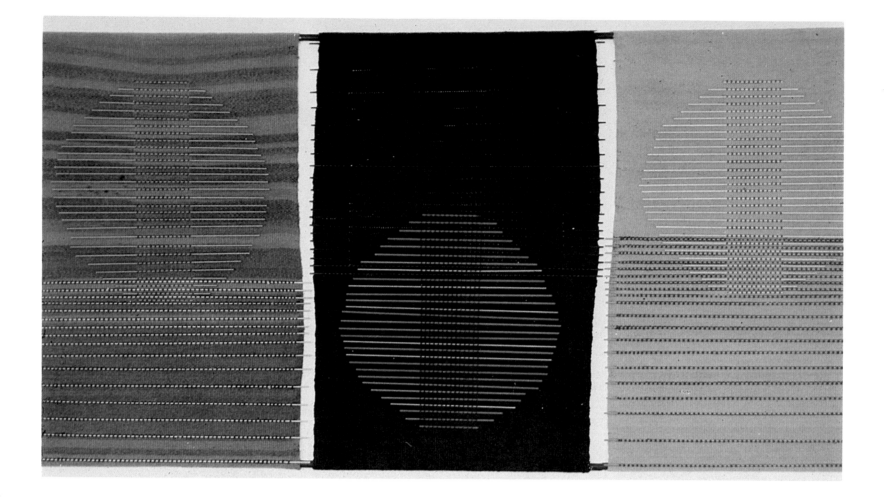

Helen Frances Gregor
Op Horizon No. 1
Wool, iodized aluminum 60″ x 120″
RCA Diploma work, deposited 1977
National Gallery of Canada

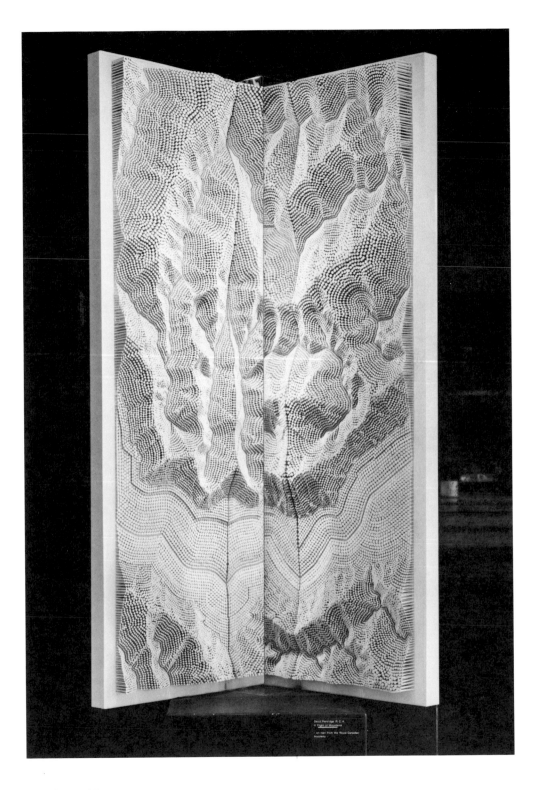

David Partridge
Flight of Mountains
Nails, wood, acrylic reflector 8'11" x 4' x 2'
Winner of RCA sculpture competition, 1978
On loan to Queen's Park, Toronto
Photograph: VIDA/Saltmarche, Toronto

269

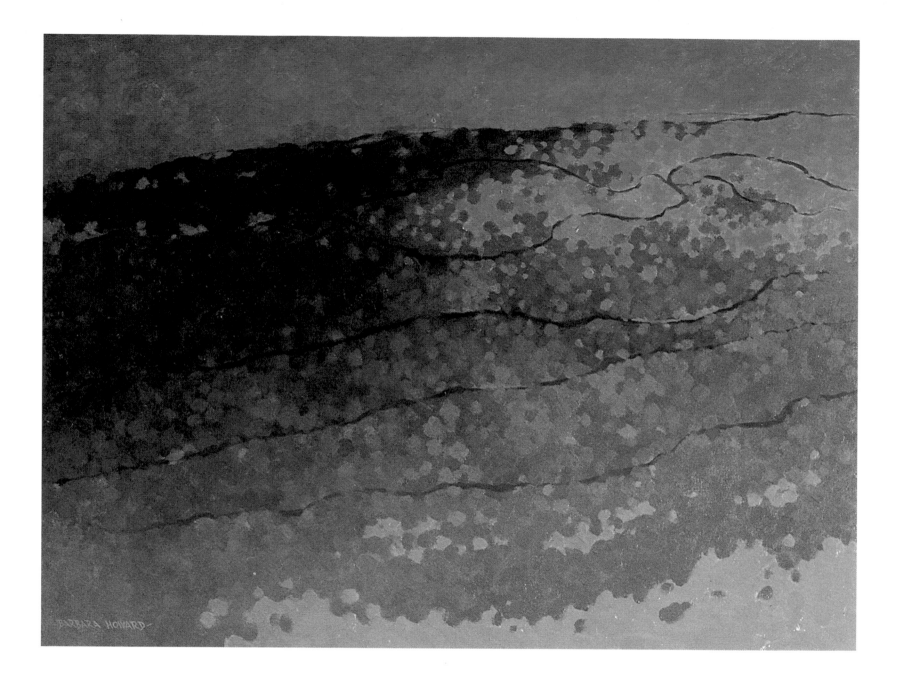

Barbara Howard
Sand and Water
Oil on canvas 24″ x 32″
RCA Diploma work, deposited 1979
Royal Canadian Academy of Arts

Roman Bartkiw
Glass Blowers Dance
Etched enamel 10″ high
Collection Finn Lynngarrd, Denmark

271

Vello Hubel
Play Cubes (industrial design)
polyethylene 15″ x 15″ x 15″

George Cuthbertson
Red Jacket (yacht)
Cored fibre glass, reinforced plastic
length: 39′9″ beam: 11′3″ draught: 6′
Airbrush rendering
Photograph: VIDA/Saltmarche, Ontario

272

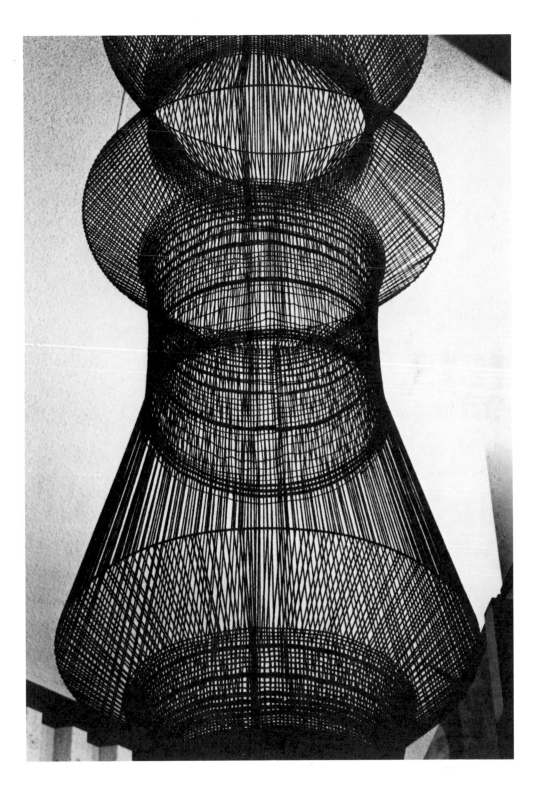

Charlotte Lindgren
Receptor
Black wool and steel 30′ long x 4′ diameter
Commissioned for CBC Building, Montreal

273

Burton Kramer
CBC Symbol (Graphic design)

Ernestine Tahedl
3 Freestanding Glass Sculptures
Glass appliqué 4'10" each
Collection Mendel Art Gallery,
Saskatoon, Saskatchewan

Lois Etherington Betteridge
Spice Shaker
Sterling silver, raised and
fabricated with chasing 3^{1}/$_{2}$″ high

Kryn Taconis
**Governor General's Garden Party,
Victoria, B.C.** (Photography)

Etienne J. Gaboury
Residence of Mr. and Mrs. E. J. Gaboury
Exhibited RCA 1970

Royal Canadian Academy of Arts

List of Presidents and Members 1880-1979

The lists of Presidents and Members are based on the dictionary catalogue, *Royal Canadian Academy of Arts: Exhibitions and Members 1880-1979*, compiled by Evelyn deRostaing McMann, published by the University of Toronto Press, 1980.

Code to Entries

ARCA	Associate Academician (prior to 1973)
RCA	Academician
RCA-e	RCA-elect, pending presentation of Diploma Work (from 1973)
C	Council Member
P	President
R	Resigned
HNR	Honorary Non-Resident
HR	Honorary Retired

Disciplines

A	Architect	I	Illustrator
AT	Architect town planner	IC	Illustrator, cartoonist
		ID	Industrial designer
BB	Book binder	IN	Interior designer
BD	Book designer	LA	Landscape architect
C	Calligrapher	P	Painter
CD	Costume designer	PH	Photographer
CE	Ceramist	PR	Printmaker
D	Designer	S	Sculptor
EN	Engraver	SD	Stage, theatre designer
ET	Etcher	SG	Stained glass designer
F	Filmmaker	T	Textile designer
G	Graphic designer		
GS	Gold/silversmith		

Presidents

1880-1890	O'Brien, Lucius Richard
1890-1893	Jacobi, Otto Reinhard
1893-1906	Harris, Robert
1906-1909	Reid, George Agnew
1909-1918	Brymner, William GMC
1918-1922	Watson, Homer Ransford
1922-1926	Russell, George Horne
1926-1929	Sproat, Henry
1929-1939	Grier, Sir Edmund Wyly DCL NA
1939-1942	Haines, Frederick Stanley
1942-1943	Nobbs, Percy Ernest, Acting Pres.
1943-1948	Fosbery, Ernest George
1948-1952	Casson, Alfred Joseph LLD NA
1952-1954	Pilot, Robert Wakeham MBE DCL NA
1954-1957	Allward, Hugh Lachlan
1957-1960	Comfort, Charles Fraser OC LLD
1960-1964	Arbuckle, George Franklin
1964-1967	Beament, Thomas Harold
1967-1970	Bice, Clare CM LLD
1970-	Parkin, John Cresswell CC

Members 1880-1979

ARCA & RCA-e	RCA	Discipline	Artist
1979		ID	Adamson, Gerald J. 1937-
1950	1956	A	Adamson, Gordon Sinclair 1904- C
1976		P	Adaskin, Gordon 1931-
1958	1966	A	Affleck, Raymond Tait 1922- C
1891-99		P	Ahrens, Carl Henry von 1863-1936
1962		P	Airola, Paavo 1915-
1975		G	Aldwinkle, Eric 1909-1980
1896-01		P	Alexander, Charles 1864-1915
1942	1959	P	Alfsen, John Martin 1902-1971 C
1967		P	Allen, Ralph 1926- C
1941	1945	A	Allward, Hugh Lachlan 1899-1971 P
1903	1920	S	Allward, Walter Seymour 1876-1955 C
1971		F	Almond, Paul 1931-
1977		P	Andrews, Stephen James 1922-
1936	1945	P	Arbuckle, George Franklin 1909- P
1966	1969	S	Archambault, Louis de Gonzaque Pascal 1915-
1978		A	Archambault, Richard Benson 1931-
1978		P	Ariss, Herbert Joshua 1917-
1880-87		P	Armstrong, William 1822-1914
1956	1964	A	Arthur, Eric Ross 1898- C
1971		G	Arthur, Paul 1924-
1975		G	Ash, Stuart 1942-
1970		A	Atkins, Gordon 1937-
1978		P	Atkinson, Eric 1928-
1894-14, 1918		P	Atkinson, William Edwin 1862-1926
1979		D	Babicki, Bogue B. 1924-
1978		G	Back, Frédéric Henri 1924-
1880-85		P	Baigent, Robert Richard 1830-1890
1880-84		A	Baillargé, Charles P. 1826-1906
1972		S	Baird, Ronald Arnott 1940- C
1880-09		A	Balfour, James 1852-1917
1975		ID	Ball, Douglas 1935-
1970	1977	A	Banz, George 1928-
1933	1936	P	Barnes, Archibald George 1887-1972 C
1920	1947	P	Barnes, Wilfred Molson 1882-1955 C
1930	1937	A	Barott, Ernest I. 1884-1966
1928		P	Barr, Robert Allan 1890-1959
1974	1975	P	Barry, Francis Leopold 1913-
1979		CE	Bartkiw, Roman 1935-
1976		G	Bartram, Edward John 1938-
1961	1971	P	Bates, Maxwell Bennett 1906-
1975		PR	Bates, Patricia Martin 1927-
1970		P	Baxter, Iain 1936-
1978		P	Baxter, Ingrid 1938-
1958		P	Bayefsky, Aba 1923- C
1936	1947	P	Beament, Thomas Harold 1898- P
1976		PR	Beament, Thomas Harold (Tib) 1941- C
1905	1913	P	Beatty, John William 1869-1941 C
1968		T	Beauchemin, Micheline 1930- C
1978		PH	Beaudin, Jean Pierre 1935-
1978		A	Beaulieu, Claude 1913-
1979		P	Beaulieu, Paul Vanier 1910-
1965		PR	Bell, Alistair Macready 1913-
1880	1886	P	Bell-Smith, Frederic Marlett 1846-1923 C
1919		P	Belle, Charles Ernest de 1873-1939
1976		G	Bellemare, Raymond 1942-
1880-81		D	Bengough, William 1857-1932
1976		S	Bentham, Douglas 1947-
1972		PH	Beny, Wilfred Roy Roloff 1924-
1974		ID	Bersudsky, Sid 1913-
1880-81		P	Berthon, George Théodore 1806-92
1978		PR	Besant, Derek Michael 1950-
1978		GS	Betteridge, Lois Etherington 1928-
1940	1966	P	Bice, Clare 1909-1976 P
1942	1959	P	Biéler, André Charles 1896-
1972		S	Biéler, André Charles Théodore (Ted) 1938- C
1954	1966	P	Binning, Bertrand Charles 1909-1976
1880-88		P	Bird, Harrington 1846-1936
1975		A	Bittorf, Donald George
1977	1978	P	Black, Samuel 1913-
1975		PR	Blackwood, David Lloyd 1941- C
1959	1967	A	Bland, John 1911-
1975		A	Blankstein, Morley
1976		S	Blazeje, Zbigniew 1942-
1970		A	Blouin, André 1920-
1975		AT	Blumenfeld, Hans
1959-63, 1972		P	Bobak, Bruno Joseph 1923-
1972		P	Bobak, Molly Joan Lamb 1922-
1885-89		P	Boisseau, Alfred 1823-1901
1963	1968	A	Bolton, Richard Ernest 1907-
1966		S	Bonet, Jordi 1932-1979
1975		S	Bonham, Donald 1940-
1943	1965	P	Bouchard, Lorne Holland 1913-1978 C
	1880-92R	P	Bourassa, Napoléon 1827-1916 C
1970		A	Bourke, Richard David 1931-
1978		PR	Boyd, James Henderson 1928-
1974		P	Boyle, John Bernard 1941-
1970		S	Braitstein, Marcel 1935-
1974		P	Breeze, Claude Herbert 1938-
1974		G	Brett, Carl 1928-

1891-92		P	Bridgman, George Brandt 1864-1940
1934	1939	P	Brigden, Frederick Henry 1871-1956 C
1978		F	Brittain, Donald 1928-
1908	1934	P	Britton, Harry 1878-1958
1978		A	Brook, Philip R. 1918-
1939		P	Brooks, Frank Leonard 1911-
1944	1975	P	Broomfield, Adolphus George 1906-
1976		I	Brown, Huntley 1932-
1943	1947	A	Brown, Murray 1884-1958 C
1898-01, 1913	1919-32R	P	Browne, Joseph Archibald 1862-1948 C
1894	1895-15R	P	Brownell, Peleg Franklin 1857-1946 C
1975		PH	Bruemmer, Fred 1930-
1891		P	Bruenech, George Robert 1851-1916
1977		P	Bruni, Umberto 1914-
1883	1886-20R	P	Brymner, William 1855-1925 P
1976		T	Bulow, Karen 1899-
1972		ID	Bulow-Hube, Sigrun 1913-
1880-90, 1908-14		A	Burke, Edmund 1850-1919
1880-88		A	Busch, Henry Frederik 1826-1902
1946-63		P	Bush, Jack Hamilton 1909-1977
1974		ID	Bush, Robin Beaufort 1921-
1976		P	Butler, Kenneth John 1937-
1956		P	Caiserman-Roth, Ghitta 1923- C
1975		F	Campbell, Norman 1924-
1897	1898-06R	A	Capper, Stewart Herbert 1859-1925 C
1972		A	Cardinal, Douglas Joseph Henry 1934-
1897-08, 1912		P	Carlyle, Florence 1864-1923
1935	1938	P	Carmichael, Franklin 1890-1945 C
1939		P	Caron, Paul Archibald 1874-1941
1976		S	Carr-Harris, Ian 1941-
1922	1928	D	Carter, Alexander Scott 1881-1968
1977		P	Carter, Harriet Estelle Manore 1929-
1926	1940	P	Casson, Alfred Joseph 1898- P
1967	1979	P	Cattell, Raymond Victor 1921- C
1891	1901	P	Challener, Frederick Sproston 1869-1959 C
1971		P	Chambers, John Richard 1931-1978 C
1925		A	Chapman, Alfred H. 1878-1949
1970	1973	F	Chapman, Christopher 1927- C
1880-88		A	Chesterton, Walter 1845-1931
1911-19		P	Clapp, William Henry 1879-1951
1956	1966	P	Clark, Paraskeva 1898- C
1974		I	Cleaver, Elizabeth Ann 1939-
1976		P	Cliff, Denis Anthony 1942-
1979		ID	Clifton, J. Terrence 1933-
1951	1958	P	Cloutier, Albert Edward 1902-1965 C
1935-74		P	Clymer, John Ford 1907-
1941		A	Cobb, Andrew Randall 1876-1943
1920	1928	P	Coburn, Frederick Simpson 1871-1960 C
1978		S	Cogswell, Barry 1939-
1956	1960	P	Collier, Alan Caswell 1911- C
1936	1945	P	Comfort, Charles Fraser 1900- P
1880	1886-94	A	Connolly, Joseph c1839-1904 C
1976		I	Cooper, Heather 1945-
1950		P	Coppold, Leslie George Murray 1914- C
1925	1932	A	Cormier, Ernest 1885-1980 C
1972		A	Corneil, Carmen Stewart 1933-
1951		P	Cosgrove, Stanley Morel 1911- C
1978		P	Coucill, Walter Jackson 1915-
1956		P	Courtice, Rody Kenny Hammond 1895-1973
1883-14		P	Cox, Arthur W. 1840-1917
1960-72		S	Cox, Elford Bradley 1914-
	1880	P	Cresswell, William Nichol 1822-1888 C
1880		P	Crocker, James A. Sydney d.1886
1937-39		P	Cross, Frederick George 1881-1941
1884	1895-19R	P	Cruikshank, William 1848-1922 C
1899	1908	P	Cullen, Maurice Galbraith 1866-1934 C
1885-97		A	Curry, Samuel George 1854-1942 C
1975		PH	Curtin, Walter Anthony 1911- C
1974		ID	Cuthbertson, George Harding 1929- C
1895		P	Cutts, Gertrude E. Spurr 1858-1941
1907		P	Cutts, William Malcolm 1857-1943
1978		A	Dalla-Lana, Alfred Bruno 1937-
1978		ID	Dallaire, Michel 1942-
1972		ID	Dallegret, François 1937- C
1947	1965	P	Daly, Kathleen Frances 1898-
1978		F	Daly, Thomas 1918-
1975		P	Danby, Kenneth Edison 1940-
1974		F	Dansereau, Mireille 1943-
1943	1952	S	Daoust, Sylvia Marie Emilienne 1902-
1880 1906	1886-89, 1907	A	Darling, Frank 1850-1923 C
			da Roza see Roza, Gustavo da
1970		S	Daudelin, Charles 1920- C
1948		A	David, Charles 1890-1962
1967		A	David, Jacques L. 1921-
1970		A	Davidson, Ian Jocelyn 1925-
1972		S	Davidson, Robert Claude (Bob) c1947-
1978		S	Davies, Haydn Llewellyn 1921-
1974		I	Davies, Will 1924-
1880	1881	P	Day, Forshaw 1837-1903 C
1946	1959	P	De Lall, Oscar Daniel 1903-1971 C
1979		PH	Delbuguet, René 1930-
1978		G	Derreth, Reinhard 1928-
1970		A	Desautels, Aimé 1921-
1970-73R		A	Desbarats, Guy
1920		P	Des Clayes, Alice 1890-
1914		P	Des Clayes, Gertrude 1879-1949

1880-88		A	Dewar, Andrew
1974	1976	A	Diamond, Abel Joseph 1932-
1880	1894-06R	A	Dick, David Brash 1846-1925 C
1978		PR	Dickson, Jennifer 1936-
1972		PH	Dille, Lutz 1922-
1972		A	Dimakopoulas, Dimitri 1929-
1975		SD	Dimitrov, Antonin 1928-
1975		CD	Dimitrov, Olga 1933-
1970	1974	G	Dimson, Théo Aeneas 1930-
1948	1968	P	Dingle, John Adrian Darley 1911-1974 C
1972		G	Doerrie, Gerhard 1936-
1974		G	Donoahue, James Thomas 1934-
1974		G	Dorn, Peter Klaus 1932-
1880		D	Doughtie, William c1846-1883
1977		S	Downing, Robert James 1935-
1970		A	Downs, Barry Vance 1930
1974		S	Drenters, Yosef Gertrudis 1929-
1976		CE	Drohan, Walter 1932-
1971	1974	PR	Drutz, June 1920-
1970		A	Dubois, Macy 1930-
1972	1974	P	Duff, Ann MacIntosh 1925- C
1979		P	Dulude, Claude 1931-
1979		P	Dumas, Antoine 1932-
1881-86		S	Dunbar, Frederick Alexander Turner 1849-1921
1880		P	Duncan, James D. 1806-1881
1883	1890	A	Dunlop, Alexander Francis 1842-1923 C
1884		A	Durand, George F. 1850-1889
1950	1957	A	Durnford, Alexander Tilloch Galt 1898-1973 C
1893	1903	P	Dyonnet, Edmond 1859-1954 C
1926		P	Earle, Paul Bernard 1872-c1955
1976		PR	Eastcott, Robert Wayne 1943-
1893-97		P	Eastlake, Mary Alexander Bell 1864-1951
1974		C	Ebsen, Alfred Karl 1908-
	1880	P	Edson, Aaron Allan 1846-1888 C
1978		PH	Ehricht, Horst
1884-88		D	Ellis, John
1974		S	Eloul, Kosso 1920-
1975		BD	Emori, Eiko 1938-
1976		ID	Ensor, Arthur John 1905-
1966	1969	A	Erickson, Arthur Charles 1924- C
1968		PR	Esler, John Kenneth 1933-
1978		G	Etienne, Errol Herbert Russell 1941-
1967		S	Etrog, Sorel 1933- C
1978		S	Etungat, Abraham 1911-
1975		P	Ewen, William Paterson 1925-
1974		P	Eyre, Ivan Kenneth, 1935-
1979		P	Fairley, Barker 1887-
1880-84		A	Fairweather, G. Ernest
1976		S	Favro, Murray 1940-
1978		P	Fenwick, William Roland 1932-
1974		F	Ferguson, Graeme 1929-
1974		P	Ferron, Marcelle 1924-
1936	1945	A	Fetherstonhaugh, Harold Lea 1887-1971 C
1950		S	Filion, Armand 1910-
1976		S	Filipovic, Augustin 1931-
1976		S	Fillion, John 1933-
1978		ID	Finkel, Henry 1910-
1949	1955	P	Finley, Frederick James 1894-1968 C
1959		P	Finley, Gerald Eric 1931-
1957	1967	A	Fiset, Edouard 1910- C
1972-80R		P	Fisher, Brian Richard 1939- C
1970		G	Fleming, Allan Robb 1929-1977 C
1976		A	Fletcher, Frederick Ernest 1923-
1944-59		P	Forbes, Jean Mary Edgell 1897-
1880	1882-13R	P	Forbes, John Colin 1846-1925 C
1928	1933-59	P	Forbes, Kenneth Keith 1892-1980
1895-99		P	Ford, Harriet Mary 1859-1939
1971		P	Forrestall, Thomas De Vany 1936-
1884-05		P	Forster, John Wycliffe Lowes 1850-1938
1942-55		P	Fortin, Marc Aurèle de Foy 1888-1970
1912	1931	P	Fosbery, Ernest George 1874-1960 P
	1880	P	Fowler, Daniel 1810-1894 C
1960	1975	A	Fowler, Gordon Lyle McLean 1909-
1959-61		P	Fox, John Richard 1927-
1902		P	Franchère, Joseph Charles 1866-1921
1961-70R		P	Franck, Albert Jacques 1899-1973
1976		P	Fraser, Carol Lucille Hoorn 1930-
	1880	P	Fraser, John Arthur 1838-1898 C
1963		P	Freifeld, Eric 1919-C
1972		A	Freschi, Bruno Basilio 1937- C
1978		S	Fulford, Patricia Parsons 1935-
	1882	A	Fuller, Thomas 1822-1898 C
1966		A	Gaboury, Etienne Joseph 1930-
1972	1977	S	Gage, Frances Marie 1924-
1880-92		A	Gage, Robert 1841-?
1880	1914	P	Gagen, Robert Ford 1847-1926 C
1970		P	Gagnon, Charles 1934- C
1909	1922	P	Gagnon, Clarence Alphonse 1881-1942 C
1955		A	Gardner, Edwin Alexander 1902-
1978		A	Garrett, Robert Michael 1931-
1945		P	Garside, Thomas Hilton 1906-
1971		PR	Garwood, Audrey Elaine 1927-
1970		P	Gaucher, Yves 1934- C
1946	1974	P	Gauthier, Joachim George 1897-
1880-13		A	Gemmell, John 1851-1915
1970		A	Gérin-Lajoie, Guy 1928- C

1975		A	Gerson, Wolfgang 1916-
1970	1976	PR	Gersovitz, Sarah Valerie Gamer 1920-
1979		S	Gilhooly, David James 1943-
1979		P	Girard, Claude 1938-
1972		ID	Girard, Marcel 1936-
1974		S	Gladstone, Gerald 1929- C
1942	1949	P	Glyde, Henry George 1906-
1976		S	Gnass, Peter 1936-
1974		P	Godwin, Edward William (Ted) 1933-
1971		P	Gordaneer, James Edward 1933-
1887-92		P	Gordon, Frederick Charles S. 1856-1924
1880-96		A	Gordon, Henry Bauld 1854-1951
1930		P	Gordon, Hortense Crompton Mattice 1889-1961
1923-39		P	Gordon, John Sloan 1868-1940
1976		P	Gorman, Richard Borthwick 1935-
1978		G	Gotthans, Manfred 1922-
1972		G	Gottschalk, Fritz 1937- C
1963-68R	1973	P	Gould, John Howard 1929-
1976		P	Goulet, Claude 1925-
1894		P	Graham, James Lillie 1873- c1971
1974		P	Graham, Kathleen Margaret Howitt 1913-
1942		P	Grandmaison, Nicolas de 1892-1978
1881-82		P	Grant, D.L.
1977		ID	Gratton, Aubry Armand 1935-
1978		S	Grauer, Gay Sherrard (Sherry) 1939-
1970		A	Greer, William Newton 1925-
1978		CE	Gregg, Erica Deichman 1914-
1970	1974	T	Gregor, Helen Frances Lorenz 1921- C
1943		P	Grier, Edmund Geoffrey 1899-1965
1893	1895	P	Grier, Sir Edmund Wyly 1862-1957 P
1931		P	Grier, Stella Evelyn 1898-
1974	1976	P	Griffith, Julius Edward Lindsay 1912-
	1880	P	Griffiths, James 1825-1896 C
1972		A	Grossman, Irving 1926-
1972		ID	Guillon, Jacques Silas 1922-
1975		S	Guite, Suzanne 1927-
1903		P	Hagarty, Clara Sophia 1871-1958
1927	1931	S	Hahn, Emanuel Otto 1881-1957
1901	1906	D	Hahn, Gustave 1866-1962 C
1919	1933	P	Haines, Frederick Stanley 1879-1960 P
1975		P	Hall, John 1943-
1943	1950	P	Hallam, Joseph Sydney 1899-1953
	1880-85R	P	Hamel, Joseph Arthur Eugene 1845-1932 C
1978		A	Hamilton, Peter Williamson 1941-
1890	1893	P	Hammond, John A. 1843-1939 C
1880		A	Hancock, Herbert 1830-1880
1961		S	Hanes, Ursula Ann 1932-
1880-88		P	Hannaford, Michael 1832-1891
1974		G	Harder, Rolf Peter 1929-
1970		S	Harman, Jack Kenneth 1927-
1943	1966	P	Harris, Lawren Phillip 1910- C
	1880	P	Harris, Robert 1849-1919 P
1881		A	Harris, William Critchlow 1854-1913
1979		P	Harrison, Allan 1911-
1970		P	Harvey, Donald 1930-
1882-01		P	Harvey, George H. 1846-1910
1972	1976	P	Hassell, Hilton Macdonald 1910-
1946	1954	P	Haworth, Peter 1889-
1948	1963	P	Haworth, Zema Barbara Cogill (Bobs) 1904-
1974		A	Hawthorn, Henry Gilbert 1939-
1975		S	Hayden, Michael 1943-
1970		P	Haynes, Douglas Hector 1936-
1978		ID	Hayward, James
1970		P	Head, George Bruce 1931-
1932	1942	P	Hébert, Adrien 1890-1967 C
1912	1922	S	Hébert, Henri 1884-1950 C
1970		ID	Hébert, Julien 1917-
1880, 1905	1886, 1906	S	Hébert, Louis Philippe 1850-1917 C
1972		P	Hedrick, Robert 1930
1934		P	Heming, Arthur Henry Howard 1870-1940
1975		A	Hemingway, Peter 1929-
1934	1941	P	Hennessey, Frank Charles 1894-1941
1978		A	Henriquez, Richard George 1941-
1921	1934	P	Hewton, Randolph Stanley 1888-1960
1972		PR	Heywood, John Carl 1941-
1908	1917	S	Hill, George William 1862-1934 C
1972		I	Hill, James Thomas 1930-
1961	1970	P	Hodgson, Thomas Sherlock 1924- C
1971	1975	S	Holbrook, Elizabeth Mary Bradford 1913-
1895-04		P	Holden, Sarah (Mrs. Hunter)
1934	1937-45, 1954	P	Holgate, Edwin Headley 1892-1977 C
1974		A	Hollingsworth, Fred Thornton 1917-
1978		PR	Holman, Donald R. 1946-
1974		P	Holmes, Reginald 1934-
1909	1921	D	Holmes, Robert H. 1861-1930 C
1948	1966	S	Hoo, Sing (Hoo Sing Yuen) 1909-
1895	1902	P	Hope, William R. 1863-1931 C
	1880	A	Hopkins, John William 1825-1905 C
1947	1951	S	Horne, Arthur Edward Cleeve 1912- C
1954-57		P	Horne, Jean Mildred 1914-
1976		P	Horne, Mercedes 1925- C
1943		EN	Hornyansky, Nicholas 1896-1965
1976		P	Horsfall, Arthur 1915-
1911		A	Horwood, Edgar Lewis 1868-1950
1976		LA	Hough, Michael 1928-

1897-02		P	Houghton, Margaret 1865-c1922
1942	1951	P	Housser, Muriel Yvonne McKague 1898- C
1960	1966	P	Houstoun, Donald Mackay 1916- C
1881	1883	D	Howard, Alfred Harold 1854-1916 C
1975	1979	P	Howard, Helen Barbara 1926- C
1880	1881-2R	A	Howard, John George 1803-90
1978		P	Howarth, Glenn Edward 1946-
1972		ID	Hubel, Vello 1927- C
1966	1969	P	Hughes, Edward John 1913-
1978		A	Hulbert, Richard Elliot 1945-
1978		S	Hung, Chung (Allan) 1946-
1956	1967	S	Hunt, Dora de Pedery 1913-
1977		PH	Hunter, George 1921-
1970		P	Hurtubise, Jacques 1939-
1936	1966	D	Hutchinson, Leonard 1896-
	1882-20R	A	Hutchison, Alexander Cowper 1838-1922 C
	1941	P	Hutchison, Frederick William 1871-1953, HNR 1937-40
1978		IN	Hymas, Jane Alison 1932-
1945		P	Iacurto, Francesco 1908-
1979		F	Ianzelo, Tony 1935-
1936		P	Innes, Alice Amelia 1890-1970
1972		S	Inukpuk, Johnny 1911-
1978		P	Irving, Daphne Butler 1931-
1880		A	Irving, William 1830-1883
1977		A	Irwin, Stephen Van Egmond 1939-
1974		P	Iskowitz, Gershon 1921-
1972		A	Izumi, Kiyoshi 1921-
1914	1919-32R, 1954	P	Jackson, Alexander Young 1882-1974 C
1880	1883	P	Jacobi, Otto Reinhold 1812-1901 P
1978		P	Jacque, Louis (Louis Jacques Beaulieu) 1919-
1979		ID	Jarry, André 1926-
1962	1967	P	Jarvis, Donald Alvin 1923-
1975		T	Jaworska, Tamara Hans 1928-
1978		F	Jaworski, Tadeusz 1926-
1978		S	Jean-Louis, Donald 1937-
1912	1927	P	Jefferys, Charles William 1869-1951 C
1978		P	Jerome, Jean Paul 1928-
1975		F	Jewison, Norman F. 1926-
1975		A	Johnson, Bradley Robert 1936-
1948	1963	P	Johnston, Frances Anne 1910-
1919-39		P	Johnston, Francis Hans (Franz) 1888-1949
1920-27		P	Johnstone, John Young 1887-1930
1882-88		P	Jones, Frances M. 1855-1940
1925	1927	A	Jones, Hugh Griffith 1872-1947 C
1943	1951	S	Jones, Phyllis Jacobine 1898-1976
1937	1940	P	Jongers, Alphonse 1872-1945
1972		P	Jorgensen, Flemming 1934-
1979		PR	Jule, Walter 1940-
1972		P	Juneau, Denis 1925-
1961-71R		S	Kahane, Anne 1924- C
1974		ID	Kaiser, Robert Joseph 1925- C
1974		PR	Kalvac, Helen c1899-
1979		PR	Kananginak, 1935-
1975		PH	Karsh, Yousuf 1908-
1978		A	Keith-King, John William 1939-
1970	1975	A	Kemble, Roger Ian 1929- C
1979		A	Kemp, Anthony Leslie 1936-
1953	1975	S	Kennedy, Sybil 1899-
1974		PR	Kenojuak 1927-
1975		P	Kergommeaux, Duncan Robert Chassin de 1927-
1975		P	Kerr, Illingworth Holey, 1905-
1976		P	Kerwin, Claire
1977		PR	Kilbourn, Rosemary Elizabeth 1931-
1975		F	King, Allan Winton 1930-
1976		P	Kingan, Edward Nathan (Ted) 1927-
1972		A	Kinoshita, Gene 1935- C
1978		P	Kipling, Barbara Ann 1934-
1974		A	Kiss, Zoltan Sandor 1924-
1978		P	Kiyooka, Harry Mitsuo 1928-
1965		P	Kiyooka, Roy Kenzie 1926-
1972		A	Klein, Jack 1927-
1908		P	Knowles, Elizabeth Annie Beach 1866-1928
1890	1898-30R	P	Knowles, Farquhar McGillivray Strachan Stewart 1859-1932 C
1976		S	Kolisnyk, Peter Henry 1934-
1974		S	Koochin, William 1927-
1974	1977	S	Kopmanis, August Arnold 1910-1976
1960-66		P	Korner, John Michael Anthony 1913-
1975		S	Kostyniuk, Ronald Peter 1941-
1975		F	Kotcheff, William Theodore (Ted) 1931-
1974		G	Kramer, Burton 1932- C
1975		IN	Kravis, Janis 1935-
1976		S	Kubota, Nobuo 1932-
1972-75R		P	Kurelek, William 1927-1977
1972		ID	Kuypers, Jan 1925- C
1912	1922-50	S	Laliberté, Alfred 1878-1953 C
1965		A	Lalonde, Jean Louis 1923- C
1979		F	Lambart, Evelyn 1914-
1977		A	Lambert, Phyllis Bronfman 1927-
	1880-05R	A	Langley, Henry 1837-1907 C
1974		P	Lansdowne, James Fenwick 1937-
1979		IC	La Palme, Robert 1908-
1970		P	La Pierre, Thomas 1930-
1919		P	Lapine, Andreas Christian Gottfried 1866-1952

1972		SD	Laufer, Murray Bernard 1929-
1972		S	Lawrence, Henry Wyndham 1924-
1881-82		P	Lawrence, William
1885-92		P	Lawson, James Kerr 1865-1939
1977		SD	Lawson, Robert Andrew 1926-
1979		F	Leaf, Caroline 1946-
1975		PR	Leathers, William Lyle 1932- C
1975		A	Lebensold, Fred David 1917-
1916		P	Leduc, Ozias 1864-1955
1971		A	Legault, Guy Robert 1932-
1935-46		P	Leighton, Alfred Crocker 1901-1965
1974		F	Leiterman, Richard 1935-
1965		A	Leithead, William Grier 1920-
1951	1966	P	Lemieux, Jean Paul 1904-
1976		P	Leonard, John C. 1944-
1880-81		A	Lepage, T. J.
1974		S	Le Roy, Hugh Alexander 1939-
1970		P	Letendre, Rita 1928- C
1880-81		A	Levesque, A.
1972		T	Lindgren, Charlotte 1931-
1977		P	Lindner, Ernest 1897-
1978		G	Lipari, François Amedeo Angeli (Frank) 1927-
1919	1947	P	Lismer, Arthur 1885-1969 C
1961		P	Little, John Geoffrey Caruthers 1928-
1974		P	Loates, Martin Glen 1945-
1922	1933	P	Long, Marion 1882-1970
1968		S	Lorcini, Gino 1923- C
1920	1947	S	Loring, Frances Norma 1887-1968 C
1920-33		P	Loveroff, Frédéric Nicholas 1894-1959
1972		F	Low, Colin Archibald 1926-
	1880-84	S	Luppen, François van 1838-1899 C
1977	1978	P	Luz, Virginia Erskine 1911-
1895		P	Lyall, Laura Adeline Muntz 1860-1930
1925	1927	A	Lyle, John MacIntosh 1872-1945 C
1951	1974	P	McCarthy, Doris Jean 1910-
1886	1892-23R	S	MacCarthy, Hamilton Thomas Carleton Plantagenet 1846-1939 C
1882-92		D	McCausland, Robert 1856-1923
1944-55		P	Macdonald, Albert Angus 1909-
1947		P	Macdonald, Evan Weekes 1905-1972
1954	1966	P	Macdonald, Grant Kenneth 1909-
1912	1932	P	McDonald, James Edward Hervey 1873-1932
1959		P	MacDonald, James Williamson Galloway (Jock) 1897-1960
1972		A	Macdonald, John Blair 1931-
1919	1948	P	MacDonald, Manly Edward 1889-1971
1947	1960	P	MacDonald, Thomas Reid 1908-1978 C
1964		A	McDonic, Henry Reed (Harry) 1904-
1970	1974	S	McElcheran, William Hadd 1927-
1964	1968	P	McEwen, Jean Albert 1923- C
1923		A	MacFarlane, David Huron 1875-1950

1925		P	McGillivray, Florence Helena 1864-1938
1939-43		P	MacGregor, Charles 1893-
1976		A	MacInnis, Garfield Allister 1936-
1974		ID	McIntosh, Lawrie Gandier 1924-
			McKague, Murial Yvonne see Housser, M.Y.
1880-88		A	MacKean, J. T. C
1971		P	MacKenzie, Hugh Seaforth 1928-
1976		CE	McKinley, Ruth Gowdy 1931-
1970	1973	F	McLaren, Norman 1914- C
1967		A	Maclennan, Ian Roy 1919- C
		S	McKenzie, Robert Tait 1867-1938, HNR 1928
1975		IN	McLoughlin, Michele 1944- C
1883-88		A	McNichol, Robert
1914		P	McNicoll, Helen Galloway 1879-1915
1972		IC	Macpherson, Duncan Ian 1924-
1903		A	MacVicar, Donald Norman 1869-1929
1890		P	Manly, Charles MacDonald 1855-1924
1978		PR	Manning, Joanne Elizabeth 1923-
1936	1947	A	Marani, Ferdinand Herbert 1893-1971
1925	1928	A	Marchand, Jean Omer 1872-1936
1971		A	Markson, Jerome 1929-
1976	1978	CE	Markson, Mayta 1931-
1880		P	Martin, Henry (Hy) c 1832-1902
1951	1965	P	Martin, John 1904-1965
	1880-18R	P	Martin, Thomas Mower 1838-1934 C
1974		F	Mason, William Clifford 1929-
1972		A	Massey, Geoffrey, 1924-
1967	1970	A	Massey, Hart 1918- C
1928	1937	A	Mathers, Alvan Sherlock 1895-1965 C
1880	1883	P	Matthews, Marmaduke 1837-1913 C
1974		PH	Max, John 1936-
1903	1908	A	Maxwell, Edward 1868-1923 C
1909	1914	A	Maxwell, William Sutherland 1874-1952 C
1915		P	May, Henrietta Mabel 1884-1971
1975		A	Mayerovitch, Harry 1910-
1974		S	Mayhew, Elza Edith Lovitt 1916- C
1978		P	Mayor, Robin 1937-
1951		A	Meadowcroft, James Curzey 1890-1969
1966		P	Menses, Jan 1933- C
1974		P	Meredith, John 1933-
1976		D	Merola, Mario Virgilio 1931-
1978		A	Merrick, Paul McCarley 1938-
1918		P	Mickle, Alfred Ernest 1869-1967
1880		P	Miles, John Christopher 1837-1911
1880		P	Millard, Charles Stuart 1837-1917, HNR 1881
1971		A	Millar, Charles Blakeway 1935- C
1943	1955	S	Miller, Herbert McRae 1895-

1911	1927	A	Miller, John Melville 1875-1948
1963-64, 1972		S	Mills, Gray Hoye 1929-
1977		P	Mitchell, Janet 1912- C
1926		P	Mitchell, Thomas Wilberforce 1879-1958
1978		A	Moffat, Donald Ormond 1933-
1966		S	Mol, Leo 1915-
1964	1969	P	Molinari, Guido 1933- C
1958	1961	A	Moody, Herbert Henry Gatenby 1903-
1970		A	Moriyama, Raymond 1929-
		P	Morrice, James Wilson 1865-1924, HNR 1913
1898		P	Morris, Edmund Montague 1871-1913
1929		P	Morris, Kathleen Moir 1893-
1954	1960	A	Morris, Robert Schofield 1898-1964
1972		P	Morrisseau, Norval 1932-
1968		P	Morton, Douglas Gibb 1926-
1897	1898	P	Moss, Charles Eugene 1860-1901 C
1939		P	Mount, Rita 1888-1967
1880-85		A	Mulligan, C. W.
			Muntz, Laura see Lyall, Laura
1941	1974	P	Murphy, Rowley Walter 1891-1975 C
1968		A	Murray, James Albert 1919-
1972		S	Murray, Robert Gray 1936-
1976		A	Myers, Barton 1934-
1976		P	Neddeau, Donald Frederick Price 1913-
1915		P	Neilson, Henry Ivan 1865-1931
1880-09		A	Nelson, James 1831-1913
1966-74		P	Nesbitt, John 1928-
1970		G	Newfeld, Frank 1928- C
1972		P	Newman, John Beatty 1933-
1923	1937	P	Newton, Lilias Torrance 1896-1980 C
1951		P	Nichols, Jack 1921- C
1976		P	Nicoll, Marion Florence S. Mackay 1909-
1972		P	Niverville, Louis de 1933-
1909	1920	A	Nobbs, Percy Erskine 1875-1963 P
1968		S	Noordhoek, Harry Cecil 1909-
1974-78		S	Norris, George 1928-
1974		IC	Norris, Leonard Matheson 1913-
1976-79R		S	Nugent, John Cullen 1921-
1929		P	Nutt, Elizabeth Styring 1870-1946
	1880	P	O'Brien, Lucius Richard 1832-1899 P
1962	1968	S	Oesterle, Leonhard Friedrich 1915- C
1970		P	Ogilvie, William Abernethy 1901-
1979		S	Ohe, Katie von der 1937-
1976		IN	Oliver, William Murray 1929-
1963		P	Onley, Norman Antonio (Toni) 1928-
1975		PR	Oonark, Jessie 1906-
1972		S	Oshooweetook "B" 1923-
1971		A	Ouellet, Jean 1922-
1979		BB	Ouvrard, Pierre 1929-
1947		A	Page, Forsey Pemberton 1885-1970

1960	1966	P	Palmer, Herbert Franklin (Frank) 1921-
1915	1934	P	Palmer, Herbert Sidney 1881-1970 C
1942		P	Panabaker, Frank Shirley 1904-
1934	1943	P	Panton, Lawrence Arthur Colley 1894-1954 C
1936		A	Parent, Lucien 1893-1956
1954	1965	A	Parkin, John Cresswell 1922- P
1962	1979	P	Partridge, David Gerry 1919- C
1882	1887-15R	A	Patterson, Andrew Dickson 1854-1930 C
1975		PH	Patterson, Freeman W. 1937-
1880-85		A	Paull, Almond E. 1824-1902
1975	1976	P	Pavelic, Myfanwy Spencer 1916-
1929	1936	A	Pearson, John Andrew 1867-1940
1882	1891	P	Peel, Paul 1860-1892
1970		P	Pellan, Alfred 1906-
1978		G	Pelletier, Pierre Yves 1938-
1906-08		P	Pemberton, Sophie Theresa 1869-1959
1976		P	Pentz, Donald Robert 1940-
1942	1957	P	Pepper, George Douglas 1903-1962 C
1968		P	Perehudoff, William 1919-
1880	1882	P	Perre, Henri 1828/or 1821-1890 C
1924		P	Perrigard, Hal Ross 1891-1960
1974		S	Perry, Frank 1923-
1974		C	Peter, Friedrich Gunther 1933-
1972		P	Peters, Gordon 1920-
1921	1934	EN	Phillips, Walter Joseph 1884-1963
1960		P	Picher, Claude 1927-
1978		P	Pichet, Roland 1936-
1970	1974	P	Pigott, Marjorie 1904-
1925	1934	P	Pilot, Robert Wakeham 1898-1967 P
1885	1897	P	Pinhey, John Charles 1860-1912 C
1974		PR	Pitseolak c1900-
	1880-81HR	P	Plamondon, Antoine Sébastien 1804-1895
1959		SG	Plamondon, Marius Gérald 1914-1976
1978		P	Plaskett, Joseph Francis 1918-
1974		F	Potterton, Gerald
1891-09		A	Power, Joseph William c1852-1925
1880		A	Power, L. John 1816-1882
1958	1966	A	Pratt, Charles Edward 1911-
1965		P	Pratt, John Christopher 1935- C
1976		P	Pratt, Mary Frances West 1935-
1979		S	Prent, Mark 1947-
1978		SD	Prevost, Robert
1948		P	Price, Addison Winchell 1907-
1960	1973	S	Price, Arthur Donald (Art) 1918-
1978		S	Prince, Richard Edmund 1949-
1970		A	Prus, Victor Marius 1917-
1978		P	Purdy, Henry Carl 1937- C
1972		S	Rabinowitch, David George 1943-

1965	1968	P	Spickett, Ronald John 1926-
1978		A	Sprachman, Mandel 1925-
1968		A	Spratley, Keith 1930-
1909	1914	A	Sproatt, Henry 1866-1934 P
1979		T	Staniszkis, Joanna 1944-
1881		A	Steele, A. D. d 1890
1971		PR	Steinhouse, Thelma Davis (Tobie) 1925-
1931	1949	P	Stevens, Dorothy 1888-1966
1974		G	Stewart, Clair 1910- C
1943-55R		S	Stewart, Donald Campbell 1912-
1972		ID	Stewart, Michael 1940-
1880-83		A	Stewart, William
1880-85		A	Stirling, D. 1822-1887
1971		A	Stokes, Peter John 1926-
	1880	A	Storm, William George 1826-1892 C
1976		A	Strasman, James Colin 1937-
1880-85		A	Strickland, Walter Reginald 1841-1915
1978		LA	Strong, Richard Allen 1930-
1978		A	Strutt, James William 1924-
1976		PH	Sugino, Shin 1946-
1978		P	Surrey, Philip Henry Howard 1910-
1911	1916	P	Suzor-Coté, Marc Aurèle de Foy 1869-1937 C
1972		PR	Swartzman, Roslyn Scheinfeld 1931-
1891-96		A	Symons, William Limbery 1862-1931
1977		PH	Szilasi, Gabor 1928-
1880-86		D	Taché, Eugene Etienne 1836-1912
1976		PH	Taconis, Kryn 1918-1979
1977		SG	Tahedl, Ernestine 1940-
1975		G	Talbot Kelly, Giles 1929-
1967-79R		P	Tanabe, Takao 1926 C
1970		P	Tascona, Antonio (Tony) 1926-
1976		PH	Tata, Samuel Bejan 1911-
1972		P	Tatossian, Armand 1948-
1976		LA	Tattersfield, Philip 1917-
1885	1890-13R	A	Taylor, Sir Andrew Thomas 1850-1937 C
1948	1967	P	Taylor, Frederick Bourchier 1906- C
1975		P	Taylor, Jocelyn 1899-
1978		PH	Taylor, Robert Ross 1940-
1974		S	Temporale, Louis 1909-
1971-76R		P	Thépot, Roger François 1925-
1979		G	Théroux, André
1971		A	Thom, Ronald 1923-
1960		D	Thomas, Lionel Arthur John 1915-
1881-84		A	Thomas, William Tutin d1892
1893-94		P	Thompson, Ernest Evan Seton 1860-1946
1957	1968	A	Thornton, Peter Muschamp 1916- C
1972		S	Tiktak 1916-
1978		F	Till, Eric 1929-
1971	1974	P	Timmas, Osvald 1919-
1953		P	Tinning, George Campbell 1910- C
1978		G	Tison, Hubert 1937-
1971		S	Tolgesy, Victor 1928-1980
1962	1969	P	Tondino, Gentile 1923- C
1970-76		P	Tonnancour, Jacques Godefroy de 1917- C
1966		G	Tooke, Gerald Ernest 1930-
1944		P	Topham, William Thurston 1888-1966
1972		S	Toulmin, Margaret 1916-
1977		P	Toupin, Fernand 1930-
1971		P	Tousignant, Claude 1932-
1978		F	Tovell, Vincent Massey 1922-
1958		P	Town, Harold Barling 1924-
1891-09		A	Townsend, Samuel Hamilton 1856-1940
1979		G	Trevor, Leslie J. 1907-
1974		S	Trudeau, Yves 1930- C
1979		T	Tudin, Tony 1930-
1890		P	Tully, Sydney Strickland 1869-1911
1977		P	Tulving, Ruth 1932-
1966-77		S	Turner, Richard Julian 1936-
1930		P	Turner, Stanley Francis 1883-1953
1978		D	Tuu'luq, Marion c1910-
1961-68		P	Urquhart Anthony Morse (Tony) 1934- C
1977		A	Valentine, Llewellyn Frederick 1939-
1925	1926	A	Vallance, Hugh 1866-1947 C
1977		P	Van Alstyne, Thelma Selina Aylma 1913-
1976		A	Van Der Meulen, Emiel George 1928-
1974		A	Van Ginkel, Blanche Lemco 1923-
1977		A	Van Ginkel, Harmen Peter Daniel 1920-
1921-39		P	Varley, Frederick Horsman 1881-1969
1972		ID	Vermette, Claude 1930-
1893		P	Verner, Frederick Arthur 1836-1928
1972	1976	PH	Visser, John de 1930- C
1976		P	Wainwright, Robert Barry 1935-
	1917	P	Walker, Horatio 1858-1938 C, HNR 1913-1916
1975		S	Wallace, George Burton 1920-
1974		P	Warkov, Esther 1941-
1975		A	Warren, Peter Haworth 1933-
1936	1952	A	Waters, Mackenzie 1894-1968
1880	1882	P	Watson, Homer Ransford 1855-1936 P
1951	1955	P	Watson, Sydney Hollinger 1911- C
1952	1962	P	Watt, Henry Robertson (Robin) 1896-1964
1880	1881	D	Watts, John William Hurrell 1850-1917 C
1880		P	Way, Charles Jones 1835-1919, HNR 1881
1977		PR	Weber, Kay Murray 1919-

1963		D	Weisman, Gustav Oswald 1926- C
1880-85		P	Weston, James L. c1815-1896
1936		P	Weston, William Percy 1879-1967
1881		P	Whale, Robert Reginald 1805-1887
1939	1954	S	Wheeler, Orson Shorey 1902- C
		P	White, George Harlow 1817-1888, HNR 1881
1978		S	Whittome, Irene 1942-
1890-01		P	Wickson, Paul Giovanni 1860-1922
1972		P	Wieland, Joyce 1931-
1970		A	Wiens, Clifford, 1926-
1943		A	Wiggs, Henry Ross 1895- C
1978		P	Wildman, Sally 1939-
1978		P	Wilkinson, John Craig Seaton (Jack) 1927-
1957	1964	SG	Williams, Yvonne 1903- C
1894	1907-34R	P	Williamson, Albert Curtis 1867-1944 C
1884-88		D	Willing, John Thompson 1860-
1937-68R		A	Wilson, Percy Roy 1900-
1945	1948	P	Wilson, Ronald York 1907- C
1887-08		P	Windeat, Emma S. d1926
1880-88		A	Windeyer, Richard Cunningham 1830-1900
1947	1954	P	Winter, William Arthur 1909-
1978		P	Wise, Jack Marlowe 1928-
1978		P	Wood, Alan 1935-
1929	1948	S	Wood, Elizabeth Wyn 1903-1966
1883	1886-34R	P	Woodcock, Percy Franklin 1855-1936 C
			Wrinch, Mary Evelyn see Reid, Mary Evelyn
1920	1938	S	Wyle, Florence 1881-1968 C
1977		G	Yaneff, Christopher 1928-
1967		S	Yarwood, Walter Hawley 1917-
1978		S	Zack, Badanna Bernice 1933-
1970		A	Zeidler, Eberhard Heinrich 1926-
1974		S	Zelenak, Edward John 1940-
1975		A	Zerafa, Boris Ernest 1933-

Honorary Academicians

1940	Richard Jack
1948	Earl Alexander of Tunis
1953	Lawrence G. White, Pres. National Academy of Design
1962	Vincent Massey
1973	Alfred Easton Poor, Pres. National Academy of Design
1973	J. Tuzo Wilson, Past Pres. Royal Society of Canada

RCA Medal Recipients

1962	Viljo Revell — Architect Norman McLaren — Animator and worker in cinematic abstraction ARCA 1970 RCA 1973 Carl Dair — Typographic designer
1963	Tanya Moseivitch — Stage and costume designer
1964	Yousuf Karsh — Photographer RCA 1975
1965	Christopher Chapman — Filmmaker ARCA 1970 RCA 1973 Allan Fleming — Typographic designer ARCA 1970
1966	Duncan Macpherson — Cartoonist ARCA 1972
1967	Pierre Dupuy — Commissioner General of Expo 67
1968	Julien Hébert — Industrial designer ARCA 1970
1969	Group of Seven (Painters) — A.J. Casson — A.Y. Jackson (posthumous) — Franklin Carmichael, Lawren Harris, Franz Johnston, Arthur Lismer, J.E.H. MacDonald, F.H. Varley
1972	Henry Moore — Sculptor
1973	Pierre Juneau — Chairman, Canadian Radio and Television Commission
1975	Moncrieff Williamson — Director, Confederation Centre of the Arts, Charlottetown, P.E.I. Gerry Moses — Corporate Fine Arts Program, Imperial Oil Ltd., (retired) Oscar Cahen — (posthumous) Painter Paul-Emile Borduas — (posthumous) Painter
1976	John Grierson — (posthumous) Filmmaker Walter Jungkind — Educator and president of INCONOGRADA
1977	Archie F. Key — Arts administrator and consultant Douglas M. Duncan — (posthumous) Collector
1978	John Crosbie Perlin — Arts administrator, Newfoundland Charles Wetmore — Educator, industrial design Emily Carr — (posthumous) Painter Albert Dumouchel — (posthumous) Printmaker Alan Jarvis — (posthumous) Arts administrator
1980	Duke of Argyll — to commemorate the founding of the Academy in 1880 by the Marquis of Lorne, later 9th Duke of Argyll

Index of Illustrations

The illustrations, except those representing the decade preceding the first exhibition of the Academy, which opened on March 6, 1880, at the Clarendon Hotel in Ottawa, are of works that have been exhibited in the RCA open-juried exhibitions over the years, or of Diploma Works of RCA members. In addition, those disciplines encompassed by the Academy in recent years, and which therefore did not appear in the regular annual exhibitions, are represented by a selection of photographs towards the end of the book.

Index

Graphic Design:
Burton Kramer Associates Limited

Typesetting:
Trigraph Inc.

Colour Separations:
Empress Litho Limited

Offset Lithography:
Sampson Matthews Limited

Binding:
T.H. Best Printing Company Limited

Endpaper:
Royal Canadian Academy Group, 1889,
Topley. Public Archives Canada, Ottawa.

Jacket:
Kaslo on Kootenay Lake by E.J. Hughes (detail)